The Enlargement of Life

The Enlargement of Life

Moral Imagination at Work

JOHN KEKES

Cornell University Press

ITHACA AND LONDON

171.3
K28en

Cau

Copyright © 2006 by Cornell University

First published 2006 by Cornell University Press

Printed in the United States of America

Library of Congress Cataloging-in-Publication Data

Kekes, John.
    The enlargement of life : moral imagination at work / John Kekes.
    p. cm.
    Includes bibliographical references and index.
    ISBN-13: 978-0-8014-4511-8 (cloth : alk. paper)
    ISBN-10: 0-8014-4511-6 (cloth : alk. paper)
    1. Imagination (Philosophy)   2. Autonomy (Philosophy)   3. Self (Philosophy)   4. Conduct of life.   5. Self-realization—Moral and ethical aspects.   6. Imagination in literature.   7. Self (Philosophy) in literature.   8. Conduct of life in literature.   9. Self-realization in literature.   I. Title.
    BH301.I53K45 2006
    171'.3—dc22   2006019343

Cornell University Press strives to use environmentally responsible suppliers and materials to the fullest extent possible in the publishing of its books. Such materials include vegetable-based, low-VOC inks and acid-free papers that are recycled, totally chlorine-free, or partly composed of nonwood fibers. For further information, visit our website at www.cornellpress.cornell.edu.

Cloth printing   10 9 8 7 6 5 4 3 2 1

for J. Y. K.

Contents

Part Three From Exploratory to Disciplined Imagination

Acknowledgments

The title of this book has been suggested to me by George Santayana, writing in *Three Philosophical Poets* of "a steady contemplation of all things in their order and worth. Such a contemplation is imaginative. No one can reach it who has not enlarged his mind and tamed his heart." Wallace Stevens consciously echoes this in *The Necessary Angel*, where he says in the introduction that imagination leads to "the enlargement of life."

My interest is in the moral importance of imagination, and this is best revealed, I think, in works of literature. The chapters that follow focus on literary works that show something important about the place of imagination in a good life. I have discussed five of these works before, but I hope that my treatment of them here reflects a deeper understanding than I had earlier. The discussions of Oedipus in chapter 4, Edith Wharton's *The Age of Innocence* in chapter 5, and Thomas More in chapter 9 use substantially revised versions of what I say about them in *The Art of Life* (Ithaca: Cornell University Press, 2002), chapters 4, 3, and 2. My reflections on Montaigne in chapter 8 draw on *Moral Wisdom and Good Lives* (Ithaca: Cornell University Press, 1995), chapter 6. And I first wrote about Herodotus's story in chapter 10 of *The Morality of Pluralism* (Princeton, N.J.: Princeton University Press, 1993), chapter 8.

Chong Kim Chong and Ann Hartle have kindly read and commented on several chapters. In revising them, I have greatly benefited from their help, and I gratefully acknowledge it.

In the book I am critical of some works of Harry G. Frankfurt, Stuart Hampshire, and Iris Murdoch. I want to make clear that I am deeply indebted to them. For many years now their writings have been part of the furniture of my mind. Their questions have been my questions, and they have remained so even when I could not accept their answers. I have learned very much from these fine thinkers.

I also want to make clear that although this book is about the constructive, sunny side of our moral life, moral life has a destructive, dark side as well. I say little about the latter here, not because I doubt its importance but because I have said about it what I could in *The Roots of Evil* (Ithaca: Cornell University Press, 2005).

My editor at Cornell was once again Roger Haydon. It has become a habit to thank him again and again for his sympathy and support for the kind of work this and previous books of mine represent. I cannot imagine a better editor than he, and I am grateful for his excellence and encouragement.

The book is dedicated to my wife, who makes it all possible and worthwhile.

J. K.

ITHAKA
Charlton, New York

Introduction

Man is a creature who makes pictures of himself and then comes
to resemble the picture. This is the process which moral
philosophy must attempt to describe and analyse.

— Iris Murdoch, "Metaphysics and Ethics"

The epigraph expresses with remarkable economy the aim of
this book. There are three processes I describe and analyze: making pictures, coming to resemble them, and reflecting in a particular way. I hope
to show that these processes jointly lead away from a widely held contemporary ideal of a good life. Its ruling ideas are freedom, choice, individuality, self-direction, and responsibility. The connecting link between them
is the importance attributed to being in control of one's life and actions.
Coercion, manipulation, obedience, authority, repression, and compulsion are its enemies. I call this the ideal of autonomy, and have serious
doubts about it.

Many people in affluent Western democracies take this ideal for
granted without having made a conscious commitment to it. It forms the
background of what they value and shapes what they expect out of life. But
when they try to live according to it, they frequently fail because misfortune, failure, boredom, confusion, hostile interference, inconsistent aspirations, communal ties, religious and political allegiances, impersonal demands by bureaucratized institutions, family and work-related obligations,
personal shortcomings, conflicting desires, and other obstacles stand in
their way. These obstacles force them to become conscious of the ideal in
the background and to examine critically their commitment to it. I think
that such critical examination discloses that although the ideal has great
attractions, it also has great problems. These problems lead to my central

concern: to show one way in which a substantially revised version of this ideal may be reasonably pursued through the three processes of which the epigraph speaks. We make pictures by means of the moral imagination. We come to resemble them by transforming ourselves. And we do so by reflective self-evaluation, which is the name I give to the revised version of the ideal of autonomy. Moral imagination, self-transformation, and reflective self-evaluation together enlarge life by enlarging its possibilities and overcoming obstacles to their realization.

To live is to act, and we act because we want to satisfy our desires and avoid their frustration. We thus aim at a future condition that we suppose would be an improvement over the present. Such activities are essential to living, and we are unavoidably engaged in them. Some people, however, succeed better than others because they reflect better on their desires, frustrations, and aims and form a more realistic view of their possibilities and limits. They show that we need not be passive subjects at the mercy of external forces, but active agents who at least sometimes decide what desires to satisfy, what frustrations to endure, and what aims to pursue. We can often make such decisions because in civilized circumstances many possibilities are available. The objects of reflective self-evaluation are these possibilities. We reflect on them in order to understand why we want to pursue some of our possibilities rather than others. The result may be to act as we want or to refrain from acting that way because we suppose it would be a mistake.

Moral imagination is one chief means by which this reflective self-evaluation proceeds. Its moral component is concerned with living a good life, understood as combining responsibility and fulfillment. Responsibility has to do with how our actions affect others. Fulfillment is overall contentment with life. Good lives require both because a responsible life may leave many important desires and aims frustrated, and a fulfilling life may be detrimental to the desires and aims of others. Frustrated lives and those lived in indifference or hostility to others are wanting in significant respects, so they fail to be good in the full sense of the word. The imaginative component of moral imagination involves both the correction of the unrealistic view we form of our limits and possibilities and the exploration of what it would be like to live according to our various possibilities. It enables us to understand how we might think, feel, and act, and how others might be affected by our actions if we were to change how we live by correcting our past mistakes and exploring particular possibilities. Moral imagination thus enlarges our understanding of the possibilities that are open to us and the limits within which we should pursue them.

This kind of imagination must be concrete and particular because our limits and possibilities differ; beliefs, emotions, and desires vary; and so do the contexts in which we live. To be sure, all of us are limited by having to conform to some universal requirements, but these constitute only a minimum. The possibilities of life are much richer than the unavoidable physiological, psychological, and social limits to which all members of our species must conform or suffer the consequences. The abundance of possibilities and the concreteness and particularity of moral imagination make it impossible to formulate rules about how it should do its work. But that does not mean that we cannot be helped by learning from the lives of others. The richest source of lives from which we can learn is literature. There is, therefore, a special affinity between literature and moral imagination—an affinity of which I make much use.

The chapters that follow focus on literary works that exemplify the success or failure of individuals as they try to correct their unrealistic view of themselves and explore more realistically their possibilities. These works, in the order in which I consider them, are John Stuart Mill's "Bentham" and *Autobiography*; Sophocles' *Oedipus the King* and *Oedipus at Colonus*; Edith Wharton's *The Age of Innocence*; Henry James's *The Golden Bowl* and *The Ambassadors*; Michel de Montaigne's *Essays*; a historical reconstruction of the life and death of Sir Thomas More; one of the remarkable stories in Herodotus's *The Histories*; and Arthur Koestler's *Arrival and Departure*. I consider these works because we can derive from them important clues about what we can do to make our lives better—more responsible and fulfilling—by improving our moral imagination and reflective self-evaluation, and thereby enlarging our possibilities in life.

The book is divided into four parts. Part I contains chapters 1 and 2. The first begins with the ideal of autonomy, shows the problems that vitiate it, indicates some of the ways in which it should be revised, and discusses how its revised version may be pursued by means of moral imagination. The second gives an account of moral imagination by distinguishing three of its modes: the corrective, the exploratory, and the disciplined. Part II is about the corrective imagination: its necessity and insufficiency for a good life and the consequences of its success or failure. Part III deals with the exploratory imagination, discussing how it can be done well and badly and how each affects the chances of living a responsible and fulfilling life. Part IV describes the disciplined imagination, which combines the corrective and exploratory modes, and explains why their reciprocal support is necessary. The last chapter makes explicit the conception of reason implicit in the discussion throughout the book.

Part One

THE IDEAL

Reflective Self-Evaluation

I wish my life and decisions to depend on myself, not on external
forces of whatever kind. I wish to be the instrument of my own,
not of other men's, acts of will. I wish to be a subject, not an
object; to be moved by reasons, conscious purposes, which are
my own, not by causes which affect me . . . from the outside.

—ISAIAH BERLIN, "Two Concepts of Liberty"

1.1 From Autonomy to Reflective Self-Evaluation

The ideal expressed in the epigraph is the ideal of autonomy. It
has emerged in the course of a long historical process culminating in Immanuel Kant's ethics.[1] Its history and Kantian context raise complex questions of interpretation, but I shall put them aside and concentrate on the
essential features of autonomy as, I believe, they now appear to those trying to understand the ideal it represents. Central to it is a particular form
of control individuals should cultivate over their lives. Choosing among alternative courses of action is a necessary part of it, but it is, by itself, not
sufficient because the choice may be among undesirable alternatives: between conversion or persecution, or life and limb. Having to make such
choices diminishes rather than increases the control individuals have over
their lives. Control depends on having unforced choices. But that is still
not sufficient because the choice may be made hastily, thoughtlessly, or
without adequate understanding of the available alternatives. Control requires, therefore, adequate understanding, but that may still fall short of
what is needed, unless the alternatives are evaluated on the basis of
whether they are conducive or detrimental to living a responsible and fulfilling life. Putting these conditions together, I will say that the desirable

3

form of control depends on reflective self-evaluation. It is *self*-evaluation because it involves the reflective evaluation of one's possible choices bearing on the kind of life one makes for oneself. The key to autonomy, then, is reflective self-evaluation.

There are numerous contemporary attempts to understand the psychological processes involved in reflective self-evaluation, but perhaps the most influential ones are those of Harry Frankfurt and Stuart Hampshire.[2] They ascribe the highest moral importance to these processes, and they claim that they are necessary for living a good—responsible and fulfilling—life.

According to Frankfurt, human beings are like animals in having desires and making choices, but unlike animals, humans can form second-order desires by reflective self-evaluation. A first-order desire is to do or not to do something. A second-order desire is to make one of the many first-order desires the object of one's will. This transforms the first-order desire into a second-order volition. Second-order volitions, Frankfurt claims, are essential to being a person. Such volitions reflect what we care about, what is important to us. They create a volitional necessity, which is a commitment to being motivated by what we regard as important, not by first-order desires inconsistent with that commitment. And he says that we act autonomously when we are guided by that commitment.

Hampshire expresses in different words the same ideas. We become free and responsible to the extent to which our actions reflect our self-conscious intentions. Our commitments are shown by the decisions about which we reflect seriously. As for Frankfurt so for Hampshire, morality is a matter of our autonomously formed will. By such acts of will we create a moral order within the natural order. And when we consciously and actively direct our intentions and actions, we are autonomous and responsible agents.

Frankfurt and Hampshire agree, then, in understanding autonomy in terms of reflective self-evaluation. Reflective self-evaluation is an essential condition of living a good life; it requires individuals to evaluate their desires by judging how well they fit in with their aspiration to live such a life; and the evaluation is deep because it concerns matters that each individual regards as most serious, most important, most worth caring about. The better individuals succeed in their reflective self-evaluations the better are their chances of living a responsible and fulfilling life. And whether they succeed depends on their will. Frankfurt and Hampshire thus put forward reflective self-evaluation both as an explanation of what a good life is for human beings and as an ideal that individuals should aim to realize. From now on I refer to this as *the voluntarist ideal* because of the pivotal role Frankfurt and Hampshire assign to the will.

The widespread appeal of this ideal is undeniable. There cannot be many people who would not like to be maximally free, responsible, and in control of their lives and actions. Who indeed would not like to have self-mastery, act only to realize favorably evaluated desires, and be moved only by motives and intentions that have passed the test of reflection? Who would not like it to be true, rather than a wry joke, that destiny is what we make of it? Who would be indifferent to having a fulfilling life or to the wonderful possibilities of life implied by this ideal? These attractions of the ideal are further strengthened by the realization that the ideal is presupposed by a variety of widely held—but not uniformly plausible—beliefs of the present age, beliefs at least some of whose influences few thoughtful people could have escaped. For the ideal is one among a small number of reasonable interpretations of the Enlightenment view of humanity. It is behind the picture of the self that motivates liberalism, the dominant political ideology in the Western world and increasingly also elsewhere. It is liberation from neurosis and anxiety that is the goal of various psychoanalytic therapies; the result of successful resistance to bad faith and inauthenticity advocated by existentialists; the state of the individual after the postmodernist deconstruction of the authority of traditions and conventions; the ideal self obscured by the distractions, self-deceptions, and unpredictability of our streams of consciousness, as depicted by Proust, Joyce, Virginia Woolf, and other writers in the genre; the secular ideal of those who have come to doubt traditional religious beliefs and yet seek to live moral lives, and of those who believe that individuals must create, rather than inherit, the values by which they live. From these attractions of the voluntarist ideal I now turn to difficulties with it.

1.2 The Problem of Exclusion

One of the lessons history teaches is that although the origin of the voluntarist ideal is not datable with precision, it is datable. "It was only from the early eighteenth century that the effort to create a theory of morality as self-governance became self-conscious." The reason for making the effort was that "moral and political concerns led increasing numbers of philosophers to think that the inherited conceptions of morality did not allow for a proper appreciation of human dignity."[3] One of these inherited conceptions was the Platonic view that the key to living a good life is knowledge of the good that exists independently of human will and whose acquisition requires exceptional talent and education. Another was the Christian view that obedience is the key to living a good life and it calls for the surrender of one's will to the will of God. Yet another was the natural law tradition according to which a good life is to live according to the scheme inherent in nature and to resist the promptings of contrary desires. A further one was a return to the pastoral simplicity of the real or imagined Garden of Eden, where living a good life depends on the rejection of the corrupting influences of civilization. And to these may be added the ideals of the Stoics, Epicureans, Confucians, Brahmins, Buddhists, Muslims, and others.

The mere existence of alternatives does not show that there is anything wrong with an ideal, but it does impose an obligation on those who champion it to explain why their ideal is preferable to the alternatives. Frankfurt and Hampshire do explain it: reflective self-evaluation, they claim, is a precondition of being a person. As Frankfurt says, "having second-order volitions . . . I regard as essential to being a person."[4] Hampshire claims that being a "free and responsible agent" requires that "he at all times knows what he is doing . . . and . . . acts with a definite and clearly formed intention."[5] If one is not a person, if one is not free and responsible, one cannot live a good life because one cannot be a moral agent. Their extremely strong claim is not merely that without reflective self-evaluation people are poor or bad moral agents, but that they are like animals, imbeciles, or the insane in not being moral agents at all. They cannot act morally, the claim is, because they lack reflective self-evaluation, upon which the very possibility of moral activity depends. Their claim denies moral status to all those simple, unreflective people who spontaneously and naturally respond to others with benevolence; who are born and raised in traditional, hierarchical societies and unquestioningly accept their inherited station in life and its duties; who are led by faith to follow the authority and morality of their religious teachers; and who are moved by unexamined compassion to do what they can to alleviate the suffering of the afflicted.

The consequences of this indefensibly exclusive claim are that all those who were and are guided by alternative ideals and are ignorant of or engage only minimally in reflective self-evaluation are not persons, fail to be free and responsible, and thus do not qualify as moral agents. Since, as the historical record testifies, the vast majority of humanity was in this position, they are not even candidates for having lived a good life. There is no need to look at how they lived and acted: if they were not reflective self-evaluators, they could not have had a good life. Such consequences, of course, are not just absurdities unintended by Frankfurt and Hampshire but also inconsistencies that cannot be reconciled with their avowed pluralism about the forms good lives may take. Unfortunately, the absurdities and the inconsistencies follow from what they say, regardless of what they intend.

What has gone wrong is that Frankfurt and Hampshire take the voluntarist ideal as the model to which all ideals of a good life must conform. Their ideal *is* attractive, but mainly for those who live in affluent, tolerant Western societies, have the leisure and inclination to reflect on their lives, and are well enough educated to know how to question, analyze, and reason. Such people constitute a very small and very fortunate minority of humanity. The forms of life, obligations, and responsibilities of the less fortunate huge majority are very different from those of reflective self-evaluators, but no worse for that.

It is reasonable to conclude, I believe, that the exclusive claim Frankfurt and Hampshire make for reflective self-evaluation is mistaken. But an exclusive claim does not invalidate the ideal on whose behalf it is mistakenly made. Why not interpret the voluntarist ideal, then, more inclusively as the claim that reflective self-evaluation is a secular ideal for well-educated, modestly affluent people living in contemporary, pluralistic, Western societies? This reinterpreted claim is compatible with the existence and acceptability of other ideals both in Western societies and elsewhere, and avoids the difficulties that follow from the exclusive claim. It is a step in the right direction, but it is not enough to make the voluntarist ideal acceptable as a guide to living a good life because it has other problems.

1.3 The Problem of Morality and Responsibility

Take people who are reflective self-evaluators—who follow Frankfurt's volitional necessity or act on Hampshire's explicit knowledge and definite and clearly formed intentions—and their actions are informed by their evaluations. There is nothing that stops these actions from being immoral, and I have found nothing in the writings of Frankfurt and Hampshire that would show that reflective self-evaluation is incompatible with immorality. They seem to assume that if reflective self-evaluation is done properly, it will lead to morally good rather than morally bad actions. But this is not so, as history, literature, and personal experience amply show. People often decide on the basis of well-conducted reflection about their lives and actions that some religious, political, or personal goal is more important to them than conformity to morality. Led by faith, ideology, or private projects, they intentionally violate elementary moral requirements in order to achieve their goals. In doing so, they inflict grave, often irreversible, harm on innocent people. Suicide bombers, ethnic cleansers, racists, witch hunters, sadists, torturers, and other malefactors may have reflected deeply on their motives and goals, endorsed them, identified their will with them, and succeeded in doing what they knew was immoral.

They may feel justified, however, because they believe on the basis of re-flective self-evaluation that the importance of their goals overrides moral scruples. Reflective self-evaluation is thus compatible with acknowledged immorality. But an ideal of a responsible life cannot be compatible with its own rejection. If reflective self-evaluation is to be a morally acceptable ideal, there must be limits built into it to rule out immoral actions. The voluntarist ideal, therefore, must be qualified further to specify what these limits should be.

The limits morality imposes on human lives and actions are very difficult to specify. I sidestep this difficulty by concentrating on minimum limits that no one committed to morality can seriously question. Good lives for human beings have certain basic requirements that must be met regardless of what other requirements there may be and how these other requirements may vary with different ideals of a good life. These basic requirements include the satisfaction of physiological needs necessary for continued existence, the protection of physical security against attacks by others, the guarantee of at least some small sphere in which individuals can obtain the necessities of life, and so on. The minimum moral limits, then, forbid depriving people of these basic requirements. None of these particular limits is unconditional be-cause the protection of the limits taken together may require the violation of a particular limit, for instance, in the case of self-defense or just punishment. But this requires justification in each case, and the only morally acceptable justification is to show that the violation is necessary for the protection of the minimum requirements in general. These minimum moral limits must be recognized by all reasonable ideals of a good life, including reflective self-evaluation, however they may differ about possibilities and limits beyond the minimum.

The protection of basic requirements by these limits is a moral neces-sity, so I will say that these limits define the domain of *moral necessity*. There is also a domain of *moral possibility*, in which individuals pursue various ideals of a good life once their basic requirements are met. In the domain of moral necessity, the central moral concern is with preventing the viola-tion of limits regardless of whether or not they result from reflective self-evaluation. The importance of protecting the limits overrides whatever importance reflective self-evaluation has. In the domain of moral neces-sity, therefore, reflective self-evaluation is neither a necessary nor a suffi-cient condition of conforming to the requirements of morality. If reflec-tive self-evaluation is the necessary condition of morality that Frankfurt and Hampshire claim for it, it can be that condition only in the domain of moral possibility, where individuals deliberate about which of the possibil-ities they should try to realize.

The same conclusion follows if we consider what Frankfurt and Hampshire say about responsibility. According to Frankfurt, the conditions of responsibility are as follows: "suppose that a person has done what he wanted to do, that he did it because he wanted to do it, and that the will by which he was moved when he did it was his will because it was the will he wanted. Then he did it freely and of his own free will."[6] Such a person, according to Frankfurt, is a responsible reflective self-evaluator because he has second-order volitions. Hampshire says that "a man becomes more and more a free and responsible agent the more he at all times knows what he is doing . . . and the more he acts with a definite and clearly formed intention."[7] The assumption that runs through this way of thinking is that responsibility depends on the presence of certain psychological activities that precede actions. Those who are engaged in the relevant sort of psychological activities are responsible; those who do not, are not. Although this assumption is not exactly false, it is seriously incomplete and misleading.

Consider two exemplary reflective self-evaluators. Having engaged in the appropriate psychological activities, they form the intention to murder a person as soon as an opportunity presents itself. The first does and the second does not because the opportunity never arose (say the intended victim died of natural causes). If responsibility depends on the psychological activities that precede action, then these two reflective self-evaluators have the same responsibility. But this is surely absurd, for the first is a murderer and the second is not. Their psychological activities may be the same, but their actions are not. What people are responsible for is not just the psychological activities that lead to their actions but also the morality of their actions. The first one acted immorally, the second did not. Their intention to commit murder may be deplorable, but only because such intentions tend to result in immoral actions. If they did not, intentions would have as tenuous a connection with responsibility as nightmares. Any acceptable view of people's responsibility must take into account the moral standing of their actions. The view held by Frankfurt and Hampshire does not, and that is another reason why the voluntarist ideal of reflective self-evaluation is incomplete. It misleads by treating responsibility as if it were merely a matter of what goes on inside people and by ignoring how their actions affect others. It concentrates on the causes of actions and ignores their effects.

It might be offered as a defense of the voluntarist ideal that its incompleteness is merely an unintended artifact of its presentation by Frankfurt and Hampshire and it can be easily remedied by adding what they have omitted. They stressed the psychological causes of actions; the remedy is to stress also the effects actions have on others. Now this certainly can and should be done, but doing it would shift the quiddity of the ideal from psychology to morality. If the effects of actions are recognized as relevant to responsibility, then reflective self-evaluation must be recognized at the same time to have limits. It is not an unqualified good, and it is not true that the greater extent individuals engage in it, the better their lives are. Reflective self-evaluation is morally acceptable only if it does not result in immoral actions. Otherwise, it is an instrument of immorality. Who could reasonably deny that good actions without reflective self-evaluation are morally better than bad actions with reflective self-evaluation? Yet this truism is incompatible with regarding reflective self-evaluation as a precondition of responsible agency. If the voluntarist ideal is to be defensible, it must recognize the central moral importance of the effects actions have on others.

But this is not all. We cannot simply add the stress on effects to the stress already placed on causes. The causes are morally important *because* of their effects. This becomes obvious if we ask why moral importance is attributed to reflective self-evaluation rather than to any one of the countless other psychological activities that precede actions. The beginning of the answer is that reflective self-evaluation enables individuals to control their desires and thus shape their lives. This, however, is only a beginning because the mere fact of control is morally indeterminate, since it is compatible with the suppression and the expression of both good and bad desires, with giving a morally good or bad shape to one's life. Reflective self-evaluation is morally important, therefore, because it enables individuals to express morally acceptable desires and to suppress morally unacceptable ones. But whether they have done so depends on their actions. The morality of individuals ultimately depends on the morality of their actions. The moral quality of the psychological activities that precede actions thus derives from the moral quality of the actions. The trouble with the voluntarist ideal is that it attributes primary moral importance to reflective self-evaluation when its moral importance is secondary. Proponents of the voluntarist ideal mistake a means for the end to which it leads. The means *is* important, but it would not be if it did not lead to the end, which is morally good actions.

Suppose, then, that the voluntarist ideal is revised to take account of the difficulties I have so far discussed. It is, then, an ideal no longer for all good lives, but only for one that appeals to fortunate and well-educated people in affluent, pluralistic societies. It is no longer an essential condition of morality in the domain of moral necessity, and whether it is that in the domain of moral possibility is an open question. Nor is it an essential condition of responsibility, but only an important means to it. The acceptance of these qualifications makes the voluntarist ideal much more defensible without detracting from its attractiveness. It is, after all, no small thing to know what people in fortunate circumstances can do to live a responsible and fulfilling life. The attractiveness of such a life is not lessened by the recognition that there must be limits within which it must be lived and that good lives may take other forms. If this were the end of the matter, there would be no need to continue with this book, but we cannot stop because the revised version of the ideal still faces a serious problem.

1.4 The Problem of Moral Obtuseness

This problem leads to my central theme, so I consider an illustrative example in some detail. The example is John Stuart Mill's portrait of Jeremy Bentham, whom he had known well. Mill writes of Bentham: with

> many of the most natural and strongest feelings of human nature he had no sympathy; from many of its graver experiences he was altogether cut off; and the faculty by which one mind understands a mind different from itself, and throws itself into the feelings of that mind, was denied him by his deficiency of imagination. . . . By these limits, accordingly, Bentham's knowledge of human nature is bounded. It is wholly empirical, and the empiricism of one who has had little experience. He had neither internal experience nor external; the quiet, even tenor of his life, and his healthiness of mind, conspired to exclude him from both. He never knew prosperity and adversity, passion nor satiety: he never had even experiences which sickness gives: he lived from childhood to the age of eighty-five in boyish health. He knew no dejection, no heaviness of heart. He never felt life a sore and a weary burthen. He was a boy to the last. . . . How much of human nature slumbered in him he knew not, neither can we know. He had never been made alive to the unseen influences which were acting on himself, nor, consequently, on his fellow-creatures. Other ages and other nations were a blank to him for purposes of instruction. He measured them by one standard—their knowledge of facts, and their capability to take correct views of utility, and merge all other objects in it. . . . He saw accordingly, in man, little but what the vulgarest eye can see; recognized no diversities of character. . . . Knowing so little of human feelings, he knew still less of the influences by which those feelings are formed; all the more subtle workings both of the mind upon itself, and of external things upon the mind, escaped him; and no one, probably, who . . . ever attempted to give a rule to all human conduct, set out with a more limited conception either of the agencies by which human conduct *is*, or of those by which it *should* be influenced.[8]

We may say, then, that Bentham was morally obtuse, but we cannot say that he was not a reflective self-evaluator. He certainly formed a second-order volition that showed, as Frankfurt says it should, a "fundamental pre-occupation with human existence—namely, *what to care about . . .* what is *important* or, rather, what is *important to us.*"[9] He was a free and responsible agent because, as Hampshire says, such an agent must act "with a definite and clearly formed intention" and his "achievements . . . [must] directly correspond to his intention."[10]

Bentham had a clear ideal of a good life (maximizing utility), he consistently and deliberately lived according to it ("having been accustomed to keep before his mind's eye the happiness of mankind"[11]), from his ideal he derived a standard (utility), and he evaluated by it not just his own desires and actions but everyone else's as well ("he measured them by one standard . . . utility"[12]). Bentham, then, qualifies as a reflective self-evaluator, given the conditions specified by Frankfurt and Hampshire. But no reasonable person can deny that Bentham's life was impoverished because he was morally obtuse about the possibilities of life other than the simple-minded pursuit of utility. If reflective self-evaluation is a reasonable ideal of a good life, it must exclude the kind of obtuseness that Bentham's life illustrates; it must include as a condition of a good life having a lively appreciation of an adequate range of possibilities that might make a life good.

Bentham did not have that. As Mill writes, he "had a phrase expressive of the view he took of all moral speculations . . . not founded on a recognition of utility as the moral standard: this phrase was 'vague generalities.' Whatever presented itself to him in such a shape he dismissed as unworthy of notice, or . . . as absurd. He did not heed, or rather the nature of his mind prevented it from occurring to him, that these generalities contained the whole unanalyzed experience of the human race."[13] Bentham was morally obtuse about the possibilities embedded in the "experience of the human race" because he lacked the appropriate kind of imagination. "The imagination, which he had not, was that . . . which enables us, by a voluntary effort, to conceive the absent as if it were present . . . and to clothe it in feelings, which, if it were indeed real, it would bring along with it. This is the power by which one human being enters the mind and circumstances of another. . . . Without it, nobody knows even his own nature, further than circumstances have actually tried it, and called it out; nor the nature of his fellow-creatures, beyond such generalizations as he may have been enabled to make from his observation of their outward conduct."[14]

It might be said in response to Mill's criticism of Bentham, and to my endorsement of it, that if a life is good because it is responsible and fulfilling, then Bentham's life was good. His reflective self-evaluation *was* impoverished because his lack of imagination *did* make him obtuse about the possibilities of life, but he found his life fulfilling, and he was a decent, if narrow, man. It is unreasonable to want more of a good life. Now this may be true in Bentham's case, but if our interest is not in Bentham but in the conditions of a good life in general, then it is reasonable to want more. This becomes apparent if we notice that Bentham was exceptionally lucky. He lived in a stable, peaceful, law-abiding society; his financial circumstances were adequate to his way of life; his health was excellent; he was able to do most of his life just what he wanted; he had great self-confidence; he worked steadily and hard at the task he set for himself, a task that interested him deeply; he was satisfied with his achievements; and he had friends and disciples who sought his company and advice. Very few people are as lucky as he was. Most people have to face misfortune, crises, adversity, failure, grief, self-doubt, betrayal, injustice, and so on. Their lives can be good only if they respond reasonably to such challenges. They can do so, however, only if they are aware of the possible responses open to them, and for that they need what Bentham neither had nor needed: imagination. If Bentham's life was good, it was because he had no need of the imagination he lacked. No reasonable account of a good life can count on such luck. Thus a good life requires more than just being a reflective self-evaluator: it requires being good enough at it to be aware of at least some of the possibilities open to one.

1.5 The Balanced Ideal

If the voluntarist ideal of reflective self-evaluation is revised in the ways I have argued it should be, it remains an ideal, but a much less ambitious one than it would appear from what Frankfurt and Hampshire say about it. First, in its revised form, reflective evaluation is an essential condition not of all good lives but only of the form that well-educated, analytical people in affluent pluralistic societies might adopt. Second, it is neither a necessary nor a sufficient condition of conduct in the domain of moral necessity. For moral necessity concerns the protection of the minimum conditions of all good lives regardless whether conformity or violation of these conditions is the result of reflective self-evaluation. The appropriate context of reflective self-evaluation is the domain of moral possibility, in which, after the minimum conditions have been secured, individuals can endeavor to realize some of the available possibilities. Third, reflective self-evaluation must also be seen as considerably less important for responsibility than it has been supposed, for responsibility depends primarily on what people do rather than on the psychological activities that lead them to do it. The moral importance these psychological activities undoubtedly have derives from how the actions to which they tend to lead affect others, not the other way around as Frankfurt and Hampshire appear to have implied. And fourth, in the normal course of events, it is not enough to be a mere reflective self-evaluator. A good life requires reflective self-evaluators to use their imagination; otherwise, they are doomed to remain unaware of possible ways in which they might cope with the adversities they are all too likely to have to face.

I do not think these revisions are contrary to the voluntarist ideal, but their acceptance requires the recognition that the revised ideal has considerably more limited scope than Frankfurt and Hampshire have supposed. Nevertheless, even if the revised ideal is not the key to all good lives, it is the key to the form that many people in our age and society recognize as their own. That, I believe, makes it sufficiently important. For reasons that will emerge only gradually, I call the revised ideal of reflective self-evaluation *the balanced ideal.*

What, then, is this balanced ideal? It is that individuals should increase the control they have over their lives and use their increased control to approximate more closely than they otherwise could their conception of a good life. It is the ideal that motivates individuals to try to overcome their dissatisfactions created by the contingent conditions of their genetic inheritance and upbringing, the political, cultural, and economic state of their society, and the private misfortunes, frustrations, and adversities they have encountered in their lives. It is the ideal of not resigning themselves to the dissatisfactions, of trying to change their contingent conditions, insofar as they can be changed, or of coping with them better than they have been doing, and of guiding both the attempted changes and improved coping by the conception of a life they suppose to be good.

This initial sketch of the balanced ideal needs to be qualified, however, to guard against attributing greater clarity to individuals than they are likely to have, especially at the stage of their development when they are beginning to be reflective about their lives. Some dissatisfactions are like toothaches, easy to identify and localize. But others are more like the memory of an oppressive dream that lingers on during waking hours. Feeling bored, listless, ignorant, fearful, inadequate, and so on are dissatisfactions much harder to be clear and articulate about. Nor is clarity about what they would regard as a good life the usual state of most people. It is easy to say that more money, a better job, more understanding friends, or a larger house would be an improvement. But this does not remove the unclarity of what would make an improved life meaningful, interesting, or fulfilling, not in its details but overall. Without clarity about their dissatisfactions and goals people cannot know where the shoe pinches or where they would go in well-fitting shoes. Part of the description of the balanced ideal must include, therefore, the endeavor to achieve greater clarity both about the nature and sources of the dissatisfactions of one's life and about the life that would be free from serious dissatisfactions and fulfilling.

One central thesis I aim to defend is that the work of moral imagination is essential to the achievement of such clarity. This is not a new idea. Bernard Williams, for instance, writing about reasons for action, says that "reflection may lead an agent to see that . . . he has in fact no reason to do something he thought he had reason to do. More subtly, he may think he has reason to promote some development because he has not exercised his imagination enough about what it would be like if it came about. . . . He may have come to have some more concrete sense of what would be involved, and lose desire for it, just as, positively, the imagination can create new possibilities and new desires."[15] He goes on to say that "practical reasoning is a heuristic process, and an imaginative one."[16] John McDowell also stresses the centrality of imagination in practical reason, although without using the word itself: "In moral upbringing what one learns is not to behave in conformity with rules of conduct, but to see situations in a special light, as constituting reasons for acting; the perceptual capacity, once acquired, can be exercised in complex novel circumstances, not necessarily capable of being foreseen and legislated for by a codifier of the conduct required by virtue."[17] Neither Williams, nor McDowell, nor, as far as I know, anyone else has shown how the imagination could do its work in these ways and by means of what processes it could provide reasons for action. This is what I aim to do in the chapters that follow. My thesis is that it is by imagining the possibilities that might overcome their dissatisfactions and the possibilities that might make their lives more fulfilling that individuals can come to understand the true nature of their dissatisfactions and arrive at a conception of a good life. The work of the imagination is thus the enlargement of life by the enlargement of its possibilities.

1.6 Imagination

The numerous attempts to account for the nature of imagination may be divided roughly into two classes, depending on how they conceive of the relation between perception and imagination. According to one, imagination relies on material supplied by perception. It reproduces what has been previously perceived by forming mental images that either copy the original or reassemble elements of the original in new configurations. The emerging account is that in one way or the other imagination is reproductive. According to the second account, imagination not only reproduces but also creates genuinely new ways of looking at the world. This gives rise to the account of imagination as the key to creativity. Empiricists by and large favor the first account; idealists and their romantic followers tend to favor the second.[18]

Both agree that imagination involves forming mental images, like the face of an absent friend; inventing new possibilities, such as models that explain previously problematic aspects of the world; and mistaking for real what is not, as in taking a shadow to be a ghost. Empiricists think that unless invention is rooted in perception, it is fantasy, whereas idealists and romantics think that genuine creativity involves invention that goes beyond perception. The history of thought about imagination is the history of conflicts between these two views.

These conflicts bear on moral imagination primarily by the odd fact that the opposing parties are alike in failing to recognize imaginative processes—of which moral imagination is one—that cannot be assimilated to image formation, invention, or delusion. A case in point is Peter Strawson, whose work on imagination is rightly respected. He distinguishes between the three usual areas of imagination: one "is linked with *image . . .* understood as *mental image*—a picture in the mind's eye"; a second "is associated with invention, and also (sometimes) with originality or insight or felicitous . . . departure from routine"; and a third "is linked with false belief, delusion, mistaken memory, or misperception."[19] The oddity is that Strawson also says in the same volume, "Men make for themselves pictures of ideal forms of life. Such pictures are various and may be in sharp opposition to each other, and one and the same individual may be captivated by different and sharply conflicting pictures at different times."[20] But the "pictures of ideal forms of life" that according to Strawson "men make for themselves" cannot be assimilated to any of the three areas of imagination he distinguishes, and yet he is quite clear that people "identify themselves imaginatively" with the pictures they make of ideal forms of life.

Consider a lawyer in his mid-thirties with a decent income and not unhappy family life. He is bored with what he sees as his humdrum existence and dissatisfied with the political conditions of his society. He is, therefore, seriously thinking about giving up his law practice and entering politics. This is not a new thought for him because he had been politically active during his college days and intended to pursue a career in politics. His present thoughts, then, go in two directions: toward the past, trying to understand why he had opted for law rather than politics, and toward the future, trying to understand what it would be like to live the life of a politician who can actually influence the state of his society. He needs to draw on his imagination to achieve the understanding he seeks.

To understand what it would be like to be a politician, he has to do more than just watch one or more in action, read biographies or memoirs, or get to know and talk about the life with an actual specimen. He has to understand what it feels like to be frequently in the public eye, to be responsive to constituents, to participate in the bargains, negotiations, and compromises that constitute daily life in politics. He has to re-create the various ways of balancing the often conflicting claims of fidelity to party, acting on principle, getting reelected, gaining power and influence, agreeing to prudent compromises, and so forth. He has to imagine how a life filled with these activities feels, what the struggle with resolving conflicts among them is like, and what effect it has on the self-respect of a successful politician to compromise on important matters. But it is crucial to realize that he has to do even more: he has to imagine what it would be like *for him* to engage in these activities, how *he* would be likely to feel about them and about *his life* if it was thus occupied. He also has to think about how the changes in his life are likely to affect his wife and children and the relationship between them and himself. And then he has to compare the satisfactions and frustrations this life might yield with those of his present life. Suppose he succeeds in this imaginative endeavor.

Difficult as that is, he has to do still more. He has to understand also his past preference for law over politics. If he finds politics more attractive now, why did he not find it so then? Why did he decide then as he did? To answer these questions, he has to re-create his past frame of mind as it was when he made the decision. Once again, mere knowledge of the facts will not give him what he wants. For essential to the frame of mind that led to his decision was how he felt about the facts and their respective importance, why he attributed the weight he did to the considerations he took into account. Say that he imaginatively re-creates his past frame of mind and arrives at the correct understanding that he opted as he did because, although he cared much about politics, he cared even more about having an orderly, secure, comfortable life. Law was more likely to give him that than politics, and that is why he opted for it. He may also come to understand that what he wanted most was the result of the uncertainties of an unhappy childhood caused by undependable parents whose existence lurched from one crisis to another. This enables him to see in the present that although he had reasons in the past to opt for security, it has become too much of a good thing. Security is fine, he now thinks, but a surfeit of it leads to boredom. Assume, then, that the lawyer puts together his well-earned imaginative understanding both of what it would be like to pursue the ideal of political life and of why he did not pursue it earlier. He then decides to leave law for politics.

The process by which the lawyer has arrived at his decision is a concrete illustration of the balanced ideal of reflective self-evaluation. A great deal remains to be said about this process—that is what this book is about—but what needs to be said immediately is that moral imagination is essential to it, although it is a process that does not fall into any one of the three areas into which imagination is customarily divided. The process need not be "linked with false belief, delusion, mistaken memory, or misperception," for it can result in genuine understanding, and although it may fail, it can also succeed, which false beliefs, delusions, and so forth cannot do. Nor is the process "associated with invention, and also (sometimes) with originality or insight," for the understanding is of the past as it was and of the true nature of a possible form of life as it might really be. Neither the past nor the form of life is invented. Each exists, and understanding either is a matter not of inventing what is not there but of feeling one's way into what is there. And the process need not be "linked with *image* . . . understood as *mental image*," because the feelings, the weighing of alternatives, and the struggles with conflicts that are understood if the process is successful are not the sorts of experiences of which mental images are normally formed.[21] It is not possible to imagine the face of an absent friend without forming a mental image of it, but it would be unusual to imagine being bored, undecided about alternative careers, or conflicted about incompatible obligations by forming a mental image. What would the image picture? As Hide Ishiguro says close to the end of her fine essay on imagination: "The fact that I picture something does not entail that I see a mental picture of the thing."[22]

The visual metaphors that permeate the language of imagination are just metaphors; they need convey no more than the understanding of what it would be like to have the imagined experiences. Moral imagination, therefore, should be recognized as a discrete area of imagination. It is perhaps because it does not fall into any of the three customarily recognized areas that the attention it has received is minute compared with the attention paid to the others.

The aim of moral imagination, then, is to understand what it would be like to live according to some ideal form of life. The description of this aim must be refined, however, because there need be nothing specifically moral in the imaginative effort to achieve the intended understanding. The next chapter is about the moral component of this imaginative effort.

CHAPTER 2

Moral Imagination

The region of the ethical, then, is a region of diverse, certainly
incompatible and possibly practically conflicting ideal images or
pictures of a human life. . . . It is a region in which many such
incompatible pictures may secure at least the imaginative . . .
allegiance of a single person. . . . Any diminution in this variety
would impoverish the human scene. The multiplicity of
conflicting pictures is itself the essential element in one of one's
picture of man.

—PETER F. STRAWSON, "Social Morality and Individual Ideal"

2.1 Characteristics

Imaginative understanding of the ideal pictures of human life
held by an individual or a society may be sought by a biographer, an an-
thropologist, a novelist, a historian, and so forth. They may want to understand in order to describe and make comprehensible someone's life and
actions, without making moral judgments about them. They may just want
to know what it would be like for someone to live by a certain ideal, but the
ideal may leave them cold or they may even find it morally deplorable.
Their moral attitude to the ideal is irrelevant to this kind of understanding
of it. But if their imaginative effort is *moral*, then their moral attitude to the
ideal is pivotal. They use their imagination in order to understand whether
the ideal is morally good or bad, or morally better or worse than another
ideal. And the ideal, it must be remembered, is of a form of life, of a way of
living and acting.

Moral imagination, understood in this way, is employed for moral purposes, but there are different moral purposes. One is to decide whether
another person, living according to some ideal, is trustworthy, culpable,

19

indoctrinated, inconsistent, admirable, or whatever. But our present concern is with the employment of moral imagination in reflective *self* evaluation. Its purpose, therefore, is the evaluation of some ideal of a good life from the point of view of those who are doing the evaluation. They would say: the aim of my evaluation is to understand what it would be like *for me*, not for anyone else, to live according to it. So the moral imagination that concerns us is *agent-centered*.

Agent-centered moral imagination may help one decide whether one would find living in a certain way good, regardless of whether others would find it the same, or whether living that way would be good for one because it would be good in general. These aims overlap, but they pull in opposite directions: the first is personal, the second impersonal. There are many ideals of a good life; people's characters, desires, and circumstances differ; consequently, an ideal that would be good to pursue for one person may not be good for another. But there are also impersonal moral requirements to which all ideals of a good life should conform, although these are minimum requirements, and ideals contain much more than the morally necessary minimum. Personal differences arise beyond the minimum requirements.

One way of expressing the difference between these two aims is in terms of the distinction drawn (in 1.3) between the contexts of moral necessity and possibility. The impersonal aim of moral imagination is pursued in the context of moral necessity, its personal aim in the context of moral possibility. In the first, ideals of good life are evaluated on the basis of universal moral requirements. In the second, they are evaluated as moral possibilities that individuals may or may not adopt as their own. Consequentialists and deontologists are typically concerned with evaluations in the first context. John Stuart Mill says, "There ought to be some fundamental principle or law at the root of all morality, or, if there be several, there should be a determinate order of preference among them; and the one principle, or the rule for deciding between the various principles when they conflict, ought to be self-evident."[1] And then he sets out to provide the principle. Kant agrees that this is the requirement, although of course not with Mill's way of meeting it: "The sole aim of the present *Groundwork* is to seek out and establish *the supreme principle of morality*. . . . Morals themselves remain exposed to corruption of all sorts as long as this guiding thread is lacking, this ultimate norm for correct moral judgment."[2] The rest of his book is devoted to stating and defending the principle.

Eudaimonists, by contrast, are concerned with the second context. As Aristotle puts it: "The purpose of our examination is not to know what virtue is, but to become good, since otherwise the inquiry would be of no benefit to us."[3] The moral imagination involved in reflective self-evaluation is eudaimonistic: individuals deliberate about possible ideals of life in order to understand whether it would be good for them personally to live according to any of these ideals. Thus we may say that the relevant kind of imagination occurs in the context of moral possibility, and it is agent-centered and deliberative.

The typical situation of those who deliberate in this context is that they are dissatisfied with their lives because their desires—understood broadly to include needs, preferences, and interests—are not met, and they have to decide which, if any, of several possible ideals of good life they should make their own in order to remove their dissatisfaction. It is crucial to understanding this kind of deliberation to bear three things in mind.

First, the imaginative understanding of a particular ideal is not merely the forward-looking one that involves exploring what it would be like for oneself to live according to the ideal in the future. People must also consider whether living according to it would better meet their desires than past or future alternatives to it. The answer requires understanding not only the ideal but also one's desires and one's estimate of their respective importance. The only way to acquire this is to look backward and imaginatively reconstruct past situations in which one has made important choices about available possibilities, and then endeavor to discover what motivated these choices. This backward-looking process cannot be just a matter of remembering the relevant facts. One must re-create how one felt about the facts, why it was that some considerations seemed to have great and others small importance, what reasons one had for the choices, and why some reasons seemed weightier than others.

There are strong reasons for making this backward-looking imaginative effort. One is that people and circumstances change and their desires may no longer be what they were. Their past choices may have satisfied them as they were then, but now they are different and what has satisfied them in the past no longer does. But to know whether this is so, they have to understand both their past and present desires; only then can they see whether their present dissatisfactions are the results of having changed. The other reason is that their present dissatisfactions may be the fruits of mistaken choices they have made in the past. Their desires have not changed, but their true nature was obscured from them by self-deception, fear, stress, indoctrination, or some other obstacle to seeing themselves as they were. If they imaginatively re-create their past frame of mind, they can perhaps understand what led their choices astray, and then they may be able to remove their present dissatisfactions by making new choices that avoid past mistakes. Moral imagination directed backward is needed, then, to guard against making mistakes in the present.[4]

The second consideration that must be borne in mind in order to understand agent-centered deliberation in typical situations concerns the forward-looking process of imagination. What usually happens is not that there is one available ideal and the imaginative task is to decide whether living according to it would be an improvement over one's present form of life. The usual situation of people living in affluent societies and civilized circumstances is to be aware of a plurality of ideals, and their task is to decide whether the adoption of one of them would be likely to lead to a life in which their present dissatisfactions would be mitigated and their desires better met. They need moral imagination, then, not just to say yes or no to a possibility, but to compare and evaluate a plurality of possibilities.

The lawyer in the earlier illustration (in 1.6) got to the point of having to choose between a continued life in law or a new life in politics only after he rejected—even if without much reflection—numerous other possibilities, such as, let us say, training for the priesthood, becoming a farmer, having a sex-change operation, working for the CIA, making himself from an amateur into a professional alto saxophonist, and so on. Now one question that reflective self-evaluators need to consider is which of the available possibilities they should take seriously, not just as a theoretical possibility but as a real practical possibility for them. And to answer that question, their moral imagination must once again be employed in two directions: toward the future, to form some initial notion of what it would be like to live according to the possibilities, and toward the past, to decide whether it would be realistic for them even to consider living that way, given their understanding of their own desires.

Let us suppose that as a result of this bidirectional imaginative process the field of possibilities is successfully narrowed to those that are correctly taken to represent possible ways of satisfying one's desires. This is by no means the end of the process because the remaining possibilities are still numerous and incompatible with one another. The decision to live according to one of them has the unavoidable consequence of not living according to the unchosen ones. But if the narrowing of the field was indeed done correctly, then, since each of the remaining possibilities would satisfy some of one's desires, the choice of one possibility over the rest means that the desires that would have been satisfied by the unchosen ones will have been doomed to remain unmet. Thus the choice of a possible ideal of life routinely involves frustration and loss. The cost of saying yes to a satisfying way of life is having to say no to others. And saying no to them is to disfavor parts of oneself that would have been favored if one had decided differently.

Making such decisions well, therefore, involves imagining not merely what it would be like to live according to an ideal, but also what it would be like to live with the frustration of some of one's genuine desires. Living a good—responsible and fulfilling—life is thus not just a matter of finding out what one wants and then doing what one can within moral limits to get it. It inevitably involves denial of part of oneself. Having a close marriage excludes carefree love affairs; a life in politics diminishes privacy; the love of comfort and security is incompatible with adventure and risk-taking.

By deciding what satisfactions to seek and what frustrations to accept, we impose a hierarchy of importance on our desires. And by living and acting in a way that reflects this hierarchy, we make ourselves into the kind of person we decided we should be. When living and acting this way become habitual—our deliberately formed second nature—we have arrived at the possession of a settled character. If the hierarchy reflects the true nature of our desires, if the ideal of a good life we have adopted does indeed provide the hoped-for satisfactions, and if our actions conform to moral limits, then we have succeeded in living a responsible and fulfilling life. The importance of moral imagination is that it makes the achievement of such a life possible.

The third consideration crucial to understanding the agent-centered deliberation in moral imagination is its psychological complexity. It has essential cognitive, emotive, and volitional components, in addition to the what-it-would-be-like form of imaginative one. The neglect of any one of them leads to a misleading view of the process. The cognitive component includes the beliefs the agents hold about their past and future possibilities and about the desires and dissatisfactions that motivate them. These beliefs may be reasonable or unreasonable, and even if reasonable, they may still be true or false. I will say more about the cognitive status of these beliefs in the next section. I should, however, stress now that although good lives depend on holding reasonable beliefs, the beliefs actually held are particularly prone to falsification. People want to think well of themselves, nurture hope about their future, and be optimistic about their prospects. This gives great scope to fantasy, self-deception, and the misinterpretation of recognized facts by focusing on their pleasant aspects and ignoring the unpleasant ones. As Iris Murdoch has again and again observed, "The human mind is naturally and largely given to fantasy. Vanity (a prime human motive) is composed of fantasy. Neurotic or vengeful fantasies, erotic fantasies, delusions of grandeur, dreams of power, can imprison the mind, impeding new understanding, new interests and affections, possibilities of fruitful and virtuous action."[5]

The beliefs involved in moral imagination have objects about which people tend to have strong feelings. For us, our ideals of a good life, the desires that motivate us to live one way or another, the frustrations and satisfactions of our way of life, our picture of ourselves and of how we would like to or ought to be are significant objects. They make us feel proud or ashamed, hopeful or hopeless, joyous or depressed, inspired or insipid; they affect our self-esteem and strengthen or weaken our self-respect. Such feelings form the emotional climate of our inner life, color our attitudes, make us wholehearted, cynical, ironic, detached, purposeful, or indifferent. Charles Taylor rightly says that "feeling is our mode of access to this entire domain of subject-referring imports, of what matters to us *qua* subjects. . . . It is only through feelings that we are capable of grasping imports of this range at all. . . . This is a domain to which there is no dispassionate access."[6] To lack feelings about what is significant in our lives is a sign of pathology. And to lack feelings because there is nothing we find significant in our lives is another way of describing lives made bad by lacking even the possibility of fulfillment.

If people believe that their important desires are best satisfied by living according to a particular ideal of a good life, and if their feelings are elicited by the motivational force of the desires they regard as important and by the attractions of their ideal of a good life, then their will naturally leads them to act so as to seek the satisfactions and pursue the ideal. Agent-centered deliberation, therefore, also has an action-guiding volitional component, even if what the will on occasion prompts is to refrain from actions that would lead to the satisfaction of the wrong desires. People want to express the results of their agent-centered deliberations in corresponding actions, but of course they may be prevented from doing so by morality, prudence, practical difficulties, or hostile interference. In the absence of self-imposed or external obstacles, however, it is normal and expected for people to act in order to pursue what they believe and feel is important in their lives.[7]

We may conclude this account of the characteristics of moral imagination and the agent-centered deliberation essentially involved in it by saying that it is individuals as reflective self-evaluators whose moral imagination makes the achievement of a good life possible. But it is essential to bear in mind that the mere possibility of its achievement falls far short of guaranteeing it because moral imagination is all too likely to go wrong. We need now to understand how it might go wrong and how that might be avoided.

2.2 Possibilities and Limits

The possibilities in question are, of course, ideals of a good life. I will consider them from the point of view of individuals who live, as we all do, in a particular society at a particular time. The ideals available to them, in their social context, constitute only a fraction of the known ideals. For ideals presuppose moral, political, cultural, economic, technological, and commercial conditions among others. These conditions vary with contexts. Homeric heroes, Confucian gentlemen, and medieval knights may be thought to represent admirable ideals, but the conditions needed for pursuing them do not exist in contemporary Western societies. I will say that the ideals available to individuals, given that suitable conditions prevail in a particular context, are their *social possibilities*.

The ideals individuals can reasonably pursue, however, are not all the socially possible ones because their reasonable pursuit depends also on the individuals' possession of suitable character traits. The clumsy cannot succeed as surgeons, the tone-deaf as musicians, the blunt as diplomats, and those who dislike children as schoolteachers. The lack of qualifications required for the successful pursuit of any particular ideal makes the ideal unattainable. Ideals for whose pursuit individuals possess the necessary qualifications are, I will say, their *personal possibilities*. Social possibilities thus depend on social conditions, personal possibilities on psychological conditions.

The ideals about which individuals may deliberate, however, are normally neither their social nor their personal possibilities but those that individuals recognize as available to them. It is most unlikely that anyone would have sufficient breadth of understanding to recognize all the ideals of a good life socially possible in a particular context. If in doubt, consider the difficulty of drawing up a complete list of socially possible ideals in our society. Who could know and how could we tell whether the list was indeed complete? It is similarly unlikely that individuals would recognize all and only ideals that are personal possibilities for them. If they were perfectly reasonable in their beliefs about their character traits and in the appropriateness of their feelings about various ideals, they would recognize only ideals that were personal possibilities for them. But who is perfectly reasonable? We are all given to inflating or doubting our talents, skills, and capacities. Our feelings tend to be colored by irrelevant considerations and apt to be stronger or weaker than what is appropriate to the ideal that is their object. And even if individuals recognized *only* personally possible ideals, who could ever know whether they recognized *all* of them? Individuals, therefore, deliberate only about ideals of a good life that are, I will say, *recognized possibilities* for them, and these possibilities are very unlikely to coincide with all and only their social and personal possibilities.

The deliberations of individuals take the form of forward-looking moral imagination by means of which they explore what it would be like for them to live in conformity to their recognized possibilities. If all goes well, they then adopt the most appealing and promising candidate for a good life. Moral imagination employed in this way, however, easily and frequently goes wrong because individuals mistakenly recognize possibilities that are socially or personally impossible for them, and because they fail to recognize all their social or personal possibilities. In the first mistake, they fail to see the limits social and psychological conditions impose on them. In the second mistake, they fail to see that what they take to be social or personal limits are in fact not limits at all. They go astray because they imagine that their possibilities are richer or poorer than they in fact are.

In order to correct such mistakes, they need to use their moral imagination also to look backward and try to re-create their past frame of mind that has led to their unrealistically inflated or deflated view of the possibilities they have recognized. By this means they can endeavor to understand which of their psychological propensities has led them not to see a limit that was there or to see a limit that was not there. The simplest case of not seeing a personal limit is to have an exaggerated estimate of one's talents, skills, or capacities, to suppose that one could do or do well what in fact one could not do at all or do only badly. Many are the dilettantes who take themselves to be professionals. A bit more complicated are cases in which passionate attachment to an ideal blinds one to the changing conditions and limits that render the ideal anachronistic. The old-time religion in which thrift was a virtue and premarital sex a vice must accommodate itself to new economic conditions that reward investment, not saving, and to the great changes in social mores brought about by effective contraception. Analogously, laziness or fear of failure may lead one to see a personal limit although it does not exist. It is easier to believe that one cannot do something than to make the strenuous effort required to do it or to damage one's self-esteem by trying and failing. And people are often led to accept as political or moral limits what are in fact arbitrary restrictions because they have been indoctrinated or cowed by some prevailing orthodoxy.

The work of moral imagination is to increase the control individuals have by enlarging their understanding of the possible ways in which their lives might be made good or better. The enlargement increases their breadth by increasing the number of possibilities they recognize, and it increases their depth by understanding the psychological obstacles that prevent them from seeing their possibilities as they are. The enlargement thus moves them toward greater realism about their social and psychological conditions. It is movement toward a broader and deeper appreciation of the truths that bear on their efforts to live a good life. And since the movement is made possible by moral imagination, it is important to break with the misleading historical view according to which imagination leads one away from the truth in a direction opposite to realism.

Although the benefits of moral imagination are considerable, there are internal forces inhibiting its use. Its backward-looking corrective use—focusing on individuals' self-imposed psychological obstacles to forming a true view of their talents, skills, and capacities—goes against the grain. For the obstacles are created by their fears, suspected weaknesses, desire for comfort, or reluctance to change, and they are often powerful enough to inhibit moral imagination, which would move them to correct their mistaken view of the recognized possibilities of life. The forward-looking exploratory use of moral imagination—individuals testing their view of social possibilities and limits—is also subversive because it tends to pit them against the prevailing consensus in their society. It is always unpopular and difficult, and often dangerous, to question the accepted limits on what can be done because it challenges widely accepted moral, political, and cultural conventions. And to question ideals of a good life that are regarded as possible in one's context is to incur the hostility of those who are trying to live according to them.

Reasonable people, however, would nevertheless use their moral imagination even in the face of such internal and external disincentives because of dissatisfaction with their lives. The dissatisfactions arise because their important desires are not met. They have needs, preferences, and interests whose satisfaction they regard as important for a fulfilling life, but some or more of them are not satisfied. They feel frustrated with the way their lives are going, and this provides a strong impetus to discover the source of their frustration. For this they need to consider whether their ideal is socially and personally possible, as well as whether there might not be some other ideal whose pursuit would be likely to satisfy their desires better. They need to consider also whether the source of their dissatisfaction might not be their own psychological propensities rather than faulty ideals. Moral imagination is needed for both these attempts, and that is a good reason for using it even if it leads to the discovery of unpleasant truths about oneself or to alienation from one's society by questioning accepted beliefs about what is and is not a possible good life. Reasonable people thus would use their moral imagination even in the face of disincentives because it is a means to the satisfaction of their desire to live a good life.

These two reasons for the employment of moral imagination will not be reasons for those who are already satisfied with their lives or who have given up trying to make their lives good. The lucky ones in the first group and the unlucky ones in the second, however, constitute only a small minority of those who live in contemporary Western societies. The remaining large majority will have good reason to employ moral imagination, and if they do not, it is because they are insufficiently reasonable.

2.3 Reason and the Voluntarist Ideal

I have been arguing that reason favors the use of moral imagination for exploring the possibilities of a good life and correcting mistakes about social, personal, and recognized limits. It should be added, as a reminder, that the possibilities and limits are in the context of moral possibility and the minimum requirements of morality are assumed to have been met in the context of moral necessity. Reason favors limiting moral imagination to the exploration of possibilities that exist within correctly recognized limits. It thus favors some uses of moral imagination and opposes others. My view is that reason guides moral imagination not by doing its work but by correcting its mistakes and identifying the limits within which its work must be done. This view, however, is opposed—in very different ways—by Frankfurt, Hampshire, and Murdoch, who nevertheless agree with me and with each other about the importance of moral imagination. Frankfurt and Hampshire think that reason is a competitor of moral imagination, not its guide. And Murdoch thinks that genuine moral imagination needs no guide. By explaining why their views are mistaken, I hope to explain further the nature of moral imagination.

Frankfurt says that the "totality of the various things that a person cares about—together with his ordering of how important to him they are—effectively specifies his answer to the question of how to live. Now suppose that he . . . becomes concerned about whether he really should care about the things that, as a matter of fact, he does care about. . . . In raising this question . . . he is asking whether there are reasons good enough to justify him in living that way, and whether there may not be better reasons for him to live in some other way instead."[8] And he says that "efforts to conduct rational inquiry into . . . [this] will inevitably be defeated." The reason Frankfurt gives for this striking claim that dismisses twenty-five centuries of moral thought is that any reason that might be given for a way of life being preferable to another presupposes the preferred way of life. All such reasons, therefore, are circular. Frankfurt denies that it is possible to adduce reasons for or against ways of life that do not presuppose some particular way of life. This is so because one's preferred way of life provides what one recognizes as reasons. According to Frankfurt's version of the voluntarist ideal, then, what we must do to live a good life is to find out what we really care about and then live that way.

Hampshire reaches the same conclusion by following a different route. He says that it is just a prejudice to suppose that the imagination must always be subordinated to the intellect. He thinks that neither should be systematically subordinated to the other.[9] In the contexts of argument, logic, mathematics, and calculation the intellect should dominate, but in what I have called the context of moral possibility our imaginative power should dominate because "we know that we in fact have essential divisions within us as persons and that we experience moral conflicts arising from them. A person hesitates between two contrasting ways of life, and sets of virtues, and he has to make a very definite, and even final, determination between them. . . . We have both to perceive and imagine the . . . actual ways of life . . . and to confront the concrete decisions which force a determination between them."[10]

The assumption on which the voluntarist ideal of Frankfurt and Hampshire rests is that reason is one psychological power; care, will, and imagination are others; and any one of them may come into conflict with reason. There is no way of resolving these conflicts without begging the question at issue, namely, whether one should be guided by reason or by care, will, or imagination. In arguing this way Frankfurt and Hampshire presuppose a particular view of reason. According to this view, reasoning is a psychological power alongside caring, willing, and imagining.

Reason, however, can be thought of in a quite different way: as a method by which the reliability of decisions about how to live and act can be tested. Reason, then, is thought of not as a psychological power but as a method for increasing the likelihood of successful action. Reason as a method does not compete with care, will, or imagination but helps to make them more likely to succeed in making one's life better. And it is, of course, the second—methodological—sense of reason I have in mind in claiming that reason should guide moral imagination. I agree with Frankfurt that finding out what we really care about is essential to living a good life. I also agree with Hampshire that the attempt by crude utilitarians and game theorists to settle questions about how one should live and act by even the most sophisticated mathematical calculation is a doomed enterprise. But I do not agree with the narrow view that identifies reason with a psychological power and takes that power to be one of calculation. The decisions prompted by care, will, or imagination should not be accepted uncritically. We should ask about them whether they would indeed lead to the satisfaction of our most important desires, whether those desires ought to be satisfied, whether all the relevant facts have been taken into account, whether it is practically feasible in the prevailing circumstances to act on the decisions, and whether there are reasons against acting on them. In normal circumstances, barring emergencies, we should not act on the decisions until these questions have been answered. But asking the questions and finding the right answers to them are done by following the method of reason. The importance of care, will, or imagination is not lessened by insisting on the importance of following the guidance of reason. I will return to this view of reason again and again, and discuss it more fully in chapter 11.

2.4 Moral Imagination and the Good

Murdoch disagrees because she thinks that if moral imagination is genuine, then it yields a vision of the good that needs no correction. At first glance, this appears to be obviously mistaken. How could it be reasonably denied that moral imagination may go wrong or that imaginative visions of the good may be deluded? But Murdoch does deny it, and she does so on two grounds. One is the "distinction between egoistic *fantasy* and liberated truth-seeking creative *imagination.*" Murdoch thus proposes to call imagination only that which is "freely and creatively exploring the world, moving toward the expression and elucidation . . . of what is true and deep. 'Deep' here involves a sense in which any serious pursuit and expression of truth moves toward fundamental questions. . . . 'Truth' is something we recognize . . . when we are led to a juster, clearer, more detailed, more refined understanding." Fantasy, by contrast, is "mechanical, egoistic, untruthful." So her view is that when imagination is, as it were, locked on the truth, it cannot go wrong or be deluded, and when it goes wrong and is deluded, it is fantasy, not imagination.[11]

If this were all to Murdoch's view of imagination, we would be justified in rejecting it as an attempt at arbitrary verbal legislation couched in overwrought language. It is part of the accepted meaning of "imagination" that it can succeed or fail, be truthful or not. Murdoch is free to stipulate that she will mean by "imagination" only successful examples of what is ordinarily called "imagination" and that she will call unsuccessful examples "fantasy." But once having proposed this ill-advised and confusing change of meaning, she should not go on to *praise* what she calls "imagination" for being true and deep since she refuses to call "imagination" what is not true and deep. In her sense, truth and depth are not achievements of imagination—as they might be achievements of beliefs or insights—but characteristics that imagination has by definition, much as triangles have three sides. But there is more than this to Murdoch's view of imagination. There is an underlying metaphysical view that explains, although fails to justify, her apparently arbitrary pronouncements. It will surprise no one familiar with her work that this metaphysical view is Platonic. It is of the "Good as absolute . . . a pure source, the principle which creatively relates the virtues to each other in our moral lives. . . . The sovereign Good . . . is something which we all experience as a creative force. . . . [The] Good is . . . clearly seen and indubitably discovered in our ordinary unmysterious experience . . . the positive experience of truth . . . which remains with us as a standard or vision, an *orientation*, a *proof* of what is possible and a vista of what might be."[12] Moral imagination, according to Murdoch, is just this clear seeing and indubitable discovering of the true and the Good. And if that were so, it would be understandable why she wants to reserve the word "imagination" for only that which is true and deep, and mean by "fantasy" what is false and shallow. We must ask, however, whether Murdoch has given any reason to accept this metaphysical view.

The answer must surely be that she has not. It is certainly not true that "the Good is . . . clearly seen and indubitably discovered in our ordinary unmysterious experience." The ordinary experience of countless people reveals that their "pictures of ideal forms of life" are "in sharp opposition to each other; and one and the same individual may be captivated by different and sharply conflicting pictures at different times," just as the epigraph to this chapter claims.[13] We get converted and lose our faith; fall in and out of love; get passionately involved with causes and embittered by the corruption of our previous causes; we change our nationality, politics, or profession; our idealism is replaced by cynicism, optimism by pessimism, philanthropy by misanthropy, or vice versa.

Murdoch may acknowledge all these changes, indeed her novels often describe them, and say that they represent stages in our pilgrimage toward the Good. But why should we suppose that the changes are for the better? Why is it a pilgrimage rather than beating a path to Hell? Whichever they are, these commonplaces of moral life render Murdoch's view untenable. If ordinary experience reveals that we are uncertain and conflicted, not that we have a clear and indubitable experience of the Good, then we must acknowledge that we are fallible about what we take to be the Good at any time, and our passionately felt visions of the Good are often mistaken. Even if Murdoch's Platonic metaphysics were true and there were such a thing as the Good, our fallibility would not be alleviated by it. Murdoch must know that reasonable and decent people have held many incompatible visions of the Good with equally great passion and conviction of their truth. The visions of the great religions of the Occident and the Orient are incompatible, as are the visions of great metaphysical systems. Classicists and romantics, theists and humanists, utilitarians and Kantians, perfectionists and pluralists are often intimately familiar with their opponents' vision and yet regard it as false and their own as true.

Visions of the Good do not carry their own warrant, and it is a dangerous mistake to believe otherwise. For the visions are not held only by reasonable and decent people, but also by fanatics, ideologues, terrorists, and religious maniacs. Stalin's Russia, Hitler's Germany, Mao's China, Pol Pot's Cambodia did not lack people with visions of the Good, and it led them to do great evil while being passionately convinced that they were on a pilgrimage to the Good. Human fallibility and depravity make it imperative that visions of the Good be subjected to the test of reason. And that means that they cannot be assumed to be genuine merely because the moral imagination of their adherents is supposed to reveal them clearly, or because they feel passionately about them, or because they believe them very strongly.

In giving these reasons against accepting Murdoch's view of moral imagination, I have not questioned her underlying metaphysical belief in the Good. But it is questionable and it has, of course, been extensively questioned. Those who hold the belief, therefore, must defend it by giving reasons for it and by explaining why the reasons against it are not telling, or they forfeit the right to claim that their belief is reasonable. It must be said, unfortunately, that Murdoch not only fails to give such reasons but denies that they could be given. She says that "the background of morals is properly some sort of mysticism, if by this is meant a non-dogmatic essentially unformulated faith in the reality of the Good. . . . This view is of course not amenable even to a persuasive philosophical proof."[14] She describes her sort of mysticism in impassioned terms that leave no doubt that she is convinced of its deepest importance and truth. But for those, like myself, who do not share her conviction, that is not enough. I must conclude, then, that Murdoch has given no reason in support of her belief; that even if the belief were true, it would not alter the fact that fallibility prevents us from knowing which, if any, of the visions of the Good on offer is the true one; and that our moral imagination of possible good lives must either be guided by reason or remain indistinguishable from fantasy.

My purpose in arguing against the views of Frankfurt, Hampshire, and Murdoch has been to resist their insistence that moral imagination ought to be independent of reason. None of them, of course, is an enemy of reason, but they all want to free the will or the imagination from limits placed on it by reason. I have argued against them that reason understood as a method of successful deliberation, not as the psychological process of calculation, does not inhibit moral imagination but helps it to do its work better. And that moral imagination unguided by reason runs the great danger of mistaking evil for good. No human activity is free from fallibility and corruption, and moral imagination is no exception. The guidance of reason helps—imperfectly—to avoid the mistakes and the pursuit of wrong ideals to which moral imagination lends itself. The sleep of reason brings forth monsters, even if reason awake does not rid the world of them.

2.5 Overview

The balanced ideal of reflective self-evaluation is the connecting link between the enlargement of life and moral imagination. Lives need to be enlarged if people are dissatisfied with them, as most people more or less are because their important desires are frustrated and some of their needs, preferences, or interests are not met. The balanced ideal aims to alleviate these dissatisfactions by means of moral imagination. It is *moral* because it is concerned with good, that is, responsible and fulfilling, lives. And it is a kind of *imagination* because it re-creates one's past frames of mind, including their cognitive, emotive, and volitional elements, and envisages what it would be like to live according to possible ideals of a good life one recognizes as such. It enlarges life by making the possibilities one recognizes coincide ever more closely with one's actual social and personal possibilities. Its work is to make reflective self-evaluation more realistic by correcting its mistakes and forming an accurate view of one's possibilities and limits. It is a personal, agent-centered, psychological activity. It increases people's control over their lives, but it ought to be kept within the limits of reason and morality.

Moral imagination does its work in three ways, which I call corrective, exploratory, and disciplined. As we have already seen, corrective imagination, which is backward-looking, toward one's past, is used first to discover why the possibilities one has recognized were different from the available social and personal possibilities and then to correct one's past mistakes. These mistakes were either to recognize as a possibility what in fact was not or to fail to recognize what in fact was a possibility. The source of these mistakes is some psychological tendency, such as self-deception, fear, or laziness, that leads to a false view of one's possibilities. Understanding and correcting them will make possible a more realistic view of one's present and future possibilities. Corrective imagination, however, being backward-looking, is of no help in forming a more realistic view of future possibilities, and that is its limitation. It can remove obstacles from the way, but it cannot help in deliberating about the possibilities one should adopt if self-imposed falsification no longer obscures one's understanding.

Exploratory imagination aims to form a realistic view of what it would be like to live according to one's recognized possibilities. This view, it should be remembered, includes not merely realistic beliefs about the possibilities, but also a realistic estimate of how one would feel while living that way and what effect living that way would have on one's motivation. Exploratory imagination, therefore, explores both the possibilities and one's likely attitude toward them, where the attitude is psychologically complex, involving cognitive, emotive, and volitional elements. Exploration can easily go wrong because one's uncorrected falsifying tendencies may prevent the forming of a realistic view of one's likely beliefs, feelings, and motives. The success of exploratory imagination thus depends on the work of corrective imagination having been done well.

Corrective and exploratory imagination are consequently interdependent: the point of correction is to make a better future possible, and the exploration of that future is reliable only if one avoids past falsifying tendencies. Each needs the other, and they should work jointly. But when they do, the perspective of each is altered. The reason for looking backward becomes not just to correct past mistakes but to correct them with an eye to the future. And the reason for looking forward is not merely to explore possibilities but to explore them as realistic possibilities for the person one believes oneself to be on the basis of one's corrected falsifying tendencies. The joint works and the altered perspectives of correction and exploration produce disciplined imagination. It is an improvement over the other two because it incorporates the correction and the exploration they make possible while avoiding the limit each has.

A further reason why disciplined imagination should be distinguished from the other two is that their temporal orientations are different. Correction is oriented toward the past, exploration toward the future. Disciplined imagination, however, is focused on the present. Its concern is with present deliberation about one's possibilities. This involves backward-looking correction and forward-looking exploration, but they are secondary and instrumental to the primary purpose, which is to deliberate well in the present. These three uses of imagination are normally indistinguishable because they tend to occur together. Their separation is only for the purpose of understanding better the work they do, the limits they have, and the mistakes to which they are liable.

The foregoing account merely introduces the characteristics and aims of moral imagination; it does not show how it actually does its work. I will attempt to do this in what follows by turning again and again to concrete cases derived from literature. These cases are intended to serve both a critical and a constructive purpose. The critical one is to show in concrete detail some particular inadequacy of the voluntarist ideal. The constructive purpose is to identify particular conditions the balanced ideal must embody. The cases thus give content to the balanced ideal by showing what conditions it must meet to make lives better.

Part Two

THE CORRECTIVE
IMAGINATION

CHAPTER 3

Understanding Life Backward

It is quite true what philosophy says: that life must be understood backwards. But then one forgets the other principle: that it must be lived forwards.

—SØREN KIERKEGAARD, *Papers and Journals*

3.1 Mill's Case

In John Stuart Mill's *Autobiography* we find an outstanding illustration of the corrective imagination.[1] Mill was driven to the imaginative re-creation of his past by what he calls "a crisis in my mental history" (86). It began when he was twenty and lasted roughly four years. Before the crisis, Mill says, "I had what might truly be called an object in life; to be the reformer of the world. My conception of my own happiness was entirely identified with this object. . . . This did very well for several years . . . [and it] seemed enough to fill up an interested and animated existence." But then, he says, "I was awakened from this as from a dream" (86). What happened was that "it occurred to me to put the question directly to myself: 'Suppose that all your objects in life were realized; that all the changes in institutions and opinions which you are looking forward to, would be completely effected at this very instant: would this be a great joy and happiness to you?' And an irrepressible self-consciousness distinctly answered, 'No!' At this my heart sank within me: the whole foundation on which my life was constructed fell down. . . . I seemed to have nothing left to live for" (87). His crisis then ensued. His state of mind, says Mill, is exactly described by a stanza in Coleridge's "Dejection":

A grief without a pang, void, dark, and drear,
A drowsy, stifled, unimpassioned grief,
Which finds no natural outlet or relief
In word, or sigh, or tear.

Reflecting on what has led to his crisis, Mill forms the surely correct view that its cause was the extraordinary education he had received from his father. At the age of three(!) he began to study ancient Greek language and literature; having achieved competence in that, at eight he was taught Latin, Euclidean geometry, and algebra; at twelve he studied Aristotelian and scholastic logic; and at thirteen his father began to read with him works on his specialty, political economy. Along the way, he picked up French and German, and he was not only well read in the serious works of literature, philosophy, history, and political economy in all these languages, but showed through his writings and conversations with numerous learned friends of his father that he understood what he had read.

Mill's moral outlook was also formed by his father, who valued "intellectual enjoyments above all others" (32); "for passionate emotions of all sorts . . . he professed the greatest contempt. He regarded them as a form of madness. 'The intense' was with him a bye-word of scornful disapprobation" (33); "the element which was chiefly deficient in his moral relation to his children was that of tenderness," and "he resembled most Englishmen in being ashamed of the signs of feeling" (34). Mill realized that his own mind was "directly formed by his [father's] instructions" (67) and that consequently he became "a mere reasoning machine," lacking in "genuine benevolence, or sympathy with mankind"; he "tended to the undervaluing of feeling" (71); "the cultivation of feeling . . . was not in much esteem among us," and from all this resulted "an undervaluing of . . . Imagination generally, as an element of human nature" (72). Mill thus falls into his crisis and concludes, "My education, which was wholly his [his father's] work, had been conducted without any regard to the possibility of its ending in this result. . . . It was however abundantly intelligible to myself; and the more I dwelt upon it, the more hopeless it appeared" (88). Suicidal thoughts came to him: "I frequently asked myself, if I could, or if I was bound to go on living, when life must be passed in this manner" (91).

Mill saw clearly the causes of his problem: "I now saw, or thought I saw, what I had before received with incredulity—that the habit of analysis has a tendency to wear away the feelings. . . . [It] fearfully undermine[s] all desires, and all pleasures" (89). It has made him "*blasé* and indifferent . . . neither selfish nor unselfish pleasures were pleasures to me"; his mind was "irretrievably analytic"; "and there seemed no power in nature sufficient to begin the formation of my character anew" (90). He concluded that "to know that a feeling would make me happy if I had it, did not give me the feeling. My education, I thought, had failed to create these feelings in sufficient strength to resist the dissolving influence of analysis. . . . The fountains of vanity and ambition seemed to have dried up within me, as completely as those of benevolence. . . . These were the thoughts which mingled with the dry heavy dejection of the melancholy winter" (90).

Mill eventually recovered, and he tells in the *Autobiography* by what means. Those familiar with his portrait in the National Portrait Gallery in London, however, may have some understandable doubts about the owner of that desiccated, bloodless, ascetic face having a life warmed by feelings. Be that as it may, my present purpose is to understand the concrete details of corrective imagination, and Mill's reflections prompted by his crisis illustrate very well what I have in mind. Mill was dissatisfied with his life, to put it mildly. He was motivated by his dissatisfactions to understand the reasons for his past decisions, why he pursued some of the possibilities he recognized and said no to others. He understood that he had decided as he did under the influence of his father and the amazing education he received. And he correctly identified the cause of his dissatisfaction as being bereft of feelings—without which life became for him an onerous burden that he conscientiously bore, while regarding all he did as Sisyphean drudgery. Mill had acted throughout in conformity with the voluntarist ideal of reflective self-evaluation, and that points to a significant and illuminating defect in that ideal, beyond the others already discussed in chapter 1.

It will be remembered that Frankfurt claims that reflective self-evaluation depends on forming and acting on second-order volitions that reveal what is important to us, what we most deeply care about,[2] and Hampshire believes that it is through reflective self-evaluation that we discover and act on fundamental beliefs.[3] Both think that acting according to this ideal is the key to a fulfilling and responsible life. Mill's *Autobiography* shows him doing just that, and what it got him was his crisis, not the fulfillment he was supposed to have. Mill certainly formed and acted on second-order volitions and reflected on what kind of person he wanted to be. His reflective self-evaluation revealed to him, however, a gaping hole at the center of his being. He had nothing where other people had feelings. He knew very well that he wanted a life rich with feelings that move him, make his existence enjoyable, and give him something to care about. But as he poignantly says, "to know that a feeling would make me happy if I had it, did not give me the feeling" (90).

This points directly to an assumption that underlies the voluntarist ideal, namely, that when reflective self-evaluation is conducted in the recommended manner, it *will* enable individuals to act on what they have found really important and worth caring about. Mill's case shows that this assumption is false. Reflective self-evaluation may reveal to individuals a deficiency in themselves that no amount of further reflective self-evaluation could possibly overcome. This is what Mill had found out about himself and what made him despair about his plight.

The false assumption is that through reflective self-evaluation individuals can discover in themselves the resources they need to overcome the obstacles to seeing their possibilities realistically. Individuals, of course, may have or develop sufficient resources for this in themselves, but they may not. For their lack of realism may be the result of an *incapacity* to appreciate their possibilities, not a misperception of them. This incapacity may be cognitive, such as stupidity, poor education, or short attention span; or it may be emotive, which in Mill's case was lack of feelings; or it may be volitional, such as a low level of energy, powerful contrary desires, or a hyperactive conscience whose scruples inhibit forming strong intentions; or, as it often happens, a combination and reciprocal reinforcement of several of these incapacities. My suggestion is not that such incapacities cannot be overcome but that individuals may lack the resources *within themselves* to overcome them. If that is the problem, further reflective self-evaluation cannot help. Outside resources are needed, and it is precisely the possibility of such resources that exploratory imagination provides, as we shall see in some detail later. Consequently, corrective imagination is not enough for a fulfilling life. It must be supplemented by exploratory imagination, which takes individuals outside themselves. This shows one of the limitations of corrective imagination.

3.2 Limitations

The voluntarist ideal of reflective self-evaluation fails to recognize the limitations of corrective imagination and the need for exploratory imagination because it attributes inflated importance to the will in living a responsible and fulfilling life. Frankfurt and Hampshire believe that the exercise of the will is the central feature of being a person who is a free and responsible agent. Why do they attribute a dominant position to the will? Why is it more important than, say, memory, knowledge, emotion, perception, reason, or, indeed, imagination? Why elevate one mental activity above the others? The point of asking is not to suggest that they elevate the wrong one but to show that the very idea of elevating any mental activity to a dominant position is faulty. All the ones mentioned above are important, and normally several of them are involved in deliberation about how to live and act. Insisting on the dominant position of one is like insisting on the dominant position of the brain, or the heart, or the lungs, or the digestive track. Surely, they all have an indispensable role. We need to understand what leads Frankfurt and Hampshire to ascribe such special importance to the will.

The explanation is that they presuppose a particular view of human beings. Murdoch, who argued against this view again and again,[4] describes it thus: "He is rational and totally free except . . . his self-awareness may vary. He is, morally speaking, monarch of all he surveys and totally responsible for his actions. Nothing transcends him. His moral language is a practical pointer, the instrument of his choices, the indication of his preferences. His inner life is resolved into his acts and choices. . . . His moral arguments are references to empirical facts backed up by decisions. . . . His rationality expresses itself in awareness of the facts, whether about the world or about himself. The virtue which is fundamental to him is sincerity."[5] The reason why will has a central place in this picture is that it is the engine that drives human beings conceived in this way. The will is the means by which they control their lives and actions and are free and responsible agents. The only question is how clear-sightedly they exercise their will. The more clear-sighted they are, the greater is their control, freedom, and responsibility. The central importance of the voluntarist ideal of reflective self-evaluation is that it is through it that self-consciousness is increased, and that is done by the corrective imagination as it overcomes one's misperceptions of the facts about oneself or about the circumstances in which one has to act.

Murdoch then asks, "What have we lost here?" and answers: "We no longer see man against a background of values . . . which transcend him. We picture man as a brave naked will surrounded by an easily comprehended empirical world. For the hard idea of truth we have substituted a facile idea of sincerity. . . . We retain a rationalistic optimism about the beneficent results of education, or rather technology. We combine this with a romantic conception of 'the human condition', a picture of the individual as stripped and solitary."[6] And what is the alternative? Murdoch says:

> We need to return from the self-centred concept of sincerity to the other-centred concept of truth. We are not isolated free choosers, monarchs of all we survey, but benighted creatures sunk in reality whose nature we are constantly and overwhelmingly tempted to deform by fantasy. . . . What we require is a renewed sense of the difficulty and complexity of the moral life and the opacity of persons. . . . We need to turn away from the consoling dream necessity of Romanticism. . . . It is here that literature is so impor-

tant, especially since it has taken over some of the tasks formerly performed by philosophy. Through literature we can re-discover a sense of density of our lives. Literature can arm us against consolation and fantasy and can help us to recover from the ailments of Romanticism.[7]

I have quoted Murdoch at length because I think she is right in her description and criticism of the view of human motivation presupposed by the voluntarist ideal. Her claims that this view substitutes sincerity for truth and that it is vitiated by romanticism are especially important because they point to ways in which the corrective imagination can go very wrong. I will now discuss these ways, but I want to stress that agreement with Murdoch's description and criticism, of course, does not commit one to the acceptance of her positive views (to which I objected in 2.4).

3.3 Sincerity

Lionel Trilling writes, "Now and then it is possible to observe the moral life in process of revising itself, perhaps by reducing the emphasis formerly placed upon one or another of its elements, perhaps by inventing and adding to itself a new element, some mode of conduct or of feeling which hitherto it had not regarded as essential to virtue." He goes on: "At a certain point in its history the moral life of Europe added to itself a new element, the state or quality of the self which we call sincerity. The word as we now use it refers primarily to a congruence between avowal and actual feeling."[8] This is right, I believe, and it is my starting point. Trilling is less than forthcoming about whether he regards the emergence of sincerity as a change for the better, but I want to make clear that I regard it, with Murdoch, as a change for the worse, and that I disagree with Frankfurt and Hampshire, who think otherwise.

To get at the basic reason for rejecting the central moral importance of sincerity, compare two ways of acting. One is hypocritical and duplicitous; the other is frank and forthright. Is it not obvious, it will be asked, that the second is better than the first? The answer is no. For it is certainly better to be insincere and cause no harm than to be sincere and cause it. Why is it virtuous to be sincere and acknowledge that selfishness, malevolence, greed, or cruelty motivate one's actions? Is it not greatly preferable if people refrain from murder and mayhem because they hypocritically and duplicitously dissimulate what they would really like to do? Is it not better, as Burke puts it, "to cover the defects of our shivering nature" by insincerity than to have "all decent draperies of life . . . rudely torn off" by sincerity?[9] Surely, what really matters about motives and actions is their true nature rather than sincerity about them. To reverse this order of importance is to rate what we say we are higher than what we in fact are. To avoid this absurdity, the primacy of truth must be recognized, and sincerity cannot be reasonably proposed as a substitute for it.

To make this clear, consider the following lines from Matthew Arnold:

> Below the surface-stream, shallow and light,
> Of what we *say* we feel—below the stream,
> As light, of what we *think* we feel—there flows
> With noiseless current strong, obscure and deep,
> The central stream of what we feel indeed.[10]

Sincerity is congruence between "what we *say* we feel" and "what we *think* we feel," but this is likely to be "shallow and light." What really matters is what is "strong, obscure and deep, / The central stream of what we feel indeed," and that is what truth is about. This is why sincerity is facile and truth hard, as Murdoch says.

Defenders of the primacy of sincerity would reply that if we knew the truth about our motives, we would be well advised to value it above sincerity, but few of us have that knowledge. Frankfurt thinks that ambivalence, rather than wholeheartedness, is our usual state: "we do not know our hearts well enough" and "our hearts are at best divided." Sincerity, then, is what can be said to move us from ambivalence to wholeheartedness.[11] Hampshire, using different words, says the same: the ideal state is a "strong sincere sentiment . . . that . . . occupies the subject's mind fully, and that displaces competing thoughts and dispositions." "Insincerity is typically a gap between what I am disposed to say about myself and what I am disposed to do," whereas "sincerity . . . amounts to the ideal of undividedness or singleness of mind."[12]

Frankfurt's wholeheartedness and Hampshire's undividedness are, of course, synonyms for sincerity, which is the aim of the voluntarist ideal of reflective self-evaluation. Their important and highly interesting description of the process of getting from ambivalence to wholeheartedness, from a divided to an undivided mind, from insincerity to sincerity, however, cannot be accepted as an adequate account of reflective self-evaluation or an adequate response to the doubts about sincerity I have voiced earlier.

According to the view of human motivation that the voluntarist ideal presupposes, our usual state of mind is to be conflicted about various possibilities. We have conflicting desires that prompt different and often incompatible actions. Our task is to clarify what we really care about, what is really important to us, then impose a hierarchical order on our desires that reflects our priorities, and then commit ourselves to acting accordingly. We have then identified ourselves with our intentions, and our actions express our intentions. That is the ideal we should aim at. The closer we get to it, the more free, responsible, and in control we are, and the more wholehearted, undivided, and sincere we become. The key to all this is the will because it is the component of our psychological constitution that is the means to obtaining the satisfactions we sincerely want. According to this view, reflective self-evaluation will make us sincere, and sincerity makes it possible to employ our will rightly.

Shaw's quip—"There are two tragedies in life. One is not to get your heart's desire. The other is to get it."[13]—rather neatly points to what is wrong with this view of human beings. Consider people on whom the second tragedy befalls. They have done all that the voluntarist ideal requires: they are sincere and wholeheartedly and undividedly employ their will to get what they really want. We should remember, but leave aside for the moment, the two problems I have already noted: people may lack the capacity to have what they want, as Mill did, and what they want may be irresponsible. Let us suppose that these exemplary people have the necessary capacities and want only what is morally acceptable.

Here are a number of adverse observations that *may* be truly made of people who actually got what Frankfurt and Hampshire say we should aim at: they are crude, vulgar, impolite, plodding, friendless, pedestrian, humorless, self-absorbed, or boring; they have no aesthetic appreciation, style, curiosity, or taste; they are ignorant of history, art, literature, music, or languages other than their own; they do not know how to have a conversation, put others at ease, take a joke, express appreciation, or be lighthearted; they are too severe, narrow, demanding, overbearing, rigid, stolid, or punctilious; and so on. I am not saying, of course, that all those who successfully follow the voluntarist ideal will acquire these unpleasing traits. My point is that there is nothing in the ideal that would rule out a life dominated by one or a cluster of them.

Moreover, it is not just others who may rightly regard these sincere and willful people as philistines. The philistines themselves may become dissatisfied with their lives despite their genuine sincerity, wholeheartedness, and undividedness, and they may want to do something about it. But if they are reasonable, they will want not to do more of what they have been doing, since that is what has led them to their present sorry pass, but to stop gazing inward and begin to look outward, toward the possibilities of life they have thus far ignored. They may conclude that what they have really wanted and got was the wrong thing because it made them unlovely bores. What brought this about was not that they misperceived their possibilities, but that they were satisfied with impoverished possibilities. The trouble was not that they were insincere about what they really wanted, but that they were sincere in having philistine wants. Seeing and wanting to avoid this possibility, among others, is what led Sartre, whose views are very similar to Frankfurt's and Hampshire's, to regard sincerity as a form of bad faith. For through sincerity people may affirm their commitment to what they are and thereby tacitly deny what they might become. As Sartre puts it: "What then is sincerity except precisely a phenomenon of bad faith? . . . One can fall into bad faith through being sincere."[14]

If it is recognized, as it surely must be, that people may care about things not worth caring about, that their will may be misdirected, and that they may be sincerely committed to wrong possibilities, then the voluntarist ideal of human motivation must be revised in a particular way to make correction possible. The revision must be in *a particular way* because Frankfurt and Hampshire themselves emphasize the necessity of correction by reflective self-evaluation that overcomes misperceptions. They are right about the importance of their kind of correction, but they are wrong to suppose that, if done well, that is all the correction needed. My objection is that another kind of correction is also needed to avoid commitment to morally unacceptable possibilities, to overcome one's incapacities, and to prevent oneself from nurturing the kind of impoverishment from which philistines suffer. The needed correction requires people to look outside themselves toward possibilities other than those they have thus far recognized. They should continue their reflective self-evaluation, but they should broaden and deepen their understanding of what it involves.

If they do this, they will realize that they have to do more than merely seek within themselves the resources for making the necessary corrections, and that they will need to look outside and explore other possibilities. As they do this, they will need to supplement their corrective imagination with exploratory imagination. In sum, I agree with Frankfurt and Hampshire about the importance of reflective self-evaluation, but I think that a more complex view of it is needed than the one they provide.

It may be asked: is there anything in their position that would prevent them from accepting this more complex view? What prevents them, I think, is a mistaken emphasis, and I doubt that they would be willing to change in this respect. Their mistake is to emphasize that people must make a commitment sincerely, wholeheartedly, and undividedly, but they emphasize that at the expense of that to which the commitment is made. My objections to their view all focused on the need to recognize that it is just as important that people should commit themselves to responsible and fulfilling possibilities as it is that they should make a commitment. Why, then, could not Frankfurt and Hampshire simply change their emphasis and stress the equal importance of making a commitment in the right way and making it to the right possibility? Because their romanticism prevents them. I will now attempt to give reasons in support of this claim.

3.4 Promethean Romanticism

It is helpful to think about moral imagination the way Aristotle thinks about virtues. We may say, then, that moral imagination can go wrong in two ways: by using it too little or too much. If too little, the result is the kind of moral obtuseness I discussed earlier (in 1.4); if too much, romanticism follows. Moral obtuseness is typically a condition in which people find themselves as a result of some cognitive, emotive, or volitional deficiency. The condition can be alleviated only by strenuous effort to compensate in some way for the deficiency that caused the trouble. Romanticism, by contrast, is a condition that has to be actively cultivated, as opposed to falling into it passively. It is a form of self-indulgence in which people take pleasure in being carried away by a combination of beliefs and feelings. Romanticism thus stands to moral imagination as recklessness does to courage, or extravagance to generosity. This self-indulgence is a temptation to which countless people who rightly value moral imagination all too willingly succumb—thereby contriving to lose what they value. Romanticism unfortunately is an extremely imprecise word. Arthur Lovejoy was right to say that "the word 'romanticism' has come to mean so many things that, by itself, it means nothing."[15] The remedy is to make clear what one means by it. In the present context, I will follow Isaiah Berlin in explaining how I use it. To distinguish my usage from others, I call it *Promethean* romanticism. (Later I will discuss other forms of romanticism.)

Berlin writes that in the early nineteenth century

> a new and immensely influential image began to take possession of the European mind. This is the image of the heroic individual, imposing his will upon nature or society: of man not as the crown of a harmonious cosmos, but as a being 'alienated' from it, and seeking to subdue and dominate it. . . . The noblest thing a man can do is to serve his own inner ideal. . . . The question of whether an ideal is true or false is no longer thought important, or indeed wholly intelligible. The ideal presents itself in the form of a categorical imperative: serve the inner light within you because it burns within you, for that reason alone. Do what you think right, make what you think beautiful, shape your life in accordance with those ends which are your ultimate purpose, to which everything else in your life is a means, to which all else must be subordinated. . . . The only principle

which must be sacredly observed is that each man shall be true to his own goals. . . . That is the romantic ideal in its fullest . . . form.[16]

The reason for calling this kind of romanticism Promethean, then, is that it postulates as an ideal for human beings a life of heroism. Like Prometheus, we are to pit ourselves against the limits of our condition. These limits may be physical, psychological, or social, they may be set by tradition, custom, or convention, but one and all, the limits weigh on us as burdens. The key to freedom and responsibility is to shake loose from them and develop our potentialities unhindered by these limits. That is why the will is the most important component of our psychological constitution. But to develop our potentialities, we have to know what they are and which of them matters to us the most. That is why reflective self-evaluation is central to human agency. To know our priorities, however, is still not enough because our actions must reflect them. That is why sincerity is crucial. And the centrality of will, reflective self-evaluation, and sincerity—the basic elements of Promethean romanticism—is precisely what Frankfurt and Hampshire have been shown to stress again and again. It is, therefore, justified to ascribe the position to them even though they do not unequivocally ascribe it to themselves. Hampshire is more explicit in this respect than Frankfurt, for he says that "the ethics of romanticism represents the man of passion as the ideal of the sincere man of undivided mind,"[17] which, of course, is the ideal he has been championing.

The widespread appeal of Promethean romanticism has far-reaching consequences. In Berlin's words: "What romanticism did was to undermine the notion that in matters of value, politics, morals, aesthetics there are such things as objective criteria which operate between human beings, such that anyone who does not use these criteria is simply either a liar or a madman. . . . This division between where objective truth obtains—in mathematics, in physics, in certain regions of common sense—and where objective truth has been compromised—in ethics, in aesthetics and the rest—is new, and has created a new attitude to life—whether good or bad, I shall not volunteer to say."[18] But I do volunteer to say that it is bad, very bad, and I will now give reasons for it.

Let us begin with objective criteria for values. To say that there are such criteria is not to say that they exist independently of human beings, as do laws of nature. Objects would fall even if humanity were to go the way of dinosaurs. But it is to say that whether or not the pursuit of some possibilities would lead to a responsible and fulfilling life is true or false regardless of what I or anyone thinks or feels about it. Everyone may think or feel alike, and everyone may be mistaken. For there are some objective conditions that must be met if life is to go well for a human being. Some of these conditions are physiological, such as having to have nutrition and rest; others are psychological, like the need for companionship and the absence of terror; yet others are social, having to do with the necessity of cooperation, the division of labor, and the adjudication of conflicts. These conditions are the same for all human beings. But there are also objective conditions that vary with individuals, depending on their characters and circumstances. The successful pursuit of some possibilities depends on abilities that individuals may or may not have, as well as on political, economic, climatic, cultural, and other factors that may or may not be present. Given these universal and variable conditions, it is obviously mistaken to hold that whether or not they are met depends on the will, reflective self-evaluation, or sincerity of anyone.

This is a conclusive reason for thinking that conformity to the Promethean romantic ideal is neither necessary nor sufficient for meeting whatever objective conditions there are. It is not sufficient because not even the strongest will, the most scrupulous reflective self-evaluation, and the utmost sincerity can guarantee that I have enough to eat, or that my life is free of the threat of torture, or that I live in a stable society, or that I have some ability I need, say, for music, learning languages, or professional basketball. And it is not necessary either, because these conditions can be met even by people who do not will it, who are not reflective at all, or who are steeped in hypocrisy.

It might be said that these objective conditions are minimum conditions, and Promethean romanticism can accept their existence without inconsistency. For the will, reflective self-evaluation, and sincerity are required for the evaluation of much more complex possibilities, such as whether I should take this lucrative but possibly corrupting job, get a divorce or stay married for the sake of the children, enter into politics and forgo privacy, or resign in protest from an unprincipled institution or continue in the hope of reforming it from the inside. For the evaluation of such possibilities, it will be said, there are no objective criteria. What we have to do to reach a decision is precisely what Promethean romanticism tells us, namely, find out what we really care about and then act on it.

Some of what it tells us is no doubt true, but that does not mean that if we find out what we really care about, then we should act on it. For what we really care about may be conquering the weak, exterminating opponents, defrauding the gullible, dominating *Untermenschen*, or persecuting religious or political dissenters. We may be motivated by cruelty, malevolence, greed, selfishness, and so forth. No one committed to morality can deny that there must be limits to what we may do if we act as prompted by our will, reflective-self-evaluation, and sincerity. So it cannot be that we should just follow the ideal of Promethean romanticism. We should follow it, if at all, only within moral limits. But this is not all because there are further limits even within moral limits.

There are many possibilities that violate no moral limit but are nevertheless detrimental to a fulfilling life. We have already seen one instance of this in the *impoverished* possibilities recognized by philistines, but there are others. People may really care about utterly *futile* possibilities, which unreasonable beliefs prevent them from recognizing as such. Passionate commitment to communicating with the dead, traveling by flying saucer to another planet, or being at two distant places simultaneously are cases in point. Nor can the pursuit of *trivial* possibilities lead to a fulfilling life. No matter how sincere commitments are to collecting burnt matchsticks or counting the number of passing pedestrians, they cannot yield more than a life filled with obsessive activity, and that of course falls far short of fulfillment. The pursuit of *demeaning* possibilities is another example showing that those who care about them more than about anything else are in some way perverse. To care most about watching sadomasochistic pornography, eating dead insects, or nurturing erotic fantasies about malodorous socks shows that there is something disordered in those whose will is focused on such pursuits, whose reflective self-evaluation reveals that that is what truly lights their fire, and who are sincere in acting accordingly. People of course can pursue such possibilities in the way Promethean romanticism recommends, and doing so may soothe their nerves, alleviate their boredom, or help them fill an otherwise empty life, but it cannot yield fulfillment.

There are, then, undeniable objective conditions that set limits to what possibilities human beings can reasonably pursue. These conditions depend on the existence of humanity in the sense that the conditions are conditions for beings like us. But they are *objective* conditions for beings like us. We can, of course, pursue possibilities and intend to transgress limits set by reason, morality, human capacity, and individual ability; we can aim at futile, trivial, or demeaning possibilities. But for beings constituted as we are, the pursuit of such possibilities cannot yield responsible and fulfilling lives no matter how strongly we will it, how positively we endorse them on the basis of the most careful reflective self-evaluation, or how sincere we are in acting as our will and reflective self-evaluation prompt. This is one reason why Promethean romanticism—urging us to strive to transgress human limits—is a bad ideal.

3.5 Transcending Limits

Another reason why the Promethean romantic ideal should be rejected follows from the existence of objective conditions to which responsible and fulfilling lives must conform. Individuals have beliefs and feelings about these conditions, and their efforts of will are guided by them. These beliefs must be reasonable, the feelings appropriate, and the efforts of will rightly directed. Human fallibility, ignorance, and poor judgment, however, often result in unreasonable beliefs, inappropriate feelings, and misdirected efforts of will. Since going wrong in these ways affects what people care about most, it is in everyone's interest to avoid such mistakes. The most obvious way in which this can be done is to learn from the examples of others who have lived the sort of life we want for ourselves and who have successfully coped with situations similar to our own, as well as from the examples of those who, as a result of some deficiency, weakness, or error, have failed. Personal acquaintance with such lives is bound to be limited, but history, literature, philosophy, religion, and the arts are rich with them. Let us call these repositories of lives from which we may be able to learn the *cultural tradition.* One way, then, of making mistakes less likely is to test our beliefs, feelings, and efforts of will by the relevant examples derived from our cultural tradition. The next two chapters begin to show how that may be done.

The cultural tradition is vast, stretching backward many centuries and containing great diversity. Individuals are bound to have a more or less limited knowledge of the riches that may be found in it. They need intermediaries whose greater knowledge enables them to interpret some area of the cultural tradition for those who know it less well. This has been one important responsibility of historians, literary and other critics, philosophers, and theologians. There still are some—all too few—among them who have not succumbed to the temptation of writing for fellow experts and who continue to discharge their traditional responsibility. Others, then, can turn to them and learn from their works about the benefits derivable from the accumulated experience of their predecessors which forms the content of the cultural tradition.

It would, of course, be very foolish not to learn in this way if we could. For it would help us to achieve better control of our lives by making us less fallible, less ignorant, less poor in judging the reliability of our beliefs, feelings, and efforts of will. But in order to do this we must look outside ourselves and explore the possibilities our cultural tradition provides. And it is precisely this foolishness, this refusal to look outside ourselves, that Promethean romantics say we must cultivate. They believe that control comes from our will, reflective self-evaluation, and sincerity, all of which are exclusively concentrated on looking within ourselves, finding what we really care about, and acting accordingly. They believe that to look outside is to jeopardize our freedom, responsibility, and control. And with this, I believe, we have finally arrived at the true center of Promethean romanticism.

We find there the conviction that to be truly ourselves, to be in control of our lives, to be a free and responsible agent depends on not being subject to the contingency of life; that is to say, not being subject to forces over which we have no control, not holding values we have not made, not recognizing limits we have not set. Promethean romantics are convinced that these requirements can be met only within our inner world, not outside it. For the forces of nature, the brute facts, are what they are and operate as they do, but our inner world we can make ourselves. There only can we be in control, and that is why we should concentrate on our will, reflective self-evaluation, and sincerity rather than explore the cultural tradition outside ourselves, which contains, at best, only other people's interpretations of how others have lived in the contingent conditions of their lives. It is this intoxication with being free of contingency that is the motivating force of Promethean romanticism.

The intoxication, however, is with an illusion. Contingency is a necessary constituent of the human condition, and it is impossible to free ourselves from it. The inner world is just as subject to it as the outer one. For it is a contingent fact where and when we were born, what our genetic inheritance is, how we were brought up, what formative experiences affected us during the early part of our lives, whether the society in which we live is peaceful, what happens to people we love, how good is our health, financial condition, or job, and so on and on for countless conditions that unavoidably influence our beliefs, feelings, and efforts of will. Forming reasonable beliefs, having appropriate feelings, and making the right efforts of will depends on our possession of many different abilities and favorable circumstances, and whether we possess them is a contingent matter.

Promethean romantics are right to stress the importance of control through efforts of will, reflective self-evaluation, and sincerity. But they are wrong to suppose that the way to achieve control is to exclude contingency from the inner world. There is no area of human life from which contingency could be excluded. No matter what we do, we can never achieve the condition in which there are no forces beyond our control that may seriously affect our lives. There will always be such forces, and they will always impinge on how we live. This is the truth that Promethean romantics are unwilling to face. They obscure it by the illusion that we could and should build an invincible inner fortress to repel the invasion of anything that we have not permitted to enter. By convincing themselves of the truth of this illusion, Promethean romantics falsely suppose that it is possible to escape human limits, to transcend our humanity, to free ourselves from the human condition. They nurture their passionate desire to reach this impossible state, and that is why they are justly charged with self-indulgently cultivating false beliefs, inappropriate feelings, and misdirected efforts of will. The overwhelming impression created by this folly masquerading as heroic effort is that of people ritually banging their heads against an unyielding wall and celebrating their self-inflicted pain as proof of their courage and dignity. The alternative is to heed the words of Wallace Stevens:

> To say more than human things with human voice,
> That cannot be; to say human things with more
> Than human voice, that, also, cannot be;
> To speak humanly from the height or from the depth
> Of human things, that is acutest speech.[19]

3.6 The Need for Balance

The discussion of corrective imagination has proceeded in two closely connected steps: by a constructive account of its use and a critical account of its misuse. The starting point is people's dissatisfaction with their lives. They have a sense that their lives are not going as they should, that their possibilities are too narrow or unlikely to satisfy their desires, that fulfillment is somehow eluding them. They need not be articulate about their dissatisfactions, which often appear as inchoate wishes for something better. If they say anything at all, it may just be in a wistful tone that there must be more to life. If their dissatisfactions are serious, they may lead them to try to understand why things have turned out as they did with their parents, children, husbands or wives, careers or jobs, interests or the lack of them, with their earlier dreams and ambitions. They may, then, start thinking about the major decisions they have made to try to realize some of their possibilities rather than others. And they may conclude that their present dissatisfactions are the results of their past mistakes. Their obvious next step is to try to understand how they came to make the mistakes, how it happened that they misperceived their possibilities. In seeking this understanding, they need to re-create both the frame of mind that led to their decisions and the true nature of the possibilities that were available to them in their past circumstances. When they try to do this, they are engaged in corrective imagination. It is a use of *imagination* because it aims to re-create how they thought and felt, what motivated them, and how, in general, the world looked to them at that time in the past. It is a *moral* use because they are asking the questions from the point of view of their attempt to live a good life, a life that is responsible and fulfilling. And it is a *corrective* use because they want not merely to understand their past mistakes but to understand them in the hope of correcting them and not making them again, and thereby making their lives better by alleviating their dissatisfactions.

In trying to do this, they can go wrong by not using their moral imagination sufficiently to reach the understanding they seek or by allowing its use to get out of hand, giving their thoughts and feelings free rein, and thus allowing their imagination to turn into fantasy. The first way of going wrong is what I have called moral obtuseness, and the second is Promethean romanticism. The two are alike in leading to the misunderstanding of the limits and possibilities that ought to be recognized. Moral obtuseness is to see as limits what are not and not to see as possibilities what are. Promethean romanticism is not to see as limits what ought to be recognized as such and to see as possibilities what are in fact impossibilities. One reason for the inadequacy of the voluntarist ideal of reflective self-evaluation is that it does not recognize that moral obtuseness and Promethean romanticism must both be excluded if reflective self-evaluation is to lead to a good life.

The emerging account of corrective imagination is balanced in several crucial respects between deficiency and excess. It avoids the deficiencies of moral obtuseness by recognizing the need for both the correction of past mistakes and the exploration of future possibilities. It also avoids the excesses of Promethean romanticism by insisting on the need for limits that keep possibilities within moral and realistic bounds. It resists the characteristic and recurrent urge of Promethean romantics not to rest content with recognizing the importance of various features crucial for the corrective use, but to exaggerate the importance of these features beyond what reason and realism can allow. Promethean romantics again and again slide from moderate and true claims to immoderate and false ones: the will is important, but it is not the most important of all mental activities; sincerity matters, but it is no substitute for truth; reflective self-evaluation is necessary for living according to a particular ideal of good life, but it is not sufficient for it; decreasing our vulnerability to contingency is necessary for having control over our lives, but no amount of control can free us from contingency; a fulfilling life depends on what goes on in our inner world, but that does not make the outer world irrelevant; we must find out what matters to us, but that does not exclude learning from and following the examples of others who have succeeded at what we are trying to do; we must make our own lives fulfilling, for if *we* do not do it, it will not be done, but that is not incompatible with making use of the riches our cultural tradition makes available; we must learn from our mistakes, but we must also be open to future possibilities to know what we should do with the lives in which mistakes have been identified and overcome.

As it stands, this balanced ideal of reflective self-evaluation, while perhaps showing what deficiencies and excesses we should avoid, is still too abstract and general. It needs to be made concrete through the consideration of detailed examples of the place of corrective imagination in it. This is the aim of the next two chapters.

From Hope and Fear Set Free

From too much love of living,
From hope and fear set free.
We thank with brief thanksgiving
Whatever gods may be
That no life lives for ever;
That even the weariest river
Winds somewhere safe to sea.

—ALGERNON SWINBURNE, "The Garden of Proserpine"

4.1 Myth and Reality

Philosophical writing is supposed to present unemotional, impersonal, closely argued conclusions that logically follow from well-established premises. Poetry, by contrast, is expected to be evocative, metaphorical, impassioned, suggestive, having little use for facts, arguments, logic, and reasoning. It is more than a little odd that these stereotypes do not fit the works of such eminent representatives of philosophy and poetry as Plato and Sophocles, whose works I shall be concerned with in this chapter.[1] Plato's allegory of the cave is one of the enduring tropes in Western literature, and Sophocles' treatment of Oedipus has been the subject of philosophical reflection for over two millennia. Contrary to the stereotypes, however, Plato's allegory of the cave is a philosophical myth and Sophocles' drama is a tragic portrayal of the reality of contingency.

One of the many reasons for their perennial appeal is that they engage our deepest hopes and fears, but Plato, the philosopher, does it poetically and Sophocles, the poet, does it philosophically. They make it hard to sustain the simpleminded stereotypes of philosophy and poetry. Both can be written in many ways, but the unmistakable sign of greatness, if they have it, is the same regardless of their varying forms: depth. That is what Plato's allegory and Sophocles' Oedipus have. The depth of understanding of the first is about human possibilities, and of the second it is about human limits. The first explains what we may reasonably hope, the second what we may reasonably fear.

Plato introduces the allegory of the cave "as an analogy for the human condition" (514a). He says that we should imagine people imprisoned in a cave from their earliest years. They are shackled and can look only straight ahead at a wall on which a fire burning behind them casts indistinct shadows of various artifacts that are being moved between the fire and their backs. The shackled people talk to each other and try to figure out the nature of their world. "The shadows of artefacts would constitute the only reality people in this situation would recognize" (515c). If they were unshackled and could turn around, they would be closer to understanding the true nature of their world. But they would still be very far from the real understanding that might be possible if they moved out of the cave and saw the world illuminated not by a flickering fire but by the bright light of the sun (especially as it is in Greece). Because they have lived in the cave for so long, using their eyes would at first cause them "pain and distress" and "they would be overwhelmed by the sun's beams" (516a). But gradually they would get used to seeing things as they are and would "think about the sun and . . . deduce that it is the source of the . . . whole of the visible realm . . . and that in a sense everything which . . . [they] used to see is its responsibility" (516b–c). They would also understand, in their new, improved situation, how pitiful was the understanding they supposed themselves to have when they were imprisoned in the cave. They did not even have access to the visible world, let alone to the intelligible world to which they were since led by understanding that the sun was responsible for the world's being visible.

If we "apply this allegory," we see the people ascending from the cave as "the mind's ascent to the intelligible realm," toward real knowledge. "In the realm of knowledge is goodness," just as in the visible realm is the sun. "And the sight of . . . goodness leads one to deduce that it is responsible for everything that is right and fine, whatever the circumstances, and that in the visible realm it is the progenitor of light and the source of light, and in the intelligible realm it is the source and provider of truth and knowledge. . . . It is a prerequisite for intelligent conduct either of one's own private affairs or of public business" (517a–c).

Plato's myth, then, is that above the natural world that imprisons us in *our* cave, there is a supernatural world that is responsible for the appearance the natural world presents to us. If we develop our capacity to reason and employ it in the right way, we come to understand this other world, realize that it is the truly real one and that the natural world is merely a shadowy appearance created by it. The supernatural world is permeated with goodness, and that is what the right use of reason will reveal to us. But to use reason rightly, we must free ourselves from *our* shackles that prevent us from seeing the world as it really is. Plato thought these shackles were our passions and appetites, interfering with reason and needing to be controlled by it. This is the task of what I, although not Plato, have called the corrective imagination. Its activity is imaginative because it re-creates our past beliefs, feelings, and motives that impeded the right use of our reason. And it is corrective because it aims to improve the frame of mind responsible for our mistaken past reactions to the world. Once this task is successfully completed, nothing stands in the way of being guided by the good, as by the light of the sun, and we will want to conform to the morally good order that informs the scheme of things. Those who live otherwise do so because they have not overcome the handicaps that prevented them from being sufficiently reasonable, and thus have been unable to understand the nature of reality. Plato makes clear that all this is an allegory, and, he says, "only God knows if it's actually true" (517c).

This, however, is a remarkable thing for Plato to say. Allegories, of course, are not literally true, but unless the symbolic representations they provide are true to what they are intended to depict, they fail as allegories. They then have nothing to do with reality; they are mere fantasies expressed in words. Plato clearly intends his words to be more than that. He wants them to convey serious moral meaning. But if that is so, how can he be so insouciant about the truth of what he is saying? Much depends on understanding Plato's attitude.

To begin with, the distinction between the natural and the supernatural worlds, and the suggestions that the supernatural world is governed by a morally good order and that the goodness of human lives depends on living in conformity to that order, are core beliefs in Judaism, Christianity, and Islam; in the great metaphysical systems not just of Plato but also of Augustine, Aquinas, Spinoza, Leibniz, Kant, Hegel, and others; and in the poetic visions, among many others, of Virgil, Dante, Pope, Goethe, and Wordsworth. As a result, they are basic constituents of the world view that has existed continuously for thousands of years. This is not to say, of course, that everyone accepts them. But it is to say that those who do not must have reasons for departing from the world view that dominated Western sensibility from the earliest times to about the eighteenth century and still commands the allegiance of many thinking people. If these core beliefs are false, then the world view that rests on them becomes untenable. Should we follow Plato in not caring about that?

There is, furthermore, also the consideration that these core beliefs sustain our hope and alleviate our fear. The fact is that in the natural world as we know it reasonable and moral actions need not lead to a good life and bad people often live contentedly enjoying their ill-gotten satisfactions until they die peacefully of old age. This frustrates our moral expectations because we believe that the world ought not to be like that. We believe that—if not immediately, then at least in the long run—people should have a good life if they are reasonable and moral and a bad life if they are not. Only if there is a morally good order governing the scheme of things will our expectation be met. This is what we hope and the opposite is what we fear. But hope and fear can be reasonable or unreasonable, warranted or chimerical. If the core beliefs are false, this hope seems to be unreasonable and we have much to fear. So, once again, how can Plato be so casual about their truth?

These doubts about the truth of the core beliefs and the reasonability of the hope based on them are strengthened by further considerations. There is no reason to believe in a supernatural world because any evidence accessible to human beings must come from the natural world and there can be no reason for believing anything unless it could be supported by evidence. This, of course, has not stopped countless people from claiming to know all kinds of things about the supernatural world, but their claims are dubious because they are conflicting and incompatible. Moreover, even assuming that the morally good order can be known, it is a plain fact that it may not always motivate those who know it because people who are bad, weak, or thoughtless often act against what they suppose to be good. It makes matters worse that human experience testifies against the very idea of there being such a thing as *the* good, conformity to which alone would make individuals or societies good, for we know that individuals and societies can be good in many different ways, conforming to many different ideas of what is good. The cumulative weight of these and other well-known reasons for regarding the core beliefs as false makes it even more pressing to understand how Plato could be indifferent to their truth.

The key to understanding Plato's attitude is that he would regard all these doubts and criticisms as irrelevant. If he had meant to describe how the world is, the objections would lead to the conclusion that he failed. What he meant to do, however, was to show how the world ought to be. He was not describing facts, but prescribing an ideal. The point of the prescription is precisely that the world is not as it ought to be, and that it ought to be changed so as to approximate the ideal more closely. Since the core beliefs are not parts of an account of the world, Plato is indifferent to whether the account is accurate. What Plato cares about is the ideal, and that is what the core beliefs are parts of. The relevant question is whether it is reasonable to accept the ideal.

The first thing that must be said in favor of it is that we do accept it. There is virtually no one who thinks about it and does not believe that the world ought to be such that people acting reasonably and morally have good lives and that bad lives result from unreasonable and immoral actions. At the same time, virtually no one believes that the world we live in and know is like that. In our world good people often suffer undeserved misfortune and bad ones often enjoy undeserved felicity. The general acknowledgment that this is so, however, is accompanied by the hope that the world might be changed for the better and the fear that it might not be. This hope and fear may take various forms, ranging from moral outrage and a passion for reform to a paralyzed will and inaction, but hardly any reflective person is without some such hope and fear. Plato's ideal, therefore, is alive and well, and most of us have hopes and fears about it. None of this shows, however, that the ideal, and the hopes and fears it elicits, are reasonable. What is reasonable cannot be settled by consensus or by how we feel, not even by a wide consensus and generally shared feelings. Part of the enduring significance of Sophocles' work is that it challenges this consensus, calls the ideal into question, and makes the hope look chimerical and the fear warranted.[2]

4.2 Contingency

We have seen (in 3.4–3.5) that Promethean romanticism aims at the impossible goal of freeing ourselves from vulnerability to contingency and achieving control over our lives. Plato's ideal requires us to pursue the same goal, but its achievement is held to depend on reason, not, as Promethean romantics think, on the will. If by corrective imagination we succeed in removing impediments that prevent us from using reason in the right way, then reason will lead us to the good and make our lives responsible and fulfilling. Sophocles' great tragedy—perhaps the greatest ever written—*Oedipus the King*, shows that Plato's ideal is rendered unattainable by the very contingency it aims to overcome. It is an illusion to suppose that reflective self-evaluation is sufficient to control our lives. To live by this illusion is to pit ourselves against the unavoidable limits of the human condition, and that is the road to disaster. Let us now consider what Sophocles shows us.

Before Oedipus was born, it was prophesied that he will kill his father and marry his mother. His parents, therefore, arranged to have the newly born Oedipus killed. But he survived and grew into adulthood, believing himself to be the son of the king and queen of Corinth, who had raised him. The prophecy was then repeated to Oedipus. To prevent it from becoming true, he exiled himself so as not to be in the proximity of his supposed parents. His effort to avoid the calamity, however, actually hastened its occurrence because it is to Thebes, to the city ruled by his real father, that his wandering brought him. On the way to Thebes, Oedipus was provoked into a fight and killed several men, not unjustifiably given the prevalent mores, one among whom was his unknown father. Upon arriving in Thebes, Oedipus, at great risk to himself, solved the riddle of the Sphinx, thus succeeding where many others had failed in liberating the city from her oppression. As a reward, he was made king and was given as a wife the widowed queen, his unknown mother. As the play opens, all these events are in the past. The action concerns Oedipus's gradual understanding that he is guilty of parricide and incest, crimes that he, in agreement with his society, finds deeply immoral. Oedipus finally realizes that he had caused the most serious and undeserved harm to Thebes, to his wife, who is his mother, to his children, who are his brothers and sisters, and to himself. Yet throughout his life Oedipus acted as well as can be expected from a reasonable and moral human being in the non-ideal conditions that prevail in the real world. Nevertheless, both he and others saw him as ruined by the grievous immorality of which he unknowingly and unintentionally became guilty. According to Plato's ideal, this could not happen.

A significant feature of Oedipus's situation is that, as he saw it, he was a plaything of the gods. He had choices, and he made them. But the alternatives among which he could choose, the conditions in which he could do so, and his doom were set by the gods. Through no fault of his own, Oedipus was manipulated by the gods for their own inscrutable purposes, and he was made to suffer a terrible fate by them. Sophocles' suggestion is that it is what befell Oedipus that reflects the human condition, not Plato's ideal. We all risk becoming the playthings of the gods, regardless of our knowledge of the good or our motivation to act according to it. It is reasonable to fear this and unreasonable to hope that life should be otherwise.

Our first reaction may well be that this cannot be the human condition because there are no such gods as Sophocles apparently believed. But this does not dispose of the matter because Sophocles' point can just as well be expressed in terms of contingency, rather than in the vocabulary of Greek polytheism. Contingency permeates human lives, including those guided by knowledge of the good and the will to pursue it. In wars, revolutions, tyrannies, natural disasters, epidemics, crimes, concentration camps, and emergencies, in acting as politicians, physicians, firefighters, officials of public health, criminal justice, or social welfare, or as parents, friends, or lovers, we have to make the weightiest choices on the basis of imperfect knowledge among noxious alternatives that circumstances force on us. Such situations are not of our making, we have not sought to be in them, and we would gladly avoid them if we could. But we cannot, we must act, and the consequence may be that we cause undeserved suffering to both ourselves and others. Human life is full of such suffering, its victims may never be compensated, knowledge of the good and a corresponding motivation are often unavailing and go unrecognized and unrewarded, and we frequently do not get what we deserve.

What emerges from this is that the natural world is indifferent to moral merit. The good may suffer and the bad may flourish, and the books may never be balanced. There is thus good reason to doubt that there is a morally good order in the natural world. The order that exists is impersonal and nonmoral. Its indifference is worse than neutrality because the latter at least implies the presence of some witnesses, even if they stand above the fray and remain uncommitted. That would permit hoping that they at least know about the human condition, and, perhaps, if things got really bad, their neutrality would be suspended. But there is no reason to suppose that this is so. There is no guarantee that what happens to us is affected by how reasonable or good we are.

But if contingency permeates life, if the connection between what happens and what ought to happen is fortuitous, then the hope that reason and morality will lead to a good life is illusory and fear of contingency is warranted. And then it becomes very hard to justify the optimism assumed by Plato's ideal. What may then follow is the state Wordsworth described:

> inwardly oppressed
> With sorrow, disappointment, vexing thoughts,
> Confusion of judgment, zeal destroyed,
> And lastly, utter loss of hope itself
> And things to hope for![3]

In this state we shall be inclined to give in to what I shall call the transcendental temptation. A particularly clear expression of it is Hegel's: "When we see . . . the evil, the vice, the ruin that has befallen the most flourishing kingdoms which the mind of man ever created, we can hardly avoid being filled with . . . a moral sadness, a revolt of good will—if indeed it has any place within us. Without rhetorical exaggeration, a simple truthful account of the miseries that have overwhelmed the noblest nations and polities and the finest exemplars of virtue forms a most fearful picture and excites emotions of the profoundest and most hopeless sadness, counter-balanced by no consoling results. . . . But in contemplating history as the slaughter-bench at which the happiness of peoples, the wisdom of states, and the virtue of individuals have been sacrificed, a question necessarily arises: To what principle, to what final purpose, have these monstrous sacrifices been offered?"[4]

Hegel's clear-sighted diagnosis is in effect denied by the assumption he drags in at the end that there is a purpose that somehow redeems the suffering human history so amply documents. This assumption, however, is merely another symptom of having succumbed to the transcendental temptation. The hope it gives is false hope, and the fear it aims to alleviate persists because there is no reason to think that a purpose exists, or that if it did, it would somehow redeem the suffering concomitant with its realization. Do the pyramids compensate the slaves who built them? Would supernatural pyramids compensate human beings? Is it plausible to suppose that the new family God gave to Job compensated him for the old one God took away?

If it is acknowledged that contingency puts human lives in jeopardy, if the false hope and equally false relief from fear created by giving in to the transcendental temptation are rejected, then what can we reasonably hope for and what can we do about our fear? Perhaps there is nothing, and then ignoring the questions may be the most reasonable course of action. A sturdy common sense may lead us to carry on with our lives, do as well as we can, and avoid these unsettling thoughts. To do otherwise, by dwelling on the hopelessness and fear produced by our vulnerability to contingency, is to sap the motivation for increasing control over our lives to the extent that it is possible.

It would nevertheless be unreasonable to proceed in this way because contingency is not just a freakish concatenation of unfavorable circumstances, as a shallow reading of *Oedipus the King* may lead one to suppose. Contingency permeates our lives as a result of genetic inheritance, upbringing, personal experiences, and social conditions, all of which easily escape our control. To foster a self-imposed blindness to the conditions that affect us and we cannot control is to collude in weakening the possibility of controlling what we can. There is, however, a more promising strategy for coping with hopelessness and fear. The fact that we are subject to contingency cannot be changed, but we can develop a reasonable reaction to it. This reaction is made possible by the corrective imagination we find Oedipus using to increasingly better effect, as shown by Sophocles in *Oedipus at Colonus*.

4.3 Oedipus's Achievement

At the beginning of the first play, Oedipus is the respected and unquestioned ruler of Thebes. His subjects tell him, "We do rate you first of men, / both in the common crises of our lives / and face-to-face encounters with the gods" (K. 42–44), because "you lifted up our lives" (K. 49). Oedipus lives the life he wants to live, and that is to be first among men. He believes that the key to it is control, and it depends on knowledge and power. He celebrates: "O power— / a wealth and empire, skill outstripping skill / in the heady rivalries of life" (K. 432–434). He is winning in the rivalries because of what he takes to be his superior character: "That is my blood, my nature—I will never betray it, / never fail to search" (K. 1193–1194), and the impetus behind the ceaseless search is a passionate desire: "I must know it all, / see the truth" (K. 1168–1169).

Reflecting on Oedipus at this stage of his life, we encounter the first sign of danger. We should always be on the alert when people say "I will never do this or that" or "I must act in this way." How could they possibly know what they might do, or might have to do, in the future? They themselves may change, or their circumstances may alter radically, and what was unthinkable before becomes thinkable. But there are questions even in the present: why *must* they act in a particular way now? what is the nature of the necessity that supposedly compels them? One answer is that they have reflected on all their possibilities, they have unequivocally committed themselves to one of them, what they must do is what their commitment requires, and what they will never do is to act contrary to it. Human fallibility, impoverished imagination, unexamined emotions, laziness, or boredom, however, may lead their reflection astray. It is much more likely that a second answer is true: their reflection is faulty, and nothing compels them to act as they feel they must or never to act as they feel they must not. Their reflection has not gone as far as it should and might have. They have just settled on the pursuit of some possibility at hand, they were reinforced in their choice by temporary success, and they stopped paying attention to other possibilities. This is reasonable to do, provided the possibility they have opted for was itself reasonable. But in Oedipus's case it was not, and its flaws soon became obvious. His declaration of "I must do . . ." and "I will never do . . ." indicate a failure of imagination rather than commitment to a truly essential condition of his identity.

If Oedipus knew what the possibility of control really requires and what other possibilities were open to him, then his "I must do . . ." and "I will never do . . ." would be far more credible. Oedipus, however, does not know; he only thinks he does, as Tiresias, who speaks for the gods, tells him: "you're blind to the corruption of your own life . . . All unknowing / you are the scourge of your own flesh and blood" (K. 471–474). As a result, "your power ends. / None of your power follows you through life" (K. 1676–1677). And soon ominous cracks begin to appear in his life, as his control slips.

As the action progresses, the superficiality of Oedipus's control is revealed. It is not that he lacks the knowledge and power he believes himself to have. Rather, the knowledge and power he has are not what is required for the control he seeks. Control *is* important and knowledge and power *are* its constituents, but their aims and objects are different from what Oedipus pursues. He thinks that the point of having knowledge and power is to control others, not himself. He thus fails to understand the true nature of control that is worth having. Understanding it would not save Oedipus from the calamity that befalls him—that he could not help. But he could have responded to the calamity in less self-destructive ways than he did if he had a deeper understanding of control.

As it is, his response to his misfortune makes matters even worse. When the feebleness of his control is revealed, Oedipus responds with a desperate reaffirmation of his misguided commitment to it. He reasserts his control by directing it against himself, his only remaining subject: in a wanton gesture, he blinds himself. When asked why he did such a horrible thing on top of all that has already happened to him, he says: "Apollo, friends, Apollo— / he ordained my agonies—these, my pains on pains! / But the hand that struck my eyes was mine / mine alone—no one else—I did it all myself" (K. 1467–1470). The chorus, beholding his misery, comments on his search for the wrong kind of control which shaped his self-destructive response: "Pitiful, you suffer so . . . / I wish you'd never known" (K. 1481–1482).

Oedipus, however, is strong, and his misfortune does not break him. He resolves to bear it and carry on because he still has a proud sense of his self: "My troubles are mine / and I am the only man alive who can sustain them" (K. 1548–1549), and "It's mine alone, my destiny—I am Oedipus!" (K. 1496). And so there he is at the end of the first play, having lost the misguided power he sought, having suffered because of the misdirected knowledge he worked so hard to acquire, and yet, for the first time, having some real control over what little is left of his previous mode of life.

The second play opens many years after the end of the first. Oedipus spent the intervening time as a blind beggar wandering in Greece, led by Antigone and Ismene, his daughters born of incest. The news of what befell him is well known, and although he is pitied, no city will accept him since he is polluted with the horrors of parricide and incest. The stage is thus set for Oedipus to try to come to terms with what happened, to understand what had gone wrong that brought him from the height of power to beggary:

> wrapped in such rags—appalling—
> the filth of years clings to his old withered body,
> wasting away the skin, the flesh on his ribs . . .
> and his face, the blind sockets of his eyes,
> and the white hair wild, flying in the wind! (C. 1421–1427)

He has become a "harried ghost of a man, / . . . Oedipus is no more / the flesh and blood of old" (C. 133–135). His dramatic physical change, however, is superficial and outward. The deep change is inward: he has become "someone sacred, filled with piety and power, bearing a great gift" (C. 312–313), which is the understanding he has reached. He now sees that the power worth having is not winning "in the heady rivalries of life" (K. 434), as he wrongly believed when he was king, but "acceptance—that is the great lesson suffering teaches" (C. 6), and he resolves, "No more fighting with necessity" (C. 210).

His attitude to knowledge also changes. The proud claims of the first play, resting on mistakes about himself, "That is my blood, my nature—I will never betray it, / never fail to search" (K. 1193–1194) and "I must know it all, / see the truth" (K. 1168–1169) are replaced by "No no! Don't ask me who I am / —no more probing, testing—stop—no more!" (C. 225–226). Instead of using his knowledge and power as instruments for the futile effort of trying to control his world, an endeavor that almost destroyed him, he now uses them to try to control himself by understanding what he did and what happened to him and by shaping his responses to both. He says, reflecting on his past, "As time wore on / and the smoldering fever broke and died at last / and I began to feel my rage has outrun my wrongs, / I'd lashed myself too much for what I'd done, once long ago" (C. 486–490).

Oedipus's acceptance of contingency, his abandonment of the restless search for some key to himself outside himself, gives him a measure of knowledge, power, and, consequently, control, and it guides his response to the world. He begins to know "the final things of life" (C. 656), and uses his limited power to scorn unworthy possibilities and to support good ones insofar as he can. What he rejects comes to him through Creon, who fraudulently attempts to enlist Oedipus's help to shore up his crumbling power (C. 865–910), and Polynices, Oedipus's son, who has abandoned his father to a miserable old age when he could have eased his plight without much trouble (C. 1524–1584). Oedipus also uses his power on the side of the good by bestowing on Athens "the power that age cannot destroy, / the heritage stored up for . . . Athens" (C. 1718–1719) that "will always form a defense . . . / a bulwark stronger than many shields" (C. 1724–1725).

Oedipus thus attains at the end of his life a considerable amount of control, a growing understanding of "the final things in life" (C. 656). "The great lesson suffering teaches" (C. 6) is that resistance is futile, "there is no escape, ever" (C. 303). He was wrong to struggle against contingency, and yet he sees that what happened to him was undeserved: "say my unwilling crimes against myself / and against my own were payments from the gods / for something criminal inside me . . . no, look hard, / you'll find no guilt to accuse me of—I'm innocent!" (C. 1101–1105). He killed his father, but he was "blind to whom I killed" (C. 1115), and he married his mother, "but I knew nothing, she knew nothing" (C. 1123). That contingency impinged on his life, that it made him suffer, that his reason and will achieved the opposite of what he intended—that, he came to understand, is just one unfortunate outcome of the human condition:

> what mortal blows can he escape
> what griefs won't stalk his days?
> Envy and enemies, rage and battles, bloodshed
> and last of all despised old age overtakes him,
> stripped of power, companions, stripped of love (C. 1393–1397)

It deepens one's appreciation of the play to realize that it was written by Sophocles the Athenian close to his death at the probable age of ninety and close also to Athens' foreseeable loss of the Peloponnesian Wars, which a few years later put an end to its glorious fifth century, during which Athens laid the foundation of our cultural life. It is important also to know that Colonus was a small village just outside Athens, where Oedipus died and where Sophocles was born. The connections and allusions are too many not to believe that what Sophocles shows Oedipus to have understood at the end of his life is not very different from the truth about the human condition Sophocles came to understand and wanted to leave to posterity. Nor is it too great a reach to conclude that the lines predicting that "the power that age cannot destroy / the heritage stored up for . . . Athens" have come true and that part of the heritage is Sophocles' Oedipus. And perhaps the parting words Sophocles gives to Oedipus:

> Dearest friend,
> you and your country and your loyal followers
> may you be blessed with greatness,
> and in your great day remember me, the dead,
> the root of all your greatness, everlasting, ever new (C.1761–1765)

are his own epitaph.

4.4 Coping with Contingency

The process of Oedipus's reflective self-evaluation that began at the end of *Oedipus the King* and was completed in his death at the end of

Oedipus at Colonus illustrates the corrective imagination at work. Sophocles shows this process, but I now want to consider it more analytically. We may begin with the question of why Oedipus's situation is so redolent with significance. It cannot merely be because he was manipulated into doing what he regarded as most seriously immoral. After all, sad as it is, people often inflict unwitting injury on those they love, and undeserved suffering and self-loathing are common enough. The source of its significance is that Sophocles depicts a conflict between his understanding of the human condition and the Platonic ideal creating the *expectation* that if the possibilities of a good life are pursued reasonably and morally, then they will be realized. The significance of Oedipus's situation is that it forces those who understand it to reflect on the discrepancy between Sophocles' understanding of the human condition and the Platonic ideal.

The expectation is that contingency will be overcome by reason and morality. Oedipus's situation is tragic because it violates this expectation. It shows the futility of living reasonably and morally, as Oedipus stumbles toward understanding his predicament. The dramatic reversal of his fortune moves us to fear, undermines our hope, and leads us to a deeper understanding of the human condition. The result of the disappointed expectation is the realization that Oedipus's situation is emblematic of the human condition. Hopelessness and fear then ensue. To see life as some tragedies suggest is to see that there is no hope and it is right to be afraid.

The first step in the work of the corrective imagination is to recognize the hold this illusory expectation has on us. The second step is to free us from the expectation by showing that it rests on our mistaken belief that reason and morality can guarantee a good life. As a result, we come to see the expectation as a lingering remnant of a state of mind that has been left behind by those who understand that contingency may frustrate even the noblest aspirations, and that the aspiration may be our own. The effect of this understanding will be to gradually wean its possessors from the expectation whose disappointment makes the human condition appear hopeless and fearful. That condition remains the same whether or not the illusory expectation is held, but understanding its illusoriness may change our reaction to it by freeing us from the hopelessness and fear that it might run afoul of reality. If we are without the expectation, we cannot hope that it will be met or fear that it might not be.

It may said against this that the possibility of arriving at this reaction is also subject to contingency, and so it is pointless to recommend its cultivation. But this is not so. The extent to which contingency affects lives varies with context and circumstance. In some cases, its effect is decisive, we are powerless to resist it, and then the recommendation *is* pointless. It would be grotesque, if not obscene, to urge people on the way to the gas chamber to abandon their illusions. But not all situations are like this. In ordinary life, it is often possible to cultivate it. Oedipus could certainly have done so before calamity overtook him. The recommendation has a point, therefore, for the vast majority of people whose lives are merely vulnerable to but not ruined by contingency.

The question should be pressed, however, of what good the reaction is if it does not change the facts. Why is it more reasonable to try to live a good life with the understanding that we may fail no matter how reasonable and moral we are than to acquire that understanding as a result of failure? There is a long and a short answer. The short one is that the understanding makes lives better. Those who have it will cope with contingency better than Oedipus did. They will see that it is better to understand one's vulnerability to contingency and to live a life informed by that understanding than to be shocked into the recognition that the expectation is illusory. The reaction frees us not just from the shock that bad things can happen to such good people as we undoubtedly are, but also from the futile response of inveighing against the gods, as Oedipus did, and from the sort of dramatic overreaction that his self-blinding illustrates.

This short answer, however, is general and does not provide much guidance about how to answer the further question that will be asked: What can *I* do in the face of the contingency of *my* life to make it good or better, given *my* character and circumstances? We all live in concrete cultural, political, and social contexts, and we are all saddled with a genetic inheritance, personal experiences, and social conditioning that decisively influence the kind of character we have or can develop. A longer answer is needed, therefore, to bring out the practical implications of this general account for concrete situations. How can this general account be applied to the daily experiences we enjoy and suffer?

If we understand that conditions beyond our control endanger our aspirations to live a good life, then it becomes possible to control our reaction to this regrettable fact. This will help us to face the realization that we are at risk, that misfortune may actually happen to anyone, including ourselves. Our control will be extended in this way by not allowing the understanding of our vulnerability to be falsified by some form of denial, or to provoke us into some sort of overreaction; or to undercut our efforts to do what is possible in pursuit of a good life, or to prevent the exacerbation of our misfortune, if it befalls us, through a mistaken reaction to it. The variety of mistaken reactions to the human condition is great. Discussing them would take a very long—and depressing—book, and this is not that book. It will suffice instead to discuss briefly four frequent, perhaps most typical, mistaken reactions: disengagement, denial, exaggeration, and resignation.

Consider this wonderfully suggestive description: "One summer . . . a large spider appeared in the urinal of the men's room. . . . When the urinal wasn't in use, he would perch on the metal drain at its base, and when it was, he would try to scramble out of the way, sometimes managing to climb an inch or two up the porcelain wall to a point that wasn't too wet. But sometimes he was caught, tumbled and drenched by the flushing torrent. He didn't seem to like it, and always got out of the way if he could. . . . Somehow he survived, presumably feeding on tiny insects attracted to the site. . . . The urinal must have been used more than a hundred times a day, and always it was the same desperate scramble to get out of the way. His life seemed miserable and exhausting."[5] If the human condition is viewed *sub specie aeternitatis*, human beings may appear as that spider. But if that perspective is truly nonanthropocentric, it will influence our emotions and will as little as does the spider's lot. We can, then, cultivate a cool, dispassionate, uncommitted reaction while observing the spectacle but remaining disengaged from it.

The cultivation of this reaction widens the distance between us as participants and as observers of our own participation. But no matter how successfully we cultivate it, we cannot cease to be participants because that would put an end to our lives. What the distance produces, therefore, is not a life of passive contemplation, for we cannot live such a life, but a life in which we disengage from participation. We cannot disengage totally, but we can reject the naiveté of wholehearted enthusiasm toward our miserable and exhausting existence in the human equivalent of the spider's urinal. The result is a frame of mind in which we react to contingency by teaching ourselves to disengage from the life that is endangered by it. We thus endeavor to cope with the human condition by distancing ourselves from it as far as we can. But the better we succeed, the less we will care about making our life good. "If *sub specie aeternitatis* there is no reason to believe that anything matters, then that does not matter either."[6]

All this, however, rests on viewing the human condition *sub specie aeternitatis*, and we should ask why that is supposed to be desirable. If we adopted that point of view, then, of course, what matters *sub specie humanitatis* would not matter. But it would be destructive of our aspirations to live a good life to disengage ourselves from it. It is a mistake to react to the realization that contingency puts us at risk by abandoning the efforts to make our lives better. The success of those efforts *is* endangered by the risk we face. But what we must face is only the *risk* of failure, not its certainty. Oedipus's situation *is* like the spider's. Our situation, however, is like Oedipus's only in the sense that everyone is as much at risk as he was before his life collapsed. Most lives, however, have not collapsed, although they may do so. Disengagement would make collapse more likely by weakening our will and desire to exercise such control over our lives as possible.

Behind the reaction of disengagement, therefore, is the mistake of taking the state of being at risk for being doomed. Risk holds out the possibility of success, not just of failure. Excessive fear of failure may lead to a loss of nerve, and that to the failure to extricate ourselves, if we can, from the risky situation. But the risk itself is integral to the human condition, so we can extricate ourselves only from particular manifestations of it. The risk itself we can only face well or badly. Disengagement leads to facing it badly because it worsens whatever chances there are of succeeding.

The strategy of viewing the world *sub specie aeternitatis* has notable successes to its credit. The great achievements of the physical and biological sciences have been made possible precisely by that objective, dispassionate, nonanthropocentric quest for understanding that also motivates disengagement. From this similarity, however, no support can be derived for disengagement. The nonanthropocentric view is appropriate to understanding nature, but not the evaluative dimension of human lives. The physical and biological sciences are not ex officio concerned with the bearing their discoveries may have on our lives. To be sure, scientists are no less interested in good lives than anyone else, but they are interested in their capacity as human beings, not as scientists. Disengagement, by contrast, is a deliberate turning away from the interests of humanity. It is not a phenomenological bracketing of the human condition for the purposes of inquiry, but a conscious effort to replace, insofar as that is possible, the anthropocentric perspective that is inevitable for human beings with an alien, nonanthropocentric one. The resulting disengagement is unavoidably committed, therefore, to downgrading the importance of what matters *sub specie humanitatis*. The strategy of coping with the prospect of failure by minimizing its importance and diverting the efforts needed for success cannot help being self-defeating.

A second mistaken reaction to the realization that it is impossible to avoid being at risk is to erect some barrier that prevents facing the full implications of that realization. The barrier may be conscious, involving a deliberate effort to ignore or to dismiss the disturbing truth. Or it may be unconscious, in which case it takes the form of self-deception. It involves persuading oneself that one is invulnerable to the risk other people face or that, although the risk is there, it is so insignificant as to be negligible. This state of mind is depicted in Tolstoy's Ivan Ilych: "In the depth of his heart he knew he was dying, but not only was he not accustomed to the thought, he simply did not and could not grasp it. The syllogism he had learnt . . . 'Caius is a man, men are mortal, therefore Caius is mortal,' has always seemed to him correct as applied to Caius, but certainly not as applied to himself. . . . Caius really was mortal, and it was right for him to die, but for me . . . with all my thoughts and emotions, it's altogether a different matter. It cannot be that I ought to die. That would be too terrible."[7]

The trouble with this reaction is that it misdirects the attention and thereby increases the liability to contingency that rightly focused attention might mitigate. If it is kept firmly in mind that contingency may destroy or damage anyone, including oneself and those one loves, it will prompt concentration on what is important and prevent the frittering away of whatever possibilities of a good life there are on trivial pursuits. The denial of risk increases our liability to it, whereas its acknowledgment strengthens our defenses against it. Its acknowledgment, however, can also go wrong because it may elicit an overreaction. This can go in the direction of heroism or despair. Both involve exaggeration, and thus the falsification of the facts that need to be faced. It may lead to an inflation of one's powers or to a pessimistic overestimation of the threat presented by contingency. The younger Oedipus is an instructive example of one who swings back and forth between these pitfalls. He vexes heroically, "My troubles are mine / and I am the only man alive who can sustain them" (K. 1548–1549), and he exaggerates in despair, declaiming that he is "the man the deathless gods hate most of all!" (K. 1480). Then the combination of these inflated passions causes him to erupt in the spectacular reaction of self-blinding, which, of course, makes matters even worse than they already were.

Realism is one of our most important resources in facing contingency. For our troubles are rarely so great and our lives rarely involve so glorious heroic struggles against overwhelming odds as it may seem to us in the throes of passion. We cannot stop having strong feelings, especially not in the midst of crises that provoke them. But we can stop them from getting out of hand. If we know the emotional excesses to which we are prone, we can recognize them when they are about to occur and we can stop ourselves from being led by them to inappropriate action, as Oedipus was to self-blinding. And then, as the old Oedipus has learned—"my rage has outrun my wrongs, / I'd lashed myself too much" (C. 488–489)—we may also learn to control their strength.

Yet even if the temptation to deny or to exaggerate what understanding contingency reveals is resisted, there remains the lure of resignation. We may come to wonder about the point of wholehearted engagement in life, if the efforts we make cannot free us from contingency. Understanding this and controlling our feelings may just sap our will. Instinct, training, the need to earn a living, small pleasures, a mild curiosity about the future, and intermittent amusement afforded by being a spectator may make us carry on, but our hearts will not be in it. We will lack enthusiasm, dedication, and seriousness, and our lives become permeated by a languid insipidity in which nothing really matters, like Eliot's J. Alfred Prufrock or the middle-aged characters of Chekhov, desultorily talking away their lives during endless barren afternoons. What results is the very misfortune whose prospect motivated resignation. For what initially disturbs us is the fear that we will not attain a good life despite our best efforts. If this leads us to make only minimal efforts, we collude in causing what we fear. The reasonable alternative is to make our best efforts, while understanding that they may be unavailing and disciplining ourselves not to allow our feelings to get out of hand if we face the likelihood of failure. What makes this alternative reasonable is that it helps to make lives good.

I have tried to show how the balanced ideal of reflective self-evaluation relying on corrective imagination may help us cope with the contingency of life. The alternative to the stark choice between succumbing to the transcendental temptation and giving in to hopelessness and fear is to understand that contingency may frustrate reasonable and moral efforts to live a good life, that the resulting hopelessness and fear are due to the unrealistic expectation that the human condition is other than it is, that abandoning this expectation is to remove the ground of hopelessness and fear, and that the key to all this is to use the corrective imagination to prevent us from forming a mistaken reaction to what we have thus understood. Thus we move toward greater realism, which acknowledges the pervasive influence of contingency but mitigates its destructive consequences. This greater realism alleviates hopelessness and excessive fear. It chastens, purifies, and strengthens us through resisting the mistaken reactions of disengagement, denial of the facts, exaggerated self-aggrandizement or despair, and resignation. It is without the expectation that everything will turn out well, and without bitterness that the world is not more hospitable to humanity.

What is left is enough to fend off despair. We are vulnerable to contingency, but it need not ruin us. And even if we are damaged by it, we need not be destroyed, as Oedipus was not. Realism avoids the futility of hounding the unresponsive heavens to relieve our misfortune, and it encourages us to pick up the damaged pieces, if they can be picked up, and go on. It does not promise that good lives pursued reasonably and morally will be realized, but it reassures us that if we do what is possible to succeed, and if we nevertheless fail despite reasonable and moral efforts, we may still survive to try another day. It promises only that if we correct our mistaken reactions, we will increase our control and thereby decrease our vulnerability to contingency.

This realism, however, is incompatible with the voluntarist ideal of reflective self-evaluation. For that ideal leads to Promethean romanticism because it assigns priority to will over reason. The realism that we have arrived at by reflecting on Oedipus's life is the result of denying that will and reason are competing sources of motivation. The will moves us to action, but as it does, it must be kept under the control of reason, which evaluates the willed action from the point of view of the goodness of one's life.

4.5 Is Realism Enough?

Let us for a moment go back to *Oedipus at Colonus*. As the play closes, Oedipus has come to terms with his past: he sees where he has gone wrong, he has corrected his mistaken reactions to control, his passions have cooled, he is finally at peace with himself, he has learned to feel and show love and generosity toward his daughters and Athens, and he is ready to die. He has put to good use what I have called the corrective imagination. It seems, then, that the play has a happy ending. This has made many attentive readers wonder why it should be thought of as a tragedy.

What makes a play a tragedy is an exceptionally difficult question, but whatever the answer is, it surely excludes a happy ending. We expect the tragic hero to suffer and come to a bad end. Oedipus, as a king, did, but Oedipus, as an old man, did not. Is it perhaps that Sophocles, as an old man, has come to the end of his talent and could no longer match the perfection of *Oedipus the King*? This has been said, more than once, but I think it is a mistake. *Oedipus at Colonus* is a tragedy. What makes it that, however, is not the suffering and bad end of its hero, for he does not suffer and his end is not bad, but what it shows *through* Oedipus's life and death. And what that is should make us suspect that realism is not enough.

Oedipus's central preoccupation after the ending of *Oedipus the King* was with using corrective imagination as a means of the reflective evaluation of his earlier self and what it was in it that had led him to actions that destroyed the moral foundation of his life. And he comes to understand that it was his misunderstanding of what kinds of knowledge, power, and control were worth having. But he does more: he corrects his misunderstanding and, as blind beggar, acquires much greater control over his life and actions than he had as a king. He is now free to go on—and then he dies. We thus see his life as an arduous quest to correct the faults that brought him to ruin, and at the successful completion of this quest what awaits him is death. Just when he could put to good use what he has learned, death deprives him of the possibility. That is what is tragic and what Sophocles shows in *Oedipus at Colonus*, through the life and death of Oedipus, about the human condition.

This prompts a number of questions: is this view of the human condition accurate? is it true that the best realism and reflective self-evaluation can bring us is a life without hopelessness and paralyzing fear? are we to be set free from hope and fear only to look forward to death? is the point of life to prevent it from getting worse? is this all we have to live *for*?

If the answer to these questions were yes, realism and reflective self-evaluation would lead to a very bleak view of our prospects. It is undoubtedly true that life without hopelessness and fear is better than a life ruled by despair, alleviated perhaps by self-deception. To avoid a bad life, however, is not to have a good one. A good life must be fulfilling. We must regard it as meaningful; we must find some of our activities worthwhile; we must enjoy or take satisfaction in how our life is going. The view of life we find in Sophocles lacks these good-making elements. Having rejected the Platonic ideal, the Sophoclean view is left without meaningful, worthwhile, satisfying possibilities. The Platonic ideal is faulty, Sophocles has shown, but faults notwithstanding, it is inspiring. It provides a positive goal to aim at, whereas the Sophoclean view merely shows how we might lessen the chances of having a bad life. But doing what it says we should—facing and correcting our misguided beliefs, feelings, and desires—is hard. What is the point of making the effort since there is a much easier way of avoiding a bad life? Why not act on the words with which Sophocles concludes *Oedipus the King*: "count no man happy till he dies, free of pain at last" (K. 1684)? Why not avoid even the chance of a bad life by suicide? As far as I can see, the consistent Sophoclean response must be: why not indeed? And this is perhaps too high a price to pay for giving up the Platonic ideal.

There is, however, an alternative to Sophoclean bleakness and Platonic illusion. We can answer no to the questions above that realism and reflective self-evaluation prompt us to ask without embracing the Platonic illusion. The alternative is to pursue the possibilities the exploratory imagination provides. This is not to deny that the corrective imagination must also do its work. For our present dissatisfactions often result from the misunderstanding of our past possibilities as a result of self-deception, fantasy, superficiality, laziness, and other defects. That is why we have pursued the wrong possibilities, and that is why we are now dissatisfied. But moral imagination can do more: it can lead us to future possibilities whose pursuit would make our lives better. This means that the work of moral imagination is not complete if it is only corrective; it must also be exploratory so that it provides possibilities to live for. Unless they are combined, the corrective imagination alone will, as the epigraph says, set us free from unrealistic hope and fear and leave us with no more than a bleak thanksgiving that no life lives forever. Realism is necessary but not sufficient.

CHAPTER 5

All Passion Spent

Calm of mind, all passion spent
—John Milton, "Samson Agonistes"

5.1 Responsibility and Fulfillment

The impetus for the use of corrective imagination is dissatisfaction with one's life. A good life is responsible and fulfilling, and dissatisfaction indicates that one or both of its requirements are to a greater or lesser extent unmet. The reasons for this are many and various. We have seen in Oedipus's case that the problem was his mistaken view of the control he took to be necessary for a fulfilling life. He was right in thinking that control depends on knowledge and power but wrong in supposing that their objects are other people rather than oneself. His dissatisfaction was a consequence of his mistake. Another, more dire consequence was that it led him to what he himself regarded as violations of fundamental moral prohibitions. In discussing his case, I aimed to show how moral imagination enabled him to understand and correct his mistake, although death prevented him from actually living the fulfilling life he sought for so long.

In this chapter I consider another case in which a fulfilling life escapes two protagonists even though they use their corrective imagination. Their reason for failure, however, is very different from Oedipus's. The protagonists of the present chapter are exemplary from the moral point of view, but that is precisely what leads to their unfulfilling lives. The two requirements of good lives can conflict: a fulfilling life may be irresponsible, and a responsible life may be unfulfilling. The fault for the conflict may lie with the conception of fulfillment or with the conception of responsibility. Moral imagination may be used to correct a conception of fulfillment by making it conform more closely to the requirements of morality, or to correct a conception of responsibility by making it more conducive to fulfillment. The *moral* use of corrective imagination thus may lead to the improvement of individuals, as in Oedipus's case, or to the improvement of moralities, as in the case I consider here, which focuses on Edith Wharton's great novel *The Age of Innocence*.[1]

The milieu of the novel is upper-middle-class society in New York during the last decades of the nineteenth century. The main protagonists are Newland Archer and Countess Olenska. Archer is a highly respectable member of this society, a lawyer, engaged to May Welland, an equally respectable young woman. Countess Olenska was born and raised in this setting, but marriage to a Polish count took her to Europe, where she and her husband had lived for many years. At the beginning of the novel, Countess Olenska returns to New York to seek the protection and comfort of her family and society, for she has left her corrupt husband and intends to divorce him. She is warmly received, but it is made clear to her that divorce is not countenanced by the prevailing moral conventions. The person who communicates this to her is Archer, who is acting both as a lawyer for her family and as a representative of their society. He explains to her in the course of several meetings that the consequences of her intended divorce would be to weaken their society, hurt her family and friends, and make her life there impossible. She ought, therefore, to give up the idea. She listens to him, upon reflection accepts the justifications he offers, and abandons the idea of divorce.

As it happens, however, in the course of their encounters, during which they discuss intimate matters normally left unsaid, Archer and Countess Olenska fall in love. Having accepted the case against divorce, she is, of course, not free to marry him. He, being engaged to May Welland, is similarly constrained. This time, however, Archer would go against the moral conventions of their society, and Countess Olenska insists that the case he had made to her earlier for conforming to them still holds. They give each other up, opt for an unfulfilling life, and accept that their love is impossible. Countess Olenska returns to Europe, where she lives out her life in dignified separation from her corrupt husband. Archer remains in New York and grows old as an exemplary but unfulfilled husband, father, lawyer, and pillar of society. There are four increasingly adequate interpretations of the significance of this simple story.

5.2 Living Responsibly

According to the first interpretation, moral conventions forbid Countess Olenska's divorce. There is a conflict between a responsible and a fulfilling life, and opting for the former, as she does, calls for a sacrifice. The following conversation between Archer and Countess Olenska may be thought to support this interpretation. She says, "I want to cast off my old life, to become just like everybody else here." And again, "I want to be free, I want to wipe out all the past." She reminds Archer, "You know my husband—my life with him?" "In this country are such things tolerated? I'm a Protestant—our church does not forbid divorce in such cases." He replies, "New York society is a very small world . . . it's ruled by . . . rather old-fashioned ideas. . . . Our ideas about marriage and divorce are particularly old-fashioned. Our legislature favours divorce—our social customs don't." She asks, "But my freedom—is that nothing?" And he says, "The individual, in such cases, is nearly always sacrificed to what is supposed to be the collective interest: people cling to any convention that keeps the family together. . . . It is my business, you know . . . to help you see these things as people who are fondest of you see them . . . all your friends here and relations: if I didn't show you honestly how they judge such questions, it wouldn't be fair of me." She considers the case he put and after a time acquiesces: "Very well; I will do what you wish" (12).

Archer's case and Countess Olenska's submission strike our modern sensibility as outrageous. Here is an admittedly injured woman, wishing to free herself from an ugly marriage, and Archer, that plenipotentiary of conventional morality, persuades her otherwise. We want to urge her to seize the day, be free, go after happiness, and sweep responsibility to superficial conventions aside. Life is to be lived, not constrained by bloodless conventions. The recognition that this is a misguided response will point the way toward a better understanding of the significance of what Wharton is showing through Archer and Countess Olenska.

Well, then, why is it misguided to see this as an obviously mistaken choice of responsibility to moral conventions over freedom, happiness, and a fulfilling life? A distinction between two attitudes toward the moral conventions of one's society will help with the answer. One attitude is conformity, which is simply to conduct oneself according to the prevailing conventions. It is to do or not to do what the conventions prescribe or prohibit; to behave appropriately, respectably. This kind of conformity to moral conventions is akin to law-abidingness. Knowledge of the relevant prescriptions and taking the corresponding actions are required and sufficient. This knowledge is not hard to obtain for anyone familiar with the social context, and the required actions are rarely demanding. Conformity is all on the surface. What matters is what is done, not why it is done, so conformity can be hypocritical.

The other attitude is identification. It is essentially connected with motivation, with the reasons for doing what the conventions prescribe. Identification is to have one's outlook informed by the prevailing conventions and act according to them because one approves of them. Those who have identified themselves with the conventions accept them, their conception of responsibility is shaped by them, their view of a fulfilling life is inseparable from them, they are comfortable with them, and they derive part of their identity from them. The attitude of identification, therefore, goes deep: it is connected with what people are and want to be. It cannot be hypocritical.

The outrage provoked in modern sensibility by Countess Olenska's decision is misguided because it sees the conflict between a responsible and a fulfilling life as juxtaposing superficial propriety to the much deeper matter of trying to live a fulfilling life. According to modern sensibility, Countess Olenska was wrong to allow herself to be persuaded by Archer's argument and he was wrong to lead her to it. They colluded in favoring superficiality over depth. The trouble with modern sensibility is that it fails to recognize the significance of the distinction between conformity to and identification with the prevailing moral conventions.

Countess Olenska's decision was motivated by her attitude of identification. She decided not to seek divorce because it would have violated the prevailing conventions of her society. The reason why Archer could persuade her was that she was committed to those conventions, although she did not realize that they prohibited divorce even in cases in which the person seeking it was injured by the marriage. Archer explained to her both that this was so and the reasons for it. Having understood that, her conflict was not between superficial conformity and the serious matter of trying to live a fulfilling life, but between alternative conceptions of a fulfilling life. She felt deep allegiance to the society whose conventions prohibited divorce, and she felt just as deeply that she wanted to be free of her ugly marriage. Her conflict was between what she saw as the good of her society and her own good, and she chose, with Archer's help, the good of her society. If her choice is seen in this light, we may still think that it was mistaken, but it would be simpleminded to regard it as outrageous. We do, after all, celebrate people who sacrifice their fulfillment for the good of their society, as Countess Olenska appears to have done. Modern sensibility prompts this simpleminded response, and that is why it is misguided. Of course, just because Countess Olenska and Archer are not obviously mistaken in favoring a responsible over a fulfilling life does not mean that they are not mistaken. Their choice requires justification, and that is what we find when we consider the second interpretation, which is better than the first but still not right.

5.3 Opting for Responsibility

According to this interpretation, there is a conflict between a responsible and a fulfilling life, but Countess Olenska and Archer have strong reasons to resolve it in favor of a responsible life. If this is understood, the conflict becomes less important and its resolution involves a much smaller sacrifice than it seemed before. After she has made her choice, Countess Olenska and Archer discuss what made her accept his argument. She says, "I felt there was no one . . . who gave me reasons that I understood for doing what at first seemed so hard and—unnecessary. The very good people didn't convince me; I felt they'd never been tempted. But you knew; you understood; you have felt the outside tugging at one with all its golden hands—and yet you hated the things it asks of one; you hated happiness bought by disloyalty and cruelty and indifference. That was what I'd never known before—and it is better than anything I've known" (18).

The essential point that Archer made and Countess Olenska accepted was that since she regards New York society as better than anything she had known, it has a claim on her allegiance. Its conventions prohibit divorce, and therefore she ought not to seek it. Reason and many of her feelings favor this conclusion. She was born and raised in that society and imbibed its conventions and the responsibility to honor them from cradle on. When she left and marriage took her to another society, she judged her husband and his society corrupt according to the conventions in which she was raised. These conventions defined her limits, not consciously or intellectually, but by making her feel that certain ways of living and acting are unthinkable. As an observer says of her, "if you are an American of *her* kind . . . things that are accepted in certain societies, or at least put up with as part of the general give-and-take—become unthinkable, simply unthinkable" (25). When she finds her husband engaged in the give-and-take as readily as she finds it unthinkable, she thinks he is corrupt, feels soiled, and leaves him. And she leaves him for her own people, her family and society, for the conventional milieu that has formed her. "New York simply meant peace and freedom to me: it was coming home. And I was so happy at being among my own people that everyone I met seemed kind and good, and glad to see me" (18). This is how many feelings prompt her decision. For how could she opt for divorce and show "disloyalty and cruelty and indifference" to her own people, whose conventions she shares and who have been so "kind and good" to her?

Yet the force of these feelings alone is not strong enough to make her give up divorce because she has feelings pulling also in the other direction. As strongly as she feels allegiance to New York society, so she feels revolted by her husband's society. One prohibits, the other demands, divorce. These conflicting feelings make her confused, indecisive, and in need of advice. Reason enters through Archer, who, at this stage, acts as her adviser. What qualifies Archer to be an adviser is that his conduct up to this point, before he falters, is exemplary, and he is reflective and articulate about the responsibility to live according to the system of conventions he accepts. He has thoroughly identified himself with the conventional morality of his society. He has compared New York society with others and found it better. And he can not only make reliable judgments but also explain the reasons for his judgments. That is just what he does to Countess Olenska.

Seen in this light, the conflict between a responsible and a fulfilling life is softened. The society to which allegiance is supposed to be their responsibility can no longer be thought of as upholding a system of trivial and old-fashioned conventions that stand in the way of freedom and fulfillment. Archer's life and conduct show that there is no sharp conflict between identification with the conventions and a fulfilling life because he is a living testimony to the possibility of having both. Countess Olenska's conception of fulfillment is inseparably connected with living according to the conventions of the society that has formed her. These conventions define for her what a fulfilling life is. Divorce is at once contrary to it and something she wishes. What Archer shows her is that the conflict she faces is not between responsibility and fulfillment but between a deeply and superficially considered conception of fulfillment. The superficial conception is connected with getting what she wants now; the shoe pinches, and she wants to take it off. Wanting that, viewed in isolation from her whole life and its context, is reasonable and understandable. The deeper view, however, moves beyond immediate satisfaction and places the conflict in the perspective of her whole life. Of course divorce would make her life better now, but it would also alienate her from her society, belonging to which is a condition of a fulfilling life for her. It would also involve a signal act of disloyalty to those who were good to her when she turned to them for help. It would be impossible, therefore, for her to have a fulfilling life if she were to divorce. So her choice is not between responsibility and fulfillment but between the possibility of a short-term relief from her misfortune and the possibility of a fulfilling life in the long run. This is what Archer leads her to see, and this is why both reason and the balance of feelings prompt her to give up the idea of divorce.

We are, however, in the hands of a master, and Wharton's vision is too cool, too ironic, too understanding of human weakness to allow us to see Archer as the paragon that he has so far appeared to be. In the course of all that advising and earnest discussion, he falls in love with Countess Olenska and she with him. But it is Archer now who is ready to go against the conventions in the name of their love. He wants her to divorce, and he is willing to break up his engagement, so that he and Countess Olenska could marry and, presumably, live happily ever after. Archer's feelings grow too strong, and they carry him away. The case he has made to Countess Olenska still holds, but he ignores it. If he were to reflect, he would realize that he is proposing to violate his own commitments, but in the grip of his feelings, he does not reflect. This time, however, Countess Olenska does for him what he previously did for her.

Archer tells her of his love, and she says, "My poor Newland—I suppose this had to be. But it doesn't in the least alter things." Archer replies, "It alters the whole world for me." Countess Olenska, then, says, "No, no—it mustn't, it can't. You are engaged to May Welland; and I am married." But he does not accept it. "He reddened under the retort, but kept his eyes on her. 'May is ready to give me up'." "What!" she says, "Three days after you've entreated her on your knees to hasten your marriage?" But, he says, the lawyer coming to the fore, "She's refused; that gives me the right—" (18). And to that, Countess Olenska has two significant rejoinders.

The first is about Archer's appeal to his rights: "you've taught me what an ugly word that is" (18). Why is *right* an ugly word? Given their conventional morality, Countess Olenska has a right to divorce, and Archer explained to her why she should not exact that right. Archer has a right to break up his engagement, and Countess Olenska explains to him why he should not take advantage of it. A right is a claim against others. This claim may or may not be cashed in. People may have a right to commit suicide, have an abortion, and see pornographic movies. But that is not an invitation to engage in these activities. There is a question of when rights should be acted on. What Countess Olenska is saying is that they should not act on theirs because it would go against the spirit, although not the letter, of their conventions. It would be irresponsible of her to divorce and of him to break up his engagement. It would make their lives better at the cost of "disloyalty and cruelty and indifference." It would offend the sensibilities of "the very good people" who have "never been tempted" and tear the fabric of their own, their families', and their friends' lives. The victims of their disloyalty, cruelty, and indifference would not just be the untempted good people but also those they love and who love them. The goodness of their own and intimates' lives would be undermined if they acted on their rights. When Archer says, we have the right, he means casuistically: we would not violate superficial conformity to conventions if we did what was necessary to get married. Countess Olenska says, in effect, exacting our rights would violate their deep identification with the conventions.

Identification involves more than merely customary conduct. It is also having good will toward others in one's society and a usually unarticulated belief that fellow members of a society share a moral outlook that governs how they should conduct themselves and treat others. Identification depends on translating this deep allegiance into practical terms. It shows itself on the surface by conformity, and more deeply by not standing on one's rights if doing so is contrary to the spirit of the shared conventions.

The second of Countess Olenska's significant replies to Archer is, "I can't love you unless I give you up" (18). She means: they love each other for what they are, and that is partly defined by their shared sense of responsibility to honor the conventions. If they violated the conventions, they would destroy part of what they found lovable in each other. Their love, therefore, requires that they should give each other up. But Archer protests, "What a life for you!" and she replies, "As long as it's part of yours." "And mine," asks Archer, "part of yours?" She nodded. "And that's to be all—for either of us?" "Well; it *is* all isn't it?" (24). The "all" is being part of the same society, sharing its conventions, its moral outlook, and a sense of identity and responsibility. That is why their lives will be part of each other's, even though they will be separated forever. She can truly say, "I shan't be lonely now. I *was* lonely; I *was* afraid. But the emptiness and darkness are gone; when I turn back into myself now I'm like a child going into a room where there's always light" (24). They give each other up, and that is a sacrifice. But they gain in return a sustained sense of worth and the disappearance of loneliness and fear. That makes their sacrifice much smaller than it has seemed before.

5.4 Going Deeper

This last remark of Countess Olenska leads to the third interpretation of the significance of their situation. According to the first, theirs is a conflict between responsibility and fulfillment, and Countess Olenska resolves it by making the great sacrifice of choosing the former over the latter. According to the second, the first is superficial. The conflict is not between responsibility and fulfillment but between a naive and a reflectively evaluated conception of fulfillment. Divorce and breaking the engagement are serious possibilities only for the naive conception. The reflective one excludes them because they would violate their shared conception of fulfillment, of which the responsibility to live according to the moral conventions of their society is an essential part. By excluding divorce and breaking the engagement, Archer and Countess Olenska make a small sacrifice. Betraying their society, friends, family, their love and self-respect would be much worse. According to the third interpretation, their situation does not involve a conflict at all. This becomes apparent if we reflect on the questions that occur naturally to modern sensibility: Why do they not leave? They are intelligent adults and have ample funds. Why do they not pack up and move to France or Italy, bask in the sun, and enjoy each other and life?

The answer is suggested by a pair of lovers who did just that: Tolstoy's Vronsky and Anna Karenina did go to Italy. And of course, what happened to them was that their love faltered. They have left behind their society and its intrusive conventions, but the anticipated joyful abandon did not occur. They soon became listless, distracted, irritable, and bored, even as they continued to love each other. Their love, however, was as troubled in Italy as it had been at home in Russia, although for different reasons. The same thing would have happened to Countess Olenska and Archer, but perhaps not so soon, for they had greater resources than Tolstoy's pair.

But the question should be pressed: Why need anything bad happen? If the love between two people is true, they want each other's company, and the world is irrelevant. Flawed love will no doubt be quickly revealed as such if the lovers are left to their own resources. Presumably, however, the love between Countess Olenska and Archer was not flawed, and if it had been, they would still be better off having found that out. If it is fear of the truth that stops them from leaving New York, they are weak and they bring their separation upon themselves. If they are strong and really love each other, then they have nothing to fear. It is in this way that modern sensibility may impatiently respond to all the nuances, fine discriminations, and interior struggles that Wharton presents. This, however, is another simple-minded response.

The mistaken supposition underlying it is that the relationship of Countess Olenska and Archer to their society and its conventions is contingent, changeable, and unimportant. It is supposed that they can abandon their allegiance with as little loss as they can change their clothes when the fashion changes. But this is not so. Countess Olenska and Archer have identified themselves with their society and its conventions. They have derived from them some of their deepest convictions about responsibility and their shared conception of fulfillment. To abandon them would be to damage themselves both psychologically and morally, since they have nothing to put in their place. They would not be converting from one conception of fulfillment to another, but abandoning the only conception they have. Moreover, their love also depends on sharing that conception. For part of the reason they love each other is that they admire and respect each other's character and sense of responsibility, and these, of course, have also been formed by the conception of fulfillment that is sustained by the society and its conventions they would be abandoning.

All this might be acknowledged by skeptical defenders of modern sensibility, but they could still ask why it is supposed that if Countess Olenska and Archer were to leave their society, they would be obliged to leave their character and sense of responsibility behind. They would presumably carry with them their deep commitments and values, and they could continue to love each other partly because of them.

This is partly true and partly false. Character and responsibility are not possessions of which customs officials could deprive Countess Olenska and Archer as they are leaving New York. But they are sustained by the conventional background they would be abandoning. Their characters are constituted of dispositions to conduct themselves in certain ways in certain situations. Leaving their society and its conventions for another involves a basic change in the situations to which they have to respond. The standards of appropriateness shift, their judgments and perceptions become unreliable, what was natural and matter of course in the old setting is no longer fitting, or fitting in the same way, in the new setting. The conventions are different because new ones are added and old ones are omitted, and because the ones that hold in both contexts have different significance and importance. If they find themselves in a new society with its conventions, they have to learn what counts there as politeness and insult, forthrightness and forwardness, mockery and compliment, supererogation and duty, irony and humor, and so forth. They would not know the signs of guilt, shame, modesty, flirtation, or sarcasm. They would not know how exactly to express gratitude, appreciation, annoyance, friendliness, resentment, or generosity. They would lack the language of conduct. They may know what they want to say, but not how to say it.

They could, of course, learn all this. But the more they learn, the more their character and responsibility will alter. The better they fit into their new society, the less remains of their previous identity. If they decide to stay aloof in order to maintain their old selves, they will fail. For the circumstances in which they could express their old selves will demand new responses, and they will alter their old selves. It is true that they can carry their character and responsibility into a new context, but the context will change them in fundamental ways over time. Since Countess Olenska and Archer love each other partly for their character and shared sense of responsibility, they show good judgment in rejecting the option of leaving behind the society and conventions that nourish their love. She is right in saying to Archer, "I can't love you unless I give you up." They cannot love and have each other in New York because the responsibility they feel to abide by its conventions makes that impossible; and they cannot love and have each other elsewhere because they would soon cease to be the people who fell in love.

Defenders of modern sensibility may still think this is making too much of changing societies. Many immigrants, exiles, and refugees have changed societies and adjusted perfectly well to the necessary changes. Countess Olenska and Archer, however, are in a different situation. For immigrants, exiles, and refugees leave behind a bad way of life and exchange it for something they believe to be better. They left because they were driven to it. But no one drives Countess Olenska and Archer, and they both believe that New York society is "better than anything I've known." Archer "had felt the outside tugging . . . with all its golden hands" and rejected it. And Countess Olenska fled in disgust from the corruption "accepted in certain societies, or at least put up with as part of the general give-and-take." They are the kind of Americans for whom certain things are "unthinkable, simply unthinkable," namely, those things that their society and its moral conventions regard as irresponsible. That is what makes it psychologically and morally impossible for them to pack up and leave.

It is a significant fact about Countess Olenska and Archer that their reflective self-evaluation and corrective imagination enable them to see this clearly. They realize that they are what they are partly because of their society and its conventions, that their identity and self-respect depend on living according to these conventions. These are conditions of a fulfilling life, as they conceive of it. When they fall in love and the conventions prohibit their love, their emotional dislocation is only temporary. Their reason and calmer feelings are powerful presences in the background awaiting the turbulence of their love to subside a little, and then they reassert themselves. They understand and feel that their love is impossible. It is not social pressure, a sense of sin, or a hyperactive conscience that stands in the way. If it were any of these, there would be a conflict between a responsible and a fulfilling life. But what really stands in the way is their realization that the fulfilling life they seek depends on meeting the responsibility they have to honoring the conventions of their society. They recognize, therefore, as illusory the possibility of a fulfilling life that involves their serious violation. For the reflective self-evaluators they are, there is only a flicker of a doubt before they understand that there is no real conflict facing them. As soon as they realize what is at stake, the supposed conflict disappears, and only the achievement of clarity involves a struggle.

It is a mistake, therefore, to think of Countess Olenska and Archer as making a big sacrifice to resolve a dramatic conflict, as the first interpretation suggests. Nor are they making a smaller sacrifice in a less dramatic conflict, as the second interpretation claims. They sacrifice nothing and face no conflict. They are momentarily tempted to betray what matters to them most, including themselves and their love, but their reflective self-evaluation, aided by their use of corrective imagination, enables them to remain true. Of course, the degree of fulfillment they desire eludes them. They settle for a less than fulfilling life in which they cannot act on their love. But they have no realistic alternative because acting on their love would deprive them of a fulfilling life, self-respect, and, therefore, worthiness to be loved by each other.

Countess Olenska returns to Europe and spends the rest of her life in Paris, separated but not divorced from her husband. Archer marries May Welland; they have three children; and he and they continue to live in New York. Countess Olenska and Archer do not meet or communicate ever again, although their memory of each other as the great but impossible love of their lives does not fade. In this manner they dutifully live their lives but—dear reader—not happily ever after.

5.5 Shortchanged by Morality

We now come to the fourth, final, and best interpretation. The last chapter of the novel takes place twenty-six years after Countess Olenska and Archer had separated. Its tone becomes elegiac, and the story concludes with Archer's reflections on his life. In giving us these reflections, Wharton comes close to abandoning the position of the omniscient narrator she had maintained throughout. She lets us know what she thinks of the moral conventions that made their love impossible. I follow Wharton and replace the internal perspective of their reflective self-evaluation with an external one that allows asking critical questions about their moral conventions and the quality of their corrective imagination.

Here, then, is Archer, age fifty-seven, sitting in the library of his mansion at East Thirty-ninth Street, New York City, reflecting on his life. He recalls that he has been spending his time with "obscure if useful municipal work, and . . . writing occasional articles in one of the reforming weeklies. . . . It was little enough to look back on. . . . He had done little in public life; he would always be by nature contemplative and a dilettante. . . . He had been . . . what people were beginning to call 'a good citizen.' . . . His days were full, and they were filled decently." Nevertheless, there was "something he knew he had missed: the flower of life. . . . When he thought of Ellen Olenska . . . she had become the composite vision of all that he had missed." Although his "marriage was a dull duty . . . it kept the dignity of a duty . . . he honoured his own past, and mourned for it." He sees clearly his wife, now two years dead, "generous, faithful, unwearied; but so lacking in imagination, so incapable of growth." And himself? "As he reviewed his past, he saw into what a deep rut he had sunk. The worst of doing one's duty was that it apparently unfitted one for doing anything else. . . . The trenchant divisions between right and wrong, honest and dishonest, respectable and the reverse, had left so little scope for . . . a man's imagination. . . . Archer hung there and wondered. . . ." But he saw that "for summer thoughts it was too late." He rejects the possibility of even visiting Countess Olenska, although both her husband and his wife are dead, and their morality would leave them free to marry if they wanted. Archer prefers the "imaginary beloved" who is, as he says, "more real to me" than actually encountering the undoubtedly changed actual person (all quotations are from 34).

It is perhaps apparent by now why the novel is called *The Age of Innocence*. The innocents are exemplary representatives of their time and place: Countess Olenska and Archer. Their innocence consists in the unquestioning acceptance of their moral conventions. They claim to know, as Countess Olenska explicitly says, that "it is better than anything I've known" (18). It does not occur to them that they do not know enough, that the fault may lie not with their love but with the moral conventions that make it impossible. Their identification with the conventions is so complete that questioning it would be questioning themselves and their milieu, and that is "unthinkable, simply unthinkable" (25). But why is it unthinkable? Because their innocence "had left little scope for . . . imagination" (34).

It will help us understand how moral conventions can curtail the scope of imagination if we return to the distinction between three kinds of possibilities (in 2.2). The possibilities are of ideals of a good life. *Social* possibilities are those available to individuals given the prevailing material and normative conditions of their society. *Personal* possibilities are ones that particular individuals have the ability to pursue. And *recognized* possibilities are those that individuals are actually aware of and deliberate about. The scope of imagination is curtailed if individuals do not recognize all their personal possibilities. The opposite error is to recognize as possibilities what are in fact personally impossible for them. The same holds for what a society acknowledges as personal possibilities. It may set its sights too high and unrealistically regard as personal possibilities ones for which no one can have the necessary abilities. Or it may be too restrictive and impoverish individuals by excluding possibilities that they actually have the abilities to pursue. One use of the moral imagination is to correct such mistakes by enabling individuals to understand why they have formed an excessive or a deficient view of their possibilities.

We have seen in the preceding chapter how Oedipus used his corrective imagination to excellent effect. He was enabled by it to understand that the possibilities he had pursued as king were unrealistic because they aimed to transcend human limits. He came to understand and accept that contingency sets limits to all human possibilities. The profundity of Sophocles' two plays is that they bring home to us with impassioned concreteness a truth that has the first importance for all human lives: reason and morality cannot overcome our vulnerability to contingency.

Wharton's novel aims lower. It is a first-rate work, but it does not match Sophocles' profundity. It tells us about the limits set by the moral conventions that prevailed at a particular place and time, not about limits set by the human condition. It shows how her protagonists have been deprived of a fulfilling life by the impoverished view of human possibilities they have unquestioningly accepted under the influence of the moral conventions of their milieu. Her protagonists are like Oedipus in using their corrective imagination, but they do not use it as well as he did. Oedipus took it to the limits of human possibilities. Archer and Countess Olenska took it only to the limits of their moral conventions. They might have gone on to question those limits, but they did not. They have accepted them, even though they should not have because the limits were too narrow and excluded fulfilling possibilities. Their morality thus shortchanged them, and they colluded in depriving themselves of a fulfilling life.

Perhaps this is too harsh a judgment of Wharton's protagonists. Perhaps they should be pitied for their plight rather than blamed for getting into it. What the right judgment is depends on whether we think that they could have freed themselves from the restrictions their moral conventions imposed on them. If they could have done so but did not, the judgment is not too harsh. If they were so totally dominated that it was psychologically impossible for them to question the conventions, then they should not be blamed for failing to do what they could not have done. It is very difficult to decide between these two alternatives. I lean toward the appropriateness of blaming them, for the following reason.

If we ask what might have brought them to question the prevailing conventional limits, we might plausibly say that if their passions had been stronger, if their circumstances had been less comfortable, if they had had friends outside their social circle, then they might have been less accepting. As passions go, theirs was pretty lame; they took much too much for granted the financial security and social preeminence they have enjoyed for life; and they were too insular in their contacts. If they had been more persistent in their reflective self-evaluation and in making their corrective imagination work, they might have realized these tendencies about themselves and might have seen that it is not the overpowering force of their conventions but their own conformist tendencies and domesticated passions that made them accept the limits. If this is right, then blaming them, and not just their moral conventions, for their lack of fulfillment is perhaps not too harsh a judgment.

Be that as it may, reflection on the novel leads to understanding that the two components of a good life—responsibility and fulfillment—tend to conflict. The key to a good life is to balance their conflicting claims and meet each as fully as possible. Their conflict is likely to occur even in fortunate circumstances because responsibility depends on conformity to moral conventions—some of which are necessary for any reasonable conception of morality whereas others vary with context—and these conventions inevitably prohibit some kinds of fulfillment: indeed, that is one main reason for having them. If the conventions prohibited only the violation of conditions that all fulfilling lives require, then there would be no serious conflict between responsibility and fulfillment. But moral conventions go far beyond this minimum. They aim to guide attitudes to sex, childrearing, illness, work, commerce, war, death, competition, taxation, punishment, violence, and so on and on. All societies have moral conventions that provide this guidance. Yet their conventions differ in the crucial respect of how far they go and how much they leave to the discretion of individuals. The distinctions between the public and the private, the social and the personal, the moral and the nonmoral, the required and the permitted are typical sources of conflict familiar from history, literature, ethnography, and philosophy.

We often face such conflicts as we are engaged in making our lives good or better. In trying, as we must, to resolve them in our own case we usually have two options: to assign priority to moral conventions or to fulfillment. Each may be reasonable or unreasonable depending on how intrusive the conventions are and on how our fulfillment affects others. Making the relevant judgments is usually difficult, they are likely to be controversial, and reasonable and morally committed people often disagree about them. This is an unavoidable part of moral life.

Countess Olenska and Archer did not recognize the complexity of these judgments. They did not allow their imaginations to explore actively alternatives to their moral conventions or to correct their unquestioning acceptance of their conventions' unreasonable intrusiveness. They simply resolved the conflict by assigning priority to the prevailing conventions. But they had to pay the price of the intrusiveness of the conventions to which they conformed: the unreasonable narrowing of their possibilities of fulfillment. They paid that price, and that is why their lives were not fulfilling. Their character and responsibility were strong enough to tame their briefly unruly passions to such an extent as to leave them eventually without any passions to tame. They ended up with calm minds and all passion spent. That was their achievement and their failure.

Their lives show, however, that the voluntarist ideal of reflective self-evaluation is not rich enough to accommodate cases like Countess Olenska and Archer. For they were assiduous reflective self-evaluators; they did not fail to do anything that Frankfurt and Hampshire say one should do; they encountered no misfortune or external obstacles; and yet the promised fulfillment eluded them. There must be more to reflective self-evaluation, therefore, than the voluntarist ideal recognizes. The more that is needed is the imaginative exploration of the possibilities of life.

5.6 Overview

There are numerous ideals of a good—responsible and fulfilling—life. I have been concentrating on a widely held contemporary version: the ideal of reflective self-evaluation. My general aim is to show that each of the three modes of moral imagination is necessary for living such a life. The specific aim of the three chapters of Part II has been to support this general view by giving concrete and detailed reasons for thinking that corrective imagination is necessary but by itself insufficient.

There are, of course, many reasons why a life may fail to be good. I have been assuming that one of its conditions, responsibility, has been met. The question then becomes one about the conditions of a fulfilling life. This is a life that a person not only lives, but lives more fully than many others do: wholeheartedly, undividedly, with satisfaction. Lasting dissatisfaction, not with details, but with one's life as a whole shows lack of fulfillment. This motivates people to look backward to discover whether the source of their present dissatisfaction may not be misinterpretations of their possibilities and limits as they were in the past when they made important decisions among whose effects is their present dissatisfaction. If they come to understand that this is the truth about themselves, they will be motivated to make such corrections as they can.

We have seen how Mill overcame his crisis in this way, how the old Oedipus finally remedied the misinterpretations of his younger self, and how Countess Olenska and Archer came to see that their very identity ruled out the consummation of their love. Of these people, Mill was by far the most successful, for he indeed went on to live a fulfilling life. But he could do that only after he had gone beyond diagnosing the source of his dissatisfaction by corrective imagination and imaginatively explored through poetry the possibilities of a life in which his feelings no longer lay fallow. Oedipus was also successful in his corrective imagination, but a fulfilling life nevertheless eluded him. Reaching the necessary reflective self-evaluation took him a lifetime, and he was old, spent, and ready to die before he could explore the possibilities that became available to him. Countess Olenska and Archer used their corrective imagination well, but not well enough. They curtailed it because they were unwilling or unable to consider whether their identity was malformed by their conventional morality. They thus denied themselves the possibilities they might have had if they had been more determined to follow where their corrective imagination might lead.

If we take a step back and reflect on what these lives and efforts show *us*, rather than how the protagonists themselves thought about it, several conclusions follow. Since there are very few lives so fortunate as to be without serious dissatisfaction, most of us have reason to use our corrective imagination. Dissatisfaction may have sources other than past misinterpretations, but fallibility, self-deception, fantasy, and timorousness make it likely that reflective self-evaluations would be improved by much-needed corrections. To understand this, however, falls short of leading to a fulfilling life. For we may know that correction is needed without having the capacity to effect it, as Mill could not give himself the feelings he knew he lacked. Even if we have the capacity, we may lack the will to make the correction because we rightly or wrongly value something more than the removal of our dissatisfactions, as Countess Olenska and Archer did. Furthermore, having both the capacity and the will may still not be enough because contingency might prevent us from having a fulfilling life, as it did Oedipus. Reflection on these lives leads us to realize that contingency permeates corrective imagination, as it does everything in human life, and places beyond our control whether we have the required capacity, whether our circumstances allow its use, and whether we live long enough to use it to good effect.

If we face the extent to which contingency permeates our lives and reduces the amount of control we have, two natural, but dangerously mistaken, reactions suggest themselves. One is to rebel against contingency and refuse to accept that we often cannot control how much control we have. This refusal makes us embark on an aggressive or a defensive quest. If aggressive, it becomes a quixotic effort to overcome human limits. The inevitable result is failure. The only consolation left for those who have thus doomed themselves is to take pride in how they bear their doom. This is what the younger Oedipus did.

If this reaction takes a defensive form, it amounts to trying to build an inner fortress in which we are in total control and from which contingency is absent. The result, once again, is guaranteed failure because our physical and psychological nature alike depend on causes external to them, and contingency enters through these causal connections. Nor are we free of contingency in how we deal with these external causal influences because that depends on our genetic inheritance, upbringing, and experiences in life, and on how far and in what direction we can develop our character and sensibility.

Both the aggressive and the defensive forms of the rebellion against contingency lead to Promethean romanticism. This is a posture full of gestures, grandstanding, and confrontation, none of which can alter our vulnerability to contingency. They are defiant protests against the human condition, like shouting orders at the storm to desist. This, I am afraid, is one result of the voluntarist ideal of reflective self-evaluation, unless it is revised in ways I have suggested.

The second natural but mistaken reaction is to conclude that our endeavors are futile, our hopes groundless, and our fears a pointless waste of energy. We want, then, calmness of mind, to be set free of hope and fear; we want to achieve a state in which all our passions will be spent. Life is bleak, we may say, getting excited about it does no good, so let us just do what our conscience dictates—and thereby sentence ourselves to a life of living death, the kind Countess Olenska and Archer lived after their separation. The root cause of people living such bleak lives is that they have nothing to live *for*. They are being realistic about human limits, but they have forgotten about human possibilities. The way out is to use their imagination not merely to correct their past mistakes but also to explore their future possibilities. How that may be done is the topic of the next part of the book.

Part Three

FROM EXPLORATORY
TO DISCIPLINED
IMAGINATION

CHAPTER 6

Registers of Consciousness

Having a consciousness highly susceptible of registration . . .
makes us see the things that may most interest us reflected in
it . . . never a whit to the prejudice of . . . being . . . a
foredoomed, entangled, embarrassed agent in the general
imbroglio.

— HENRY JAMES, preface to *The Golden Bowl*

6.1 The Approach

In contrast with backward-looking corrective imagination, exploratory imagination looks forward toward future possibilities. It is an attempt by particular people in particular circumstances to understand what
it would be like for them to realize some possibility that significantly affects how they live. The understanding they seek is motivated by dissatisfaction with their present life. It seems desirable to them to change how
they live. It is obviously prudent to want to understand, before embarking
on it, what the changed life would be like: what it would be like to marry
or leave that person, adopt or abandon that cause, forgive or condemn
that action, make or not make that sacrifice, and so on.

This use of imagination is moral if people aim to evaluate their possibil-
it es by considering what effect their realization might have on their responsibilities to others and on fulfillment for themselves. It is surely reasonable to use imagination for this purpose, but just as surely its use can
go wrong and lead to mistakes, such as treating as possibilities what are in
fact socially or personally impossible, failing to recognize possibilities that
are in fact available, or forming a false view of what it would be like to live
according to particular possibilities. It may lead to wrong beliefs, inappro-

priate feelings, misdirected attitudes, or a failure to appreciate how particular possibilities might affect other areas of their lives. I rely on Henry James's complex masterpiece, *The Golden Bowl*,[1] to make concrete the possibilities and failures of the exploratory use of moral imagination. In doing so I offer an interpretation of this difficult novel. My modest claim for it is merely that it is a possible interpretation, not that it is the only one. Its aim is not to supersede the voluminous critical literature but to contribute to understanding exploratory imagination.

The complexity of the novel and the difficulty of James's style are the result of what James is trying to convey. James explains in the preface that the "marked inveteracy of a certain indirect and oblique view of my presented action" is "the very straightest and closest possible" (7). For he is presenting the action as it appears "to the register . . . of the consciousness of . . . the characters." Each "virtually represents to himself everything that concerns us. . . . Having a consciousness highly susceptible of registration, he thus makes us see things that may most interest us reflected on it," even as each is, as James says of one of them, "a foredoomed, entangled, embarrassed agent in the general imbroglio" (8–9). The consciousness of each registers his or her impression of what the others believe or feel, but these impressions are colored by their own beliefs and feelings and rendered uncertain by the imperfect information on which they are based. It adds to the already great complexity that each character has good reasons to disguise from at least some of the others his or her own beliefs, feelings, and lack of adequate information. What the consciousness of each registers, therefore, is highly fallible, and each knows that. Consequently, uncertainty permeates everyone's consciousness. James's "indirect and oblique view" is "the very straightest and closest possible," given this uncertainty.

One may justifiably wonder why one should undertake the undeniably hard work of penetrating this style, which leads, in the words of a most sympathetic commentator, to "perpetually losing one's way amidst the qualifications and parentheses, struggling to keep a hold on the proliferating subtleties of analysis . . . the tormenting crypto-statements of the elliptical, allusive, digressive dialogues."[2] The answer must be that what James shows in this manner has great enough interest to reward the effort needed to understand it. I believe it has that interest, and I hope to make that convincing by considering the story James tells.

6.2 The General Imbroglio

The story has four main characters. Adam Verver is an immensely rich American who has come, once again, to Europe with his daughter,

Maggie, intending to spend huge amounts of money to add to his already large collection of works of art. He ships his acquisitions back to "American City" for the museum he is founding. Verver's wife died years ago, and father and daughter have an exceptionally intimate relationship, which excludes others and renders their contacts with everyone else superficial. Prince Amerigo is the scion of one of Italy's ancient aristocratic families, an appealing, gracious example of the best that nobility and civilization can produce. He and Charlotte Stant have been lovers, connected by passion and affection, hers considerably more ardent than his. She is brilliant, accomplished, beautiful, a thoroughly Europeanized American and a fitting partner for the Prince. Amerigo and Charlotte, however, were forced to end their affair, although their love and passion have not cooled, because they realized that they have to make good marriages to individuals who have the wealth they lack so they can continue to live in the style to which they are accustomed. Charlotte and Maggie know each other through having been in school together in Switzerland. In addition to these four, there are two observers, Fanny Assingham and her husband, who know everyone and who discuss and interpret the imbroglio in which the four are involved.

Maggie and the Prince meet, marry, and have a child. Maggie is afraid that the marriage will alter her relationship with her father. She thinks that her father should also marry, partly to give him a partner as a substitute for herself, and encourages him to marry Charlotte. At this point, neither she nor her father knows about the past affair of the Prince and Charlotte. Verver marries Charlotte, but the relationship between Maggie and her father remains unaltered. They spend as much time in each other's company as before, enjoy it as much as before, and, in their ignorance, exclude Maggie's husband, the Prince, and Verver's wife, Charlotte, and urge the ex-lovers to entertain each other and take part in the social whirl they, but not Verver and Maggie, enjoy. After a while, the Prince and Charlotte resume their affair. Maggie eventually becomes suspicious, her suspicion grows, and it shatters her innocence. She feels compelled to do something, but she does not know what because she is confused and divided.

Part of James's art is to show the state of each character's consciousness and how they seem to others. Consider first Maggie and Verver. Maggie was "prim," "resembled a nun" (154); "her imagination was clearly never ruffled by the sense of any anomaly" (252); she "was the person in the world to whom a wrong thing could least be communicated. It was as if her imagination had been closed to it, her sense altogether sealed" (286). As Maggie and her father were, "knowledge wasn't one of their needs and . . . they were in fact constitutionally inaccessible to it. They were good children, bless their hearts, and the children of good children" (252). Maggie, however, is losing her innocence. On the one hand, she is sexually awakened by the Prince. "He had . . . unfailing magic. He *knew* how to resort to it—he could be, on occasion, as she had lately more than ever learned, so munificent a lover." She admired "his genius for charm, for intercourse, for expression, for life" (338). On the other hand, she has become suspicious of the Prince and Charlotte, and she is jealous. She finds in herself "vertiginous moments, that fascination of the monstrous, that temptation of the horribly possible" (456). There are also "the straight vindictive view, the rights of resentment, the rages of jealousy, the protests of passion" elicited by "the first sharp falsity she had known in her life," which she found "behind so much trusted, so much pretended, nobleness, cleverness, tenderness," and which "made everything that was accustomed in her cry out with pain" at "the horror of finding evil seated, all at its ease, where she had only dreamed of good" (459). The suspected affair between Charlotte and the Prince shatters Maggie's innocence and changes her forever by showing her possibilities she never even dreamed of before.

Mercenary detachment is a central feature of Adam Verver's consciousness. It makes him calculating, impersonally polite, and cold to everyone but Maggie. "The luxurious side of his personal existence was . . . furnished . . . with the thing classed and stamped as 'real'. . . . The note of reality . . . had occasionally been reached in his great 'finds'." These finds "continued, beyond any other, to keep him attentive and gratified" (159). Verver, in other words, was a collector, but of a peculiar sort: "Nothing perhaps might affect us as queerer . . . than this application of the same measure of value to such different pieces of property as old Persian carpets, say, and new human acquisitions; all the more indeed that the amiable man was not without an inkling, on his own side, that he was, as a taster of life, economically constructed" (159–160). It was in this spirit that he aimed "to satisfy himself, so to speak, both about Amerigo and about the Bernardo Luini he had happened to come to knowledge of at the same time he was consenting to the announcement of his daughter's betrothal, so it served him at present to satisfy himself about Charlotte Stant and an extraordinary set of oriental tiles" (160). The Prince was a beautiful thing Verver bought for Maggie, and Charlotte was a beautiful thing he bought for himself. The Prince saw that Verver regarded him "much of the same order as any glance directed . . . to the figure of a cheque received in the course of business. . . . It made sure of the amount—and just so, from time to time, the amount of the Prince was made sure. He was . . . already reposed in the bank as a value, but subject . . . to repeated, to infinite endorsement" (245–246).

The Prince, in turn, was willing to play his part. He "had no wish to see his value diminish. He himself, after all, had not fixed it—the 'figure' was a conception all of Mr Verver's own. Certainly, however, everything must be kept up to it" (246). The Prince "knew why, from the first of his marriage, he had tried with such patience for such conformity; he knew why he had given up so much and bored himself so much; he knew why he . . . sold himself" (268). It was for "a bottomless bag of solid shining British sovereigns" (251). Having made his bargain with a world "governed by . . . the smile of the gods and the favour of the powers," what was left to him was "intelligent acceptance," "faith in its guarantees and a high spirit for its chances. Its demand . . . was above all for courage and good humour" (251). Nevertheless, he felt "reduced," "held cheap and made light of," but "there was a spirit in him that could rise above it." Still, he did not understand "the fathomless depths of English equivocation. He knew them . . . [had] lived with them, stayed with them, hunted, shot and done various other things with them; but the number of questions about them he couldn't have answered had much rather grown than shrunken" (265). Perhaps what stood in the way, although the Prince only vaguely suspected it, was that he lacked a moral sense, as he himself says in response to Mrs. Assingham: "'I should be interested,' she presently remarked, 'to see some sense *you* don't possess.' Well, he produced one on the spot. 'The moral, dear Mrs Assingham.' . . . 'Machiavelli!' she simply exclaimed. 'You do me too much honour. I wish indeed I had his genius'" (48).

In Charlotte's consciousness "the knowledge of how and where and the habit, founded on experience, of not being afraid" (58) occupied an important place. She was "strong-minded . . . but it would never interfere with the play of her extremely personal, her always amusing taste. This . . . she threw out positively . . . like a light" (58). She was like "some wonderful finished instrument, something made for exhibition, for a prize" (59). "She always dressed her act up . . . showing in fact in those dissimulations a cleverness equal to but one thing in the world, equal to her abjection. She was . . . possessed by her doom, but her doom was also to arrange appearances" (59). "Nothing in her definitely placed her; she was a rare, a special product. Her singleness, her solitude, her want of means . . . and other advantages contributed to enrich her somehow with an odd, precious neutrality, to constitute for her, so detached yet so aware, a sort of small social capital. It was the only one she had" (64). She returns from America to Italy, and her ex-lover, the Prince, says to her: "I've been thinking . . . that you would have seen your way to marrying." "To marrying whom?" Charlotte asked. "Why, some good, kind, clever, rich American," says the Prince, who has succeeded in doing just that. To which she replies: "'I tried everyone I came across. I did my best. I showed I had come, quite publicly, *for* that. Perhaps I showed it too much. At any rate it was no use. I had to recognize it. No one would have me.' Then she seemed . . . sorry

for his having to hear of her anything so disconcerting" (66). But she finally succeeds, and marries Verver. What she says to being asked by "the
clever, rich American" she had sought, to the man old enough to be her
father, is revealing: "I won't pretend I don't think it would be good for me
to marry. . . . I am so awfully unattached. I should like to be a little less
adrift. I should like to have a home. . . . I don't want to be a horrible English old-maid" (175). And it is equally revealing what Verver says when
she questions why he wants to marry at all: she wonders "why you're not
happy, as you are. . . . Oughtn't we . . . think of Maggie? . . . She's everything to you—she has always been. Are you certain that there's room in
your life—?" He completes her question: "For another daughter?—is that
what you mean? . . . Can't a man be, all his life then . . . anything but a father? . . . You talk about differences, but they have already been made—as
no one knows better than Maggie. She feels the one she made herself by
her own marriage—made, I mean, for me. She constantly thinks of it—it
allows her no rest. To put her at peace is therefore . . . what I'm trying to
do. I can't do it alone, but I can do it with your help" (177–178). So, as the
Prince has done, Charlotte and Verver make their loveless bargain: security for Charlotte, relief of Maggie's worries for Verver. Both marriages are
instrumental to the partners' purposes, and all of the partners use one another.

Now that we have these four registers of consciousness before us, let us
see what they do. The ex-lovers, the Prince and Charlotte, are practically
forced into each other's arms by the obtuseness of Maggie and Verver, who
prefer to be together and who urge the other two to entertain each other.
The old flames naturally enough revive, and having achieved their goal of
a marriage that provides for their style, pleasure, and luxury, they see no
obstacle to taking up where they left off. "They stood together, as strongly
held and closely confronted as any hour of their earliest past even had
seen them. They were . . . grasping and grasped . . . meeting and met. 'It's
sacred,' he said at last. 'It's sacred,' she breathed back to him. . . . Their
lips sought their lips, their pressure their response and their response
their pressure; with a violence that had sighed itself the next moment to
the longest and deepest stillness they passionately sealed their pledge"
(237).

Far more complicated are Maggie's actions after having learned that
her suspicions and jealousy were warranted. She tells the Prince that she
knows of his affair with Charlotte, her father's wife. I know, she says, "of
your having, and of your having for a long time had, *two* relations with
Charlotte. . . . 'One kind,' she went on, 'was there before us; we took that
fully for granted. . . . We never thought of there being another, kept out of
our sight" (429). In saying this, it seemed to the Prince, she was "speaking

more or less for her father as well," and thereby "she put before him [something] that he was afraid directly to touch" (430). And that, of course, was that since both Charlotte and he had defaulted on the bargain they have made, they were liable to lose the riches for which they had sold themselves. Maggie, knowing that the implied threat had sunk in, says no more, and leaves him stewing with the knowledge that she knows and the ignorance of what she might do about it.

Maggie, in fact, has hatched a plot. Its goals were to keep her husband, since his sexual appeal has not diminished; separate the Prince from Charlotte by making her father take Charlotte back to America; punish Charlotte by dooming her to a provincial life without access to her lover; and hide from her father the knowledge of Charlotte's infidelity and the Prince's betrayal. She wants the status quo ante reestablished, the bought Prince and Charlotte to stay bought. She succeeds remarkably well, although she must deceive everybody: the Prince by holding over him the threat of her father's retribution, although she in fact wants to hide everything from her father; Charlotte by keeping her ignorant of the causes of the Prince's hasty retreat from their mutual pledge and of the causes of her exile to America; and her father by hiding from him his wife's and son-in-law's faithlessness. The result is that the Prince is "a proud man reduced to abjection" (453); Charlotte is in "a spacious but suspended cage, the home of eternal unrest, of pacings, beatings, shakings, all so vain . . . a prisoner looking through the bars" (454); and she and her father can agree that "Charlotte . . . only wants to know what *we* want. Which is what we have got her for!" (364). She and her father, then, can delight in the works of art they have secured: "She had passed her arm into his, and the other objects in the room, the other pictures . . . the 'important' pieces, supreme in their way, stood out, round them, consciously, for recognition and applause. . . . The two noble persons seated, in conversation, at tea, felt thus the splendid effect and the general harmony: Mrs Verver and the Prince fairly 'placed' themselves, however unwittingly, as high expressions of the kind of human furniture required, aesthetically, by such a scene. The fusion of their presence with the decorative elements, their contribution to the triumph of selection, was complete and admirable; though, to . . . a view more penetrating than the occasion really demanded, they also might have figured as concrete attestations of a rare power of purchase" (541). Beholding it all, Maggie can say: "It's success, father," and he can reply: "It's success" (545).

If we mean by success that the four protagonists got what they wanted, then it was indeed success. The Prince and Charlotte got the marriage to the rich Americans who provided them with a luxurious life. Maggie got a jewel of a man securely tied to herself, satisfying her awakened sexual needs, and she got also her revenge over the woman who provoked her jealousy. Verver got to add two highly accomplished and aesthetically pleasing human "finds" to his fabulous collection. But their success exacted a heavy cost from each. They had to live with poisoned marriages in which Maggie and Verver subjugated the Prince and Charlotte by a combination of threat and bribery to do their bidding. They were separated from the person to whom they were most deeply attached because Verver took Charlotte back to America and Maggie stayed in Europe with the Prince. And they had to sustain their relationships by a web of ceaseless deception while pretending that all was idyllic.

Part of James's great achievement is showing how the failings of each of these people have led to an outcome that none of them could desire or welcome; how that outcome was reached by each working very hard to sustain the very deception that doomed all of them to a life of pretense and dissimulation; and how each of these cunning and clever people, acutely registering what each could glean of the reverberations of the consciousness of the others, became "a foredoomed, entangled, embarrassed agent in the general imbroglio" (8–9).

6.3 The Failure and Its Sources

If, however, by success we mean living a good life, then it is obvious that they have not succeeded. They were unable to reach fulfillment or meet their responsibilities because they failed both in their reflective self-evaluation and in their understanding of others. Their failure resulted from the deficiency of their exploratory imagination, which prevented them from forming a reasonable views of their possibilities. We need to see now why this is the correct diagnosis in each of the four cases.

The failures of the Prince and Charlotte were very similar. Each supposed that a fulfilling life, at any rate for themselves, had to be luxurious. They were willing to, and did, subordinate everything else to the realization of that possibility. To that end they twice broke up their affair, violated their solemn pledge to each other, and frustrated their reciprocal sexual passion. The Prince put up with abjection, boredom, and living with people he could not understand, with the ruin of his pride, with the shame of being found out in a lie, with being bought, and with a marriage in which he must, when the chips are down, do his wife's bidding. And Charlotte put up with her husband "holding in one of his pocketed hands the end of a long silken halter looped around her beautiful neck. He didn't twitch it, yet it was there; he didn't drag her, but she came" (493). She put up with not really knowing why the Prince broke up their affair, with not knowing what Maggie and Verver knew, and with being sentenced to what seemed to her a life of living death in American City, deprived of the cultural and social life for the sake of which she had sold herself.

The Prince and Charlotte failed to understand that the cumulative effect of their compromises and of the injuries to their self-respect was not to bring fulfillment closer but to make it less and less likely. They did not see that the luxurious life for which they sacrificed everything will not provide the fulfillment with which they have mistakenly identified it. They got what they wanted, but they wanted the wrong thing. Their imagination was misled by the glitter of luxuries and their fear of losing them. Thus misled, they failed to understand both themselves and their possibilities.

They also failed to understand the people they married. They expected Maggie and Verver to be putty in the hands of such charming and accomplished manipulators as they took themselves to be. They falsely supposed that under Maggie and Verver's unsophisticated exterior there were awe and admiration of themselves, pliability, and inhibitions. They found out to their chagrin just how badly they misunderstood father and daughter when they were manipulated by them into submission, forced to live up to the responsibilities they undertook as part of the bargain they made, and their vaunted charm and sophistication treated as pleasing aesthetic qualities having only the lightest weight in serious practical affairs. They underestimated Maggie and Verver because their own superficiality prevented them from seeing the strength below the surface. The Prince and Charlotte thus misunderstood both themselves and the other two because their desire for luxury and their inflated estimate of their own appeal made them misunderstand the possibilities inherent in their situation.

Of the four protagonists, Verver is the least developed. He is, when present, enigmatic because it is unclear how much he knows and suspects of what is going on. It is clear that his ruling passion is his collection and that he has developed sufficient taste to distinguish between the fine and the tawdry. But it is also clear that such delight as he takes in works of art is to a considerable extent the delight of possessing fine things of great commercial value. Nor is there any doubt that Verver loves Maggie and wishes the best for her. Their relationship is the only intimate one he is shown to have. He is willing to speak plainly when the occasion warrants, as to Charlotte when he asks her to marry him, but otherwise he is cold, remote, and calculating, and maintains a polite distance from everyone but Maggie. He appraises people as he appraises art works, and treats them all, except Maggie, with mercenary detachment.

Perhaps the key to understanding him is the suggestion made by several critics that James intended him to represent the American myth of a new beginning, in separation from Europe and its decadent traditions, customs, manners, and mores. The myth projected "an individual emancipated from history, bereft of ancestry, untouched and undefiled by the usual inheritances of family and race; an individual standing alone, self-sufficient and self-propelling, ready to confront whatever awaited him with the aid of his unique and inherent resources. . . . The new hero . . . was . . . Adam before the Fall. . . . His moral position was prior to experience, and in his very newness he was fundamentally innocent."[3] It is not an accident that he was called Adam or that Verver suggests the verdant freshness of unspoiled nature. James, however, is a thoughtful critic of this myth, for he saw "that innocence could be cruel as well as vulnerable; that the condition prior to conscience might have insidious undertones of the amoral as well as the beguiling naiveté of the premoral."[4]

Verver seems enigmatic only to those who expect him to have the depth that he in fact lacks. He sees only surfaces, and he has no knowledge to disguise from others. He says little because he has little to say. "He was simple, he was a revelation of simplicity, and that was the end of him" (244–245). He was "in a state of innocence, the state of our primitive parents before the Fall" (253). In his simplicity and innocence, he did not see the possibilities life holds out or how his mercenary bluntness affected the Prince and Charlotte, who saw some few of those possibilities and reveled in them. Verver did not see that the bargain he had made with the Prince and Charlotte included not only money but also recognition of them as human beings rather than as handsome acquisitions. He violated the terms of the bargain as much as they did, not because he was immoral but because he was in a premoral state of moral obtuseness (see 1.4), unaware of having those responsibilities. And it was also moral obtuseness that prevented him from recognizing that his life was impoverished, lacking in grace and humanity, excepting his love of Maggie. He supposed he was fulfilled, but only because he failed to see possibilities whose recognition would have shown him how deprived he was. He was smug because he did not miss what he did not know he lacked. But the Prince and Charlotte knew. It could not have failed to rankle them to be in the power of such a simpleton, as they took him to be, or to add the fillip of sweet revenge to their resumed love affair.

The characters of the Prince, Charlotte, and Verver are formed. They are what they are, and they want what they want. They confront the situations in which they find themselves, and they respond in characteristic ways. Maggie is different. At first she is unformed, has no characteristic responses and no experience of the world. She has not been seriously challenged yet because her father's love and money protected her. When she has to confront the Prince's infidelity, Charlotte's change from friend to rival, the threat to both her own and her father's sense of fulfillment, and her own raging, confused, and contrary emotions, Maggie realizes that she is now alone, that she has to act, and that whatever she does will have serious consequences for all four of them. This situation and her attempts to come to terms with its implications transform her from a naive girl into a scheming, manipulating woman. She enjoys the transformation: "She could at all events not remember a time at which she had felt so excited and certainly none . . . that brought with it the necessity of concealing excitement. This . . . became a high pastime . . . a private and absorbing exercise" (303). But it was not just a pastime, for she was deadly serious about it. "She was no longer playing with blunt and idle tools, with weapons that did not cut. There passed across her vision ten times a day the gleam of a bare blade" (305). The aim of the plot she hatches is "happiness without a hole in it. . . . The golden bowl—as it *was* to have been. . . . The bowl with all happiness in it. The bowl without the crack" (445). What she wants is the same as what the innocent girl she had been had wanted. But Maggie—sexually awakened, newly accessible to knowledge, imagination no longer closed to the possibility of wrongdoing by her and to her, vindictive, jealous, resentful, mature Maggie—nevertheless wants, really wants, the same impossible dream as her earlier self had wanted. The difference is that she is now willing to do what seems to her necessary to get it.

What she does is "to exploit . . . her husband's and her friend's terror of exposure . . . exploit their compunction at what they have done . . . hold them in an unbroken suspense . . . keep them always in the wrong . . . never provoke the kind of show-down in which they would certainly gain mastery over her."[5] She has become "consummately, diabolically . . . audacious and impudent" (294), a shrewd "mistress of shades" (396). She has acquired the "dissimulated arts" and "egoism," and she is "as hard . . . as a little pointed diamond" (398). She is "humbugging . . . her father" (439). She found that "here reigned for her . . . that fascination of the monstrous, that temptation of the horribly possible" (456). She learns that giving up the resentment of "innocence outraged and generosity betrayed . . . [was] not to be thought of" (459). Armed with these newly acquired arts, she weaves a web of deception to mislead her husband, whom she wants to keep; her rival, whom she wants to punish; and her father, whom she continues to love. In words or actions, explicitly or by omission, she lies to and manipulates everyone in order to realize her impossible dream.

James masterfully shows, however, that she deceives herself as well. "Her little lucidities . . . were really so divinely blind" (294). She says that she is deceiving everyone for love (379), but what motivates her is possessiveness and revenge. "In reclaiming her husband, Maggie seeks revenge upon his mistress. . . . Charlotte's crime in Maggie's eyes is twofold. Charlotte took something away from her that belonged to her—*that* Maggie can right by taking it back. And Charlotte did so by exploiting Maggie's ignorance. To right this Maggie . . . starves Charlotte of knowledge."[6] In Maggie's fantasy, she hears her father saying to her about taking Charlotte back to America: "Yes, you see—I lead her now by the neck, I lead her to her doom, and she doesn't so much as know what it is; though she has a fear in her heart. . . . She thinks it *may* be her doom, the awful place over there—awful for *her*; but she's afraid to ask . . . just as she is afraid of not asking; just as she's afraid of so many other things that she sees multiplied round her now as portents and betrayals" (494). Maggie, having succeeded in her revenge over Charlotte and in repossessing her husband, says to herself, "Yes, she had done all" (514). But what she takes to be her triumph in fact makes a good life for her, as well as for the others, impossible.

In the first place, her dream, "the bowl with all happiness in it. The bowl without the crack" (445), is unattainable. She has lost her innocence, became manipulative, and the cost of that for her personally is that the unquestioning trust she had before in her husband, in her friend, in her father's and Charlotte's marriage, in the four of them living harmoniously, amicably together became impossible. The snake of "the horribly possible" has entered her fantasy Garden of Eden, and she ate from the tree of knowledge. The difference between the naive girl she was and the scheming woman she became is that her later self knows good and evil and the "horribly possible" tempts her. And even if she could resist its temptation in the future, she would not be able to silence her suspicion that the others, especially her husband, will succumb to it, as he and Charlotte did before. But it is not just that she is now incapable of having all happiness. It would be impossible even if she were capable of having it. For all the happiness includes for her both a fulfilling marriage and the loving intimacy with her father that excludes the rest of the world. Scheming for a fulfilling marriage meant manipulating her father into removing her rival from the scene, and that required his own removal and separation from Maggie. She had to decide whether it was a fulfilling marriage or the loving presence of her father she really wanted. Having all the happiness required both, and that was no longer possible for her. The dream she has nurtured, for the sake of which she became a little monster, was made unattainable by her own transformation and actions.

In the second place, her success in regaining the Prince and punishing Charlotte could not be expected to last. The Prince may temporarily play the role of the dedicated lover to his wife, but he is a proud man, well versed in the ingenuities of clandestine love affairs, and does not share his wife's moral outrage at extramarital affairs. He is bored even during the events described in the novel, and his boredom is bound to increase with Charlotte's removal and the routines of married life setting in. He will no doubt be much more circumspect in future love affairs, will be more careful not to arouse his wife's suspicions, but he will have them. It is natural and expected for a Roman aristocrat of his time and sensibility to add spice to life by having amorous flings. And Charlotte is a resourceful person. She is no doubt temporarily cowed and tortured by the agonies of not knowing what really has happened to her and why. But she will recover and find some way to persuade her husband that at least her place, if not his, is in Europe. There are many small ways in which a wife can make life unpleasant for her husband, and such stratagems may well make the always calculating Verver conclude that it is easier to let her have what she wants.

In the third place, it must be said that if a good life is not only fulfilling but also responsible, then none of the four can be said to have it, regardless of how fulfilling they might find their lives. Verver treated everyone but Maggie impersonally, expediently using them as his purposes dictated. The Prince and Charlotte sold themselves, made a bargain, violated its terms, and did their best to exploit their exploiters. They were unscrupulous opportunists, ready to take advantage of the supposed gullibility of Verver and Maggie, and it was their bad luck that they were outmaneuvered by an even more unscrupulous schemer. And Maggie made herself into a self-righteous harridan who by threats and bribery made people do her bidding as she was taking pleasure in hatching and executing her unlovely schemes.

The picture that emerges from James's novel is of four unlikable people trying as best as they can to get through life in an agreeable manner, but their character defects doom them to failure. One of these defects is the poverty of their exploratory imagination. It prevents them from forming an accurate judgment of the possibilities they are so busily engaged in trying to realize. They do not see that the possibilities they pursue will not yield them fulfillment, or that in pursuing them they will violate their responsibility to those on whom their fulfillment depends. The Prince and Charlotte fail to see that a luxurious life will not be enough to fulfill them and that the pursuit of it will ruin their pride, shame them, and cause grave damage to their self-esteem. Verver is morally obtuse to such an extent that he fails even to be aware of possibilities he might pursue, let alone choose among them intelligently. And Maggie does not see that her self-righteousness and manipulativeness alter her relationship to her father, husband, and erstwhile friend, on all of whom she believes her fulfillment, in one way or another, depends.

6.4 Aesthetic Romanticism and Its Snares

In the preceding discussion, I have found three ways in which the exploratory imagination can go wrong. One is through moral obtuseness, which prevents people from recognizing possibilities whose realization may make their lives better. This was illustrated by Verver. Another is through making serious mistakes in judging what life would be like if certain possibilities were realized. This was illustrated by the Prince and Charlotte, who were blind to the destructive consequences of selling themselves for a luxurious life. A third way of going wrong is to pursue a possibility in violation of moral limits. This, I believe, is what James shows Maggie to be doing. In what follows, I concentrate on her misuse of exploratory imagination. It has a larger significance than the mere failings of a character in a novel.

Maggie, of course, was less than fully aware of what she was doing. Self-deception and passionate involvement in the imbroglio have directed her attention elsewhere. But Martha Nussbaum decided to speak for Maggie in two essays that present Maggie and her actions in a favorable light.[7] Nussbaum, in my opinion, has succumbed to the snares of aesthetic romanticism, and this leads her to a bad misunderstanding of the novel, Maggie, and the morality of her actions. Before I give reasons for this, I should say that I completely agree with Nussbaum about the importance of literature and the particularity of moral judgments for understanding the nature of morality.

One clue to Nussbaum's misunderstanding is her claim that "this novel . . . is about the development of a woman."[8] Given the complexity of *The Golden Bowl*, this is an odd claim. Surely, the novel is about many things, among them, American innocence meeting European sophistication, the corrupting effect of money on human relationships, how people's perceptions of one another affect their lives and actions, the relation between the aesthetic and the moral dimensions of life, the varieties of love, the corruption of innocence, the wages of betrayal, and so on and on. Why does Nussbaum single out one of many themes in the novel and claim that *it* is what the novel is about? Because she thinks that the theme of Maggie's development reveals something crucial about morality: namely, that "meaningful commitment to a love can require the sacrifice of one's own moral purity . . . the breaking of moral rules." And that doing this is nothing less than "a new way of getting at perfection."[9]

Nussbaum explains what this new way is: "See clearly and with high intelligence. Respond with vibrant sympathy of a vividly active imagination. If there are conflicts, face them squarely and with keen perception.

Choose as well as you can for overt action, but at every moment remember the more comprehensive duties of the imagination and emotions. If love of your husband requires hurting and lying to Charlotte, then do these cruel things. . . . Maggie's keen sensibility to the values of love and friendship, which she herself is violating, redeems and transfigures the cruelty of her act. If she acts badly of necessity, at least she takes upon herself the conscious guilt for that badness."[10]

Now the view expressed by these lines is extraordinary: cruelty, harm, lies, and the violation of love and friendship may be dictated by "the more comprehensive duties of the imagination and emotions." What this means in plain language is that if you fancy doing it and it feels good, then it is not just all right but your duty—your duty!—to do it. And this is presented as a "new way of getting at perfection"—at perfection, no less! It is allowed that you should feel guilty when you subjugate your husband, enjoy taking revenge on your rival, and manipulate the father you love, as Maggie has done, but they are just the broken eggs the making of Maggie's omelet requires. Love indeed conquers all, morality apparently included.

Nussbaum thinks this follows because "life is a tragedy." You should "respond to that fact with pity for others and fear for yourself," but "never for a moment close your eyes or dull your feelings."[11] Provided people pity their victims, fear for themselves, and feel guilty that their imagination and emotions prompt them to inflict grievous injury on others, it is their duty, their way to perfection to cause the injuries. Life is a tragedy because the promptings of imagination and emotions often conflict with the requirements of morality. Nussbaum appears to think that such conflicts should be resolved in favor of the imagination and emotions, and one should feel guilty for injuring others. She does not go so far as to give reasons for rejecting the view defended throughout the history of moral thought that part of the purpose of morality is to set limits to what people might be led to do by their imagination and emotions. She simply shunts aside this basic moral view in the course of reflecting on what she misperceives as Maggie's development toward the acceptance of the tragic view of life.

Let us ask, therefore, whether life has appeared tragic for scheming Maggie. Maggie says to herself, after she has surveyed with no small satisfaction the results of her plot, that "she has done all" (514), and she says to her father, who agrees with her, "It's success, father" (545). I suppose it might be said, if one works hard to keep a straight face, that Maggie's life was tragic because she could not enjoy sexual fulfillment provided by her husband unless she reclaimed his attention from his mistress. It must not be forgotten, however, that the moral cost she was all too willing to pay for this and for succeeding at the plot she hatched was created only by what she wanted, not by any tragic necessity intrinsic to life. And her compunctions were more than outweighed by the "wonderful excitement" and the "high pastime" (303) she found in scheming. It may be said, just short of a joke, that it was tragic for Maggie not to get everything she wanted, but to call *life* tragic on that account shows a badly skewed judgment.

Nussbaum's judgment is skewed by the ideal she claims to find in *The Golden Bowl*. When "we study the loves and attentions of a finely responsive mind such as Maggie's, through all the contingent complexities of a tangled life . . . when we see that even for such a consciousness the golden bowl is broken—then we have something like a persuasive argument that these features hold of human life in general. It is . . . the presence of a character who will count as a high case of human response to value, that creates the telling argument."[12] This argument says "that human deliberation is constantly an *adventure* of the personality, undertaken against terrific odds among frightening mysteries, *and* that this is, in fact, the source of much of its beauty and richness."[13]

There are three consideration I want to set against this ideal and what Nussbaum regards as a telling argument for it. First, when people refrain from violence, although provoked; keep promises, although it is onerous; pay bills, although short of money; or are polite, although it is to a stranger, then we look in vain for adventure, terrific odds, or frightening mysteries. We just find plain common decency. Moral conduct is usually and generally like that. And moral transgressions are likewise banal failures to control one's temper, keep a promise, pay a debt, or be civil. The complexities James conveys in *The Golden Bowl* are certainly morally instructive, but it is grotesquely at odds with common human experience to suppose, as James does not, that they "hold of human life in general" or that Maggie—cruel, lying, scheming, vengeful, jealous, resentful—is a moral exemplar.

Second, the ideal is not one that James holds in *The Golden Bowl* or, as far as I know, anywhere else. Ascribing the ideal to him involves an extremely implausible interpretation. In one of the two essays, Nussbaum uses James's phrase "finely aware and richly responsible" as a shorthand to refer to James's view. I am willing to accept it as a convenient label, but I am not willing to accept Nussbaum's interpretation of what it means to be responsible. To say of people that they are responsible is normally to say that they are accountable for their actions; it is appropriate to praise or blame, reward or punish them for what they do. They are held accountable for meeting or failing to meet requirements, rules, obligations, or standards. When James talks about being richly responsible as part of moral life, he uses these words in their ordinary sense to mean paying particularly close attention to doing the right thing. In precisely this sense, none of the four protagonists in *The Golden Bowl* was richly responsible. Even if they were finely aware, which is doubtful, they used such awareness as they had to deceive others and satisfy themselves. James has richly responsible characters in other novels—Isabel Archer in *The Portrait of a Lady* and Lambert Strether in *The Ambassadors*, for instance—but in *The Golden Bowl* it is the failure of being richly responsible that he is, among other things, describing.

Nussbaum denies this because she understands by responsibility something very different from its ordinary sense and from the sense in which, I believe, James uses it. She thinks that being responsible is being responsive. "Moral knowledge," Nussbaum says, "is seeing a complex reality in a highly lucid and richly responsive way; it is taking in what is there, with imagination and feeling." The measure of Maggie's "moral adequacy" is the "fullness and richness of her imaginings," which "achieves its moral goal in the finding of the right way of seeing."[14] "Responsible action, as James conceives it," says Nussbaum, "is a highly context-specific and nuanced and responsive thing."[15] Speaking of Verver, Nussbaum says, "He is responsible . . . for making sure that nothing is lost on him, for feeling fully, for getting the tone right."[16] And she says that "the most exact and responsible way of doing is, in fact . . . an achievement of the precisely right description, the correct nuance of tone."[17]

I will shortly give reasons for rejecting this view of responsibility, but let us suppose for the moment that it is correct and that Maggie has "a finely responsive mind." It would still have to be recognized that fine responsiveness is only a very partial description of Maggie's morally relevant psychological states. She is "consummately, diabolically . . . audacious and impudent" (294); she finds her revenge plot "a high pastime . . . a private and absorbing exercise" (303); she is jealous and tormented (375); she is "bewildered" (379); a "mistress of shades" (396) and of the "dissimulated arts" (398); she is "humbugging . . . her father" (439); and she feels the "fascination of the monstrous, that temptation of the horribly possible" (456). To speak of Maggie's "moral adequacy" without taking into account these psychological states, as Nussbaum does, is to form a false picture of her by ignoring or misinterpreting textual evidence.

But Nussbaum's view, according to which responsibility has to do with being in a particular psychological state, namely, being imaginative, feelingful, nuanced, and responsive, is very much mistaken. In the first place, people in such a psychological state may go on to perform morally right actions, morally wrong actions, or no action at all. Surely, what they do is an essential part of their responsibility, and whether their psychological state is refined enough to satisfy this odd requirement that Nussbaum lays on them is irrelevant. If it were not irrelevant, the absurd conclusion would follow that very few people were ever responsible. Second, people are rightly held responsible for their actions even if they are unimaginative, emotionally dull, crude, and unresponsive. Murderers, torturers, fanatics, ideologues are often like this, but that does not acquit them from responsibility. Third, being in the psychological state Nussbaum requires for responsibility carries with it no guarantee that people's imaginations, feelings, discriminations, and responsive reverberations are accurate reactions to the real world. There is immense scope here for self-deception, fantasy, self-serving falsification, being led astray by one's hopes, fears, prejudices, pride, jealousy, envy, and so forth. The fact is that responsibility has mostly to do with meeting obligations that are usually plain, simple, and require no fine discrimination. Paying debts, keeping promises, being helpful, and doing one's job rarely and only exceptionally call for the kind of refinement that Nussbaum mistakenly regards as essential to responsibility.

Nussbaum does say that "fine-tuned perceiving" does not displace "standing obligations, some particular and some general." But she goes on, "Duty without perception is blunt and blind. The right 'basis' for action is found in the loving dialogue of the two [i.e., of duty and perception]."[18] This means, of course, that without fine-tuned perception people are blind to their duty, since one component of the supposedly necessary loving dialogue is missing. And that is just the untenable view to which I have been objecting, on the ground that the loving dialogue is neither necessary nor sufficient for right action. A fine-tuned perception may lead to violation of responsibility, responsibility can be and often is met without fine-tuned perception, and fine-tuned perceptions are not exempt from fallibility. It needs to be added that Nussbaum provides no convincing reason to think that her mistaken view of responsibility is actually held by James. She thinks that being finely aware *is* being richly responsible, and that this is what James also thinks. She is wrong on both accounts, however, and even if she were right in attributing this view to James, all that would follow is that both Nussbaum and James hold an untenable view about responsibility.

Let us go a step deeper and ask about the source of Nussbaum's mistake. Why think that responsibility has an intimate connection with responsiveness? Why is being finely aware essential to being richly responsible? This brings us to the third consideration I want to set against Nussbaum's ideal. It also brings us, finally, to aesthetic romanticism. At the root of Nussbaum's ideal is the assumption that the moral imagination is a kind of creative imagination. She says: "The work of moral imagination is in some manner like the work of creative imagination, especially that of the novelist. I want to study this analogy and to see how it is more than analogy. . . .

More: why according to this conception, the novel is itself a moral achievement, and the well-lived life is a work of literary art."[19]

The obvious objection to this view is that there is a crucial difference between moral and creative imagination. Creative imagination ought to be freer to explore whatever possibility interests the novelist in particular or artists in general than moral imagination, which ought to be constrained by moral limits, because there are morally deplorable possibilities that ought not to be explored. The reason why creative imagination ought to be freer of limits than moral imagination is that exploration in literature and arts leads to producing works of art that have only a tenuous and indirect connection with actions that may harm others, whereas exploration in human lives directly prompts actions that may harm others. Moral imagination is moral because it is conducted with the purpose of trying to make human lives better. The exploration of morally deplorable, cruel, unjust, destructive possibilities makes lives worse. The idea that living a good life is like creating a work of art, that moral imagination is a species of creative imagination in which the artists work in the medium of their own lives, is pernicious because it leads to the rejection of moral limits.

Aesthetic romanticism is a response to this objection. It has a radical version, represented by, among others, Nietzsche, and a moderate version, which may or may not be held by Nussbaum. Neither version is tenable. The radical version calls for the transvaluation of values, as Nietzsche put it. It rejects any conception of morality that places limits on the creative development of individuals. True morality is to find out what sort of life one wants to live and then use one's resources to the fullest to achieve it. Individuals should be as little curtailed in this endeavor as artists in producing works of art. Good lives are the results of creative efforts. They are made from the resources individuals find in themselves. Not everyone has the resources necessary to live this way, but those who do and who use them represent the great achievements of humanity. Morality is false if it obstructs this endeavor; it is a life-denying obstacle erected by the weak to prevent the strong from achieving what the weak can only envy.

The objections to the radical version of aesthetic romanticism are decisive. First, it identifies good lives with fulfilling lives and ignores that good lives must also be responsible. It is thus committed to regarding immoral lives as good, provided they are found fulfilling by the malefactors. Second, there is no more reason to suppose that the creative efforts of individuals will produce a fulfilling life than to suppose that the creative efforts of artists will produce anything worthwhile. The creative efforts of artists often produce kitsch, just as the creative efforts of individuals often produce unfulfilling lives. Third, fulfilling lives require a hospitable social context and at least some intimate relationships. They require also the cooperation of countless strangers who supply the food, medical care, housing, education, security, the amenities of civilized existence, without which a fulfilling life is impossible. These requirements impose unavoidable constraints on what a fulfilling life could be. Reasonable moral rules embody these constraints. Violating them is to violate the conditions that make a fulfilling life possible. Consequently, the ideal of being free of constraints—the ideal of the radical version of aesthetic romanticism—is self-defeating.[20]

Nussbaum appears to reject this version because she rejects "the aestheticization of the moral."[21] Her "ideal makes room . . . for a norm or norms of rightness and for a substantial account of ethical objectivity."[22] It appears, therefore, that she accepts that a good life must be both fulfilling, by which she means that it must be guided by imagination and emotions, and responsible, that is, constrained by objective norms of rightness. This may be thought of as a moderate version of aesthetic romanticism. I said of it above that she may or may not hold it. My reason for saying this is that moderate aestheticism faces a dilemma, and Nussbaum says nothing about how she would try to resolve it.

The two requirements of good life often conflict. Fulfillment aimed at by the free and creative play of the imagination and emotions often requires actions that violate objective norms of rightness and are thus irresponsible. And responsibility often requires curtailing actions prompted by imagination and emotions. At the end of the "loving dialogue" between them that Nussbaum recommends, the conflict must still be resolved. If it is resolved in favor of fulfillment and against responsibility—in favor of Nussbaum's "more comprehensive duties of the imagination and emotions"[23]—then moderate aesthetic romanticism is abandoned in favor of the untenable radical version. If the conflicts are resolved in favor of responsibility, then moderate aesthetic romanticism is abandoned in favor of the usual view that actions ought to conform to moral rules. But this is just the view that Nussbaum is arguing against in the two essays I have been discussing. Recall her claims that "life is a tragedy" because it "can require the sacrifice of one's own moral purity . . . the breaking of moral rules" and that this is "a new way of getting at perfection."[24] So one does not know whether Nussbaum is really a closet Nietzschean or whether her overheated prose disguises the familiar, conventionally held moral position. Whichever it is, however, her interpretation of *The Golden Bowl* is indefensible. If her position is Nietzschean, then she should not think that Maggie sacrificed her moral purity; for moral purity, then, is to follow the promptings of one's imagination and emotions, which is what Maggie did. If Nussbaum's position is conventional, then she should condemn Maggie for violating moral rules rather than hold her up as an admirable moral exemplar.

It is, of course, the latter alternative that I have been defending. But the aim of my defense is not to make a case for condemning Maggie, who is after all a fictional character, but to get at perhaps the main danger that the exploratory imagination faces. This danger is that the exploration of one's possibilities turns into aesthetic romanticism and undermines responsibility. In the closing section I make some further remarks about this.

6.5 Exploratory Imagination and Aesthetic Romanticism

Exploratory imagination can go wrong by being insufficient. This leads to moral obtuseness, to trying to realize possibilities of life without an effort to understand what they are. It can also go wrong even if its quantity is adequate but its quality is defective. This leads to misunderstanding the possibilities one has explored because of self-deception, fantasy, fear, hope, or some other psychological interference with realistic understanding. But the way of going wrong that is the besetting vice of exploratory imagination is to use it so well as to allow it to become a delight in itself. The delight is of doing something difficult well. It may make its user forgetful of the reason for using it in the first place, which is to explore possibilities that may make one's life better, and better means more fulfilling and more responsible.

The danger is that the pleasures of exploration—the satisfaction taken in the free play of one's mind, in the keenness of one's perception, in the acuity of one's sensibility—are found to be so fulfilling as to carry with them a sense of their obvious justification. But although the pleasures of exploration are undeniable, they are not thereby justified. They tend to divert attention from responsibility, which is as important for the evaluation of possibilities as fulfillment is. For responsibility is indispensable to protecting the conditions that make fulfillment possible.

Aesthetic romanticism is the attitude that privileges the pleasures of imagination and regards responsibility as a life-denying interference with it. This attitude may be justifiable in literary and artistic creativity and appreciation, but it is unjustifiable in the context of trying to live a good life. To deny this is to assimilate exploratory imagination to creative imagination, to repudiate limits in the name of freedom and creativity, to regard a good life as a work of art. This is why aesthetic romanticism in morality—which aims at protecting the conditions of good lives—is always a vice. The exploratory imagination easily leads to this vice, and that is one of the most serious threats its users must guard against. Part of James's achievement in *The Golden Bowl* is to show through Maggie what a life can be like if this danger is not avoided.

James also shows that exploratory imagination faces two other threats. Both have to do with its failure: one in quantity, the other in quality. Verver's moral obtuseness was the result of his failure to use his exploratory imagination to a sufficient extent. He was simply disinterested in the possibilities of life other than those he spent his time, money, and energy realizing. His life was impoverished by a self-imposed blindness to ways in which it might have been immeasurably enriched, such as viewing people other than means to satisfying his mercenary passion of acquisition. If he had used his exploratory imagination more, he would have had a more fulfilling and more responsible life.

The Prince and Charlotte cannot be faulted for underemploying their exploratory imagination. Their mistake was to use it badly. They were seriously wrong about the possibility that they imagined would give them a fulfilling life. The conclusive proof is that they got the luxurious life they had wanted and connived for, but it utterly failed to yield the hoped-for fulfillment.

Although all four protagonists failed to achieve the good life they wanted, they all conformed to the voluntarist ideal of reflective self-evaluation. They had, as Frankfurt recommends, controlled their first-order volitions by their second-order volitions. Or, as Hampshire prescribes, their actions faithfully expressed their intentions. It follows that if the ideal of reflective self-evaluation is to lead to the good life it promises, it must meet conditions in addition to those Frankfurt and Hampshire recognize. We learn from Maggie's case that the ideal must include the recognition of one's responsibilities; from the Prince's and Charlotte's case that it must include the successful imaginative exploration of the possibilities one intends to realize; and from Verver's case that the lack of exploratory imagination is most likely to lead to the pursuit of possibilities whose realization will not be fulfilling.

CHAPTER 7

This Process of Vision

> *Would* there yet perhaps be time for reparation?—reparation,
> that is, for the injury done his character; for the affront, he is
> quite ready to say, so stupidly put upon it and in which he has
> even himself had so clumsy a hand?
> The answer to which is that he now at all events *sees*; so that . . .
> the precious moral of everything is just my demonstration of this
> process of vision.
>
> —HENRY JAMES, preface to *The Ambassadors*

7.1 Halfway to Fulfillment

In the preceding chapter I was concerned with showing how the four main characters in *The Golden Bowl* failed in the exploratory use of moral imagination and how this contributed to their failure to achieve the good life they wanted. Because of moral obtuseness (Verver), inadequate understanding of the possibility for which they sold their souls (the Prince and Charlotte), and selfishness and self-deception (Maggie), they lived irresponsibly and without fulfillment. In this chapter I consider someone going through the process of mastering exploratory imagination and illustrating concretely how to use it well. He achieves remarkable success, he is exemplary in meeting his responsibilities, but fulfillment still eludes him. He cannot live according to the possibility he has learned through exploratory imagination to value. This person is Lewis Lambert Strether in Henry James's *The Ambassadors*,[1] of which James says, "I am able to estimate this as, frankly, quite the best, 'all round' of my productions" (1:vii).

Strether is a fifty-five-year-old American from Woollett, Massachusetts. His wife and son died many years ago. He is the editor of a small cultural-literary review whose expenses are underwritten by the widowed Mrs.

Newsome, a rich lady of Woollett to whom Strether is engaged. Strether is the first ambassador of the novel. At the end of the nineteenth century he travels to Paris at Mrs. Newsome's behest to persuade Chad, her twenty-eight-year-old son, to return to Woollett after several years in Paris and assume his responsibility in the family business. Chad's family suspects that he is in the clutches of some wicked Frenchwoman. Strether is to talk sense to Chad, remind him of his responsibilities, and make him return home.

Strether meets Maria Gostrey and Little Bilham, expatriate Americans who introduce him to life in Paris and interpret for him the attractions and subtleties that life there involves. Strether is a quick, sensitive learner. He is beguiled and charmed by what he is shown. He comes to see the great contrast between the utilitarian mode of existence in Woollett, devoid of joy, grace, taste, and discrimination, and the aesthetically rich, refined life in Paris. He contrasts the rigid moralism, determined money-making, and philistine crudity he left behind with the free, lighthearted, nonjudgmental, cultivated ease of his newfound Parisian society. He sees how much richer are the possibilities of life in Paris than in Woollett.

Strether then meets Chad, and finds him transformed from the crude, unlikable, callow youth he was in Woollett to a gracious, tactful, and civilized young man. Strether sees the change and cannot but applaud it. The more time he spends with Chad, the better he appreciates the superiority of the milieu of Paris to that of Woollett. He begins to see why Chad has been reluctant to give it up and go home for a life in commerce. He gains the young man's trust, and Chad introduces him to Madame de Vionnet, a French comtesse and Chad's special friend. Strether is uncertain about the nature of their friendship, but he understands that the transformation in Chad is the result of Madame de Vionnet's influence. As Strether comes to know her better, he sees that she exemplifies the possibility of gracious life he has begun to discern behind the changes in Chad.

During the weeks that pass there is a steady exchange of letters between Strether and Mrs. Newsome, to whom Strether faithfully conveys his impressions of what he is finding. These letters alarm Mrs. Newsome because she perceives a change in Strether that is leading to his equivocal attitude to getting Chad to return home. She thinks he is succumbing to the corrupting allure of Paris and is being seduced by it in the same way as Chad has been. This may be a forgivable weakness in a young man, but it is inexcusable in the fifty-five-year-old Strether, who is tied to her by affection and obligation. Mrs. Newsome then dispatches a second group of ambassadors, the most formidable of whom is her daughter, a younger version of herself. And Mrs. Newsome summons Strether to return to Woollett.

Strether temporizes. Mrs. Newsome's daughter then gives him the ultimatum: bring Chad home or his ties to Mrs. Newsome and to all she offers him will be severed. Strether chooses the latter and advises Chad to stay in Paris. He does this even though he has come to understand that Chad's friendship with Madame de Vionnet is a sexual liaison that is immoral according to Woollett. This, however, is no longer a judgment Strether shares. He sees that such liaisons have a very different significance in Paris from what they have in Woollett. The facts are what they are, but Strether now understands how differently their moral significance can be viewed. And he is no longer clear how he views them. He does know, however, that his very uncertainty and his answer to the ultimatum have put an end to his previous existence in Woollett.

At this point two events occur. Chad ignores Strether's advice; decides to go home; abandons Madame de Vionnet, who loves him; and accepts the responsibilities he, in agreement with his family's and Woollett's morality, now acknowledges to have. He has sown his wild oats, and the time has come to turn to the serious business of making money. The other event is that Strether also decides to go back to Woollett, even though he knows that he cannot resume his old life. He knows as well that his guide to Paris, Maria Gostrey, loves him, wants to marry him and share a life with him in Paris, but he does not accept what she offers.

7.2 Growing in Appreciation of Life

Central to the novel are several ironic transformations. All of them reflect the shifting point of view of Strether as he is being transformed by what he sees. He arrives to champion the cause of Woollett and learns to appreciate the attractions of Paris; he starts with the conviction that he should persuade Chad to go home and ends with trying to persuade him to stay in Paris; he comes expecting to find a wicked woman who has ensnared Chad and finds a charming, gracious lady in love with Chad, who spurns her; he learns to appreciate the richness of life Paris offers in comparison with the rigidity of Woollett, and yet he chooses life in Woollett over one in Paris; he begins with affection and admiration for Mrs. Newsome and ends with doubts about her dogmatism, authority, and intransigence; he views Little Bilham at first as an amiable idler and learns to see him as a younger version of himself who is making the sort of mistake he himself has made; he encourages and values the deepening relationship between Maria Gostrey and himself, and yet he repudiates it and the life it offers; he learns that a fulfilling life depends on active engagement, but he decides to go back to Woollett to a life of passivity. To understand the novel and the central role of exploratory imagination in it requires understanding these transformations. In this we have the invaluable help James himself provides in the preface.

James says that the following remarks of Strether to Little Bilham "contain the essence of 'The Ambassadors'. . . . Live all you can; it's a mistake not to. It doesn't so much matter what you do in particular so long as you have your life. If you haven't had that what *have* you had? I'm too old—too old at any rate for what I see. What one loses one loses; make no mistake about that. . . . I'm a case of reaction against the mistake. Do what you like so long as you don't make it. For it *was* a mistake. Live, live!" (1:v–vi and 1:217–218; it is interesting that James is not quite accurate in quoting himself). The key to the novel, I think, is to understand that behind the transformations is Strether's changing view of life, and his view changes as his exploratory imagination improves.[2]

The view of life with which Strether begins emerges in one of the first conversations he has with Maria. He says that his mission is to take Chad back to Woollett and to "a lot of advantages," which include not just a great deal of money but also "consideration and comfort and security— the general safety of being anchored by a strong chain . . . to be protected. Protected I mean from life" (1:71). Life, then, is something to be protected from, and that is what money, comfort, and security are for. This view begins to shift after Strether has spent a few weeks in Paris under the tutelage of Maria and encountered the changed Chad: "his changed state, his lovely home, his beautiful things, his easy talk. . . . Chad's case . . . was first and foremost a miracle. . . . It was the alteration of the entire man" (1:165, 1:167). Strether beholds the change and reflects on it: "One wants, confound it . . . one wants to enjoy anything so rare. Call it then life . . . call it poor dear old life simply that springs the surprise. Nothing alters the fact that the surprise is . . . engrossing . . . that one sees, that one *can* see" (1:167–168). Life has become surprising, engrossing, something he wants to enjoy. And what makes it possible is his capacity to see and the pleasure it gives him to be able to see.

Strether, however, reflects further on what he sees and on his own life, and then occurs the conversation with Little Bilham that I cited earlier as expressing the essence of the novel. He sees that life is not to be protected from, nor merely to be observed, but actually to be lived. "Live all you can; it's a mistake not to" (1:217), he tells Little Bilham, and then he goes on reflecting about himself: "This place and these impressions . . . all my impressions of Chad and of people I've seen at *his* place—well, have had their abundant message for me. . . . I see it now. I haven't done so before—and now I'm too old; too old at any rate for what I see. Oh I *do* see, at least. . . . It's too late. . . . The affair—I mean the affair of life—couldn't, no doubt, have been different for me. . . . At present I'm a case of reaction against the mistake" (1:217–218). And Strether looks wistfully at the changed, refined, and young Chad standing at some distance, and says, "Oh Chad!—it was that rare youth he should have enjoyed being 'like' " (1:220).

The reality, however, is that "he has . . . missed too much, though perhaps after all constitutionally qualified for a better part" (1:vi). Or as Strether puts it in another conversation: "he thinks, you know, that *I've* a life of my own. And I haven't! . . . I seem to have a life only for other people" (1:269). And Strether blames himself "for the injury done to his character . . . in which he has even himself had so clumsy a hand." Nevertheless, he has something: "he now at all events *sees*," and as James puts it, "the business of my tale . . . the precious moral of everything is . . . this process of vision" (1:vi). Strether is "a man of imagination" (1:viii); he is, James says, "my man of imagination" (1:xi); his life is "the drama of discrimination . . . [it was] his blest imagination . . . that helped him to discriminate" (1:xiii).

We can, I think, trace the upward trajectory of Strether's imagination in his shifting view of life. At first he sees the possibilities of life as threatening, then as enjoyable; and then he sees that because of his past mistakes the pleasures of having and using his imagination are the only pleasures left to him. But is this view that Strether ends up having of the possibilities of his own life realistic? Why can he not act on the possibilities open to him? In particular, why can he not abandon Woollett, marry Maria, and live in Paris with her? Why does he think and feel that it is too late, that he is too old to act on what he has learned to see? Because, he says to Maria, "all the same I must go. . . . To be right." But, she asks, "why should you be so dreadfully right?" Strether's reply is "I can't do anything else." And she says, having accepted it, "It isn't so much your *being* 'right'—it's your horrible sharp eye for what makes you so" (2:326–327). What, then, does Strether see with his horrible sharp eye that warrants his decision?

7.3 Seeing Things as They Are

Strether's decision is warranted by several things he sees. Each acts as a counterweight to the attractive possibilities life in Paris offers. One concerns the expatriate life he finds in Paris, another is what he glimpses at in French mores, and the third has to do with himself. It is a noteworthy feature of the novel that although its setting is Paris, apart from a brief early period in England and an interlude in the French countryside, Madame de Vionnet and her daughter are the only French people in it. All the other characters are Americans, either visiting Paris or expatriates living there. Strether sees that these expatriates are united by saying yes and no to the same things. They form an "aesthetic fraternity"

(1:115) and live an "irregular life" with only "indirect" connections to the surrounding society (1:117). They are "intense Americans together" (1:125), "ingenuous compatriots," living a "makeshift life" that "twang[s] with a vengeance the aesthetic lyre" (1:128), has an "overflow of taste," but suffers from the "lack of nearly all else" (1:127). They hold no jobs, practice no professions, cultivate no talents. They are, as it is said of another group of aesthetes, "water-spiders, gracefully skimming, as light . . . as air, the surface of the stream without any contacts with the eddies and currents underneath."[3]

Strether sees them as they are, charming, perceptive dilettantes, taking pleasure in beauty, living superficially, unengaged in life, and lacking in seriousness and depth. The closest they come to depth is their passionate rejection of all that Woollett stands for. Little Bilham speaks for all of them when he says to Strether that he would "rather die than go home" (1:178). These are the people with whom Strether would have to live if he married Maria and stayed in Paris. He sees that "one of the platitudes of the human comedy [is] that people's moral scheme *does* break down in Paris . . . that hundreds of thousands of more or less hypocritical or more or less cynical persons annually visit the place for the sake of the probable catastrophe." Strether wanted to have no part of this "association, one of the vulgarest in the world" (1:xiii–xiv).

The second thing Strether sees is a mere glimpse, but it is enough to put him off French mores. Chad makes clear to Strether "that his social relations . . . were perhaps not to the extent Strether supposed with the rising flood of their compatriots" and "that he went about little in the 'colony' " (1:163). His social relations are with the French through Madame de Vionnet. Madame de Vionnet tells Strether that Chad has been instrumental in arranging the marriage of her young daughter to a French aristocrat. The daughter, Jeanne, barely knows her husband-to-be. The marriage is for Madame de Vionnet's convenience: it enhances her social position, it is agreeable to have Chad use part of his wealth to make the arranged marriage attractive to the future husband, and Jeanne is inconveniently in love with Chad. Madame de Vionnet is jealous, and Chad wishes to reassure her.

Strether is shocked by the mores that permit disposing of Jeanne in this manner. "He had allowed for depths, but these were greater. . . . It was— through something ancient and cold in it—what he would have called the real thing. In short his hostess's [Madame de Vionnet's] news . . . was a sensible shock." Madame de Vionnet asks him, "Do I seem to you very awful?" And he answers, " 'Awful? Why so?' But he called it to himself, even as he spoke, his biggest insincerity yet." She explains, "Our arrangements are so different from yours" (1:129–130). He concedes later in a conversation with Maria that the engagement "simplifies" (1:138), but he is appalled by the cold, calculating expediency and the absence of sentiment that the simplification involves. He begins to see the duplicity underneath Madame de Vionnet's charm and exquisite manners, and he sees that whatever may be said for them, her ways are not his.

The third thing that disposes Strether against staying in Paris is his realization that "I've been sacrificing so to strange gods that I feel I want to put on record, somehow, my fidelity—fundamentally unchanged after all—to our own" (2:167). Strether has a moral center, a core that ultimately sets the possibilities and limits that are possibilities and limits *for him*, regardless of how others may see them. What he comes to see is that "he mustn't dispossess himself of the faculty of seeing things as they were" (1:118), "for keeping things straight, for the happy forestalment of error" (1:141). It is, then, the combination of this moral core at the center of his being and his ability to see, through his imagination, the possibilities of Woollett and Paris as they were that set for him what he must and must not do. Attractive as the possibilities of Paris were, and unattractive as the narrow-minded, joyless rigidity of Woollett was, Strether's fundamental allegiance was nevertheless with Woollett. His imagination enabled him to explore sympathetically the possibilities of Paris, but it also enabled him to forestall the error of confusing them with possibilities he might make his own. Because he saw clearly, he knew how he must live, what he must and must not do to remain true to himself.

As Iris Murdoch says: "We are not free in the sense of being able suddenly to alter ourselves since we cannot suddenly alter what we can see and ergo what we desire and are compelled by. In a way, explicit choice seems now less important: less decisive (since much of the 'decision' lies elsewhere) and less obviously something to be 'cultivated'. If I attend properly I will have no choices and this is the ultimate condition to be aimed at."[4] And that is the condition Strether had finally reached. His exploratory imagination enabled him to realize that he had no choice, he had to go home to Woollett, he had to do what is right because "I can't do anything else" (2:327). "His supreme scruple" was "not to do anything because he had missed something else, because he was sore or sorry or impoverished, because he was maltreated or desperate; he wished to do everything because he was lucid and quiet, just the same . . . on all essential points as he had always been" (2:294–295). His decision was reinforced by his distaste for the lives of the expatriates and the mores of the French. But he also saw that going home will doom him to a life without fulfillment; nevertheless, that is what he resolved to do.

Aided by his exploratory imagination, Strether acted responsibly, but why did that preclude fulfillment? Because at the core of the self to which he so admirably remained true there was a conflict. His morality, essentially formed by Woollett, was incompatible with his imagination, which allowed him to see things as they are. His moral values pulled him one way, and his understanding of the significance of facts revealed by his imaginative explorations pulled him in the other. He valued the conscientiousness and principled conduct expected in Woollett, but he saw that its cost was narrow-mindedness, rigidity, and the exclusion of possibilities of life that did not fit in with it. He condemned Chad's irresponsibility, but he could not help admiring his fineness, taste, good manners, and graciousness. He was a little bit in love with Madame de Vionnet, who was born and bred to an aristocratic life of which beauty, elegance, and refinement were integral parts, but he saw the coldness and calculation under the glittering surface. He responded with fondness to Maria and Little Bilham, but he saw their superficiality and disengagement from life. He was perfectly clear about the embarrassing, brash crudity of the American visitors to Paris, but he saw the value of forthrightness and lack of pretense that motivated it. He saw himself as having been formed by Woollett, and yet, having lost the unquestioning acceptance of the mores that would have made him feel at home there, he still regarded it as his home. As James tells us, Strether was in a "false position" because he was "primed with a moral scheme . . . which was yet framed to break down on any approach to vivid facts," provided one had, as Strether did, "any at all liberal appreciation of them" (1:xiii).

The moral scheme of Woollett set the responsibility that Strether had recognized and honored. His imaginative capacity for a liberal appreciation of the facts showed him possibilities of life whose realization would have brought him fulfillment. Discharging his responsibility, however, precluded fulfillment, and Strether, seeing things as they were, doomed himself to a responsible and unfulfilled life. He saw that the way his character has been formed left him no choice in the matter; that he himself actively participated in making his character what it was; and that he was past the age at which what has been done could be undone. That is what he says to Little Bilham in the conversation that James says expresses the essence of the novel: "Live all you can; it's a mistake not to. . . . It's as if the train had fairly waited at the station for me without my having the gumption to know it was there. Now I hear its faint receding whistle miles and miles down the line. What one loses one loses; make no mistake about that" (1:217–218). And he asks himself the "terrible question": "*Would* there perhaps be time for reparation . . . for the injury done his character . . . and in which he has himself had so clumsy a hand?" The answer Strether gives himself is "that he now at all events *sees*." And that, as James says about the novel, is "the precious moral of everything . . . this process of vision" (1:v–vi).

But why does Strether's seeing—his process of vision—constitute anything like an answer to the terrible question of whether reparation is possible for his past mistake? Because seeing is his way out of the conflict between his morality and imagination. It is his modus vivendi, what he will
have left after he returns to Woollett. One result of Strether's conflict is
that it prevents him from active participation in life. He cannot take part
in the expatriates' life in Paris because he cannot join them in renouncing
Woollett and he cannot be satisfied with the unanchored superficiality of
their existence. Nor can he be part of the life of Woollett because, having
seen its narrow, dogmatic rigidity, he cannot join the members of that society in excluding all they exclude or in wholeheartedly taking for granted
all they take for granted. His imagination has made him reflective; with reflectiveness came loss of innocence, spontaneity, and wholeheartedness;
and he found no way back from reflectiveness. Strether sees all this, and
that is why the novel, showing him seeing it, is aptly described by James as
a "drama of discrimination" (1:xiii).

It is important that it is a *drama*, not a tragedy. Strether's position is
different from Oedipus's at Colonus. Oedipus is tragic because by the
time he came to terms with his past, death prevented him from enjoying
the fruits of his hard-earned lesson. Strether is not at death's door, and he
is prevented only from active participation. That still leaves for him a possibility he is particularly well suited to realize: a life of reflection in which
he is an imaginative but detached observer of the shifting scene around
him. He knows that "I'm not in real harmony with what surrounds me"
(2:320), but with the possibility of his "wonderful impression" he has, and
will have, a great deal (2:326). The life ahead of him, then, will be of one

> who hath watch'd, not shared, the strife,
> Knows how the day hath gone.
> He only lives with the world's life,
> Who hath renounced his own.[5]

It will be a life of responsibility, but not of fulfillment. It will not be bleak
because "one wants to enjoy anything so rare" as his ability to see, and the
shifting spectacle will be "engrossing" and surprising because it will be
"poor dear old life simply that springs the surprise" (1:167–168).

7.4 Integrated Lives

Strether's life was doomed to remain unfulfilled because of the
"injury done to his character . . . in which he has himself had so clumsy a

hand" (1:v–vi). His taking a hand in injuring his character was the ir-reparable mistake he made. In order to understand what exactly that mistake was, we need to understand the psychological requirement of fulfill-ment that Strether failed to meet. This requirement is to have an integrated life. A fulfilling life, of course, has other requirements as well.

Let us approach what an integrated life is by considering people's eval-uation of their own lives.[6] Such evaluations need not be expressed in a propositional form; they need not be reflective—indeed, one may not even be aware of having them. The evaluation may simply be an unarticu-lated feeling of satisfaction, dissatisfaction, or ambivalence regarding how one's life in general is going. It may reflect an unconscious wish that everything should go on by and large the same way as it has been going, or it may be the inchoate wish that it should be changed in some important ways. The signs of satisfaction may be tranquillity, wholehearted engage-ment in one's projects, or a benign and generous view of other people. Dissatisfaction may show itself in boredom, irritable restlessness, unfo-cused anxiety, or what Nietzsche perceptively described as *ressentiment*.

Although the realistic evaluation of one's life does not require knowing articulation, serious dissatisfaction normally leads to wanting to change how one lives, and then clarity about the source of one's dissatisfaction be-comes important. Because few lives are so fortunate as to be without seri-ous dissatisfactions, clarity and articulation are often desirable. But they are desirable for overcoming dissatisfactions, not as conditions of fulfill-ment. The desirability of overcoming dissatisfactions should not be con-fused with the desirability of being without them. Socrates, therefore, was wrong to say that the unexamined life is not worth living.[7] What he should have said is that examination—reflective self-evaluation—may make many lives more worth living.

Regardless, however, of the degree of clarity, articulation, and reflection involved in people's evaluations of their lives, the evaluations have cogni-tive, emotive, and motivational components. The cognitive component comprises people's beliefs about themselves, their lives, and circum-stances. These beliefs may be true or false. If false, they may be so because some internal psychological obstacle, such as self-deception, fear, hope, stupidity, laziness, fatigue, and so forth, has interfered with forming a re-alistic view. Such obstacles range from reasonable defenses against the aw-fulness of one's circumstances, through nonculpable weaknesses and shortcomings, to culpable vices. It may or may not be reasonable to try to overcome these obstacles, for the effort may be futile or the false belief may help one cope with an unbearable truth. It is normally reasonable, however, to aim to hold true beliefs about one's life, for the successful pur-suit of whatever one wants depends on the truth of the relevant beliefs.

Only in exceptional cases do falsifications escape being unreasonable. The source of false beliefs, however, may also be mistakes that result not from psychological obstacles but from physiological limits, physical illness, deception by others, manipulation, adverse external conditions, or the ambiguity or complexity of the relevant facts.

It is not only factual mistakes, however, that account for having false beliefs about one's life. The mistake may be one of judgment, in which accurately perceived facts are ascribed the wrong significance. In this way people may over- or underestimate the importance of something they lack or have, such as money; or they may be beguiled by some features of their life while overlooking other, no less important features, such as being attracted by the glamour of fame and missing the lack of privacy that goes with it; or they may be so wrapped up in their pursuit that they lose sight of the moral and political implications of what they are doing.

In people's evaluations of their own lives emotions are normally present.[8] It is natural to feel optimistic or pessimistic, hopeful or fearful, pleased or apprehensive, proud or ashamed, satisfied or guilty, contented or frustrated, joyful or depressed, enthusiastic or bored about one's life. Having such emotions is readily understandable, and it is their absence that requires explanation. Such an explanation typically reveals that something has gone very wrong in the lives of those who have no emotional reaction to how their lives are going. Extreme hardship, constant struggle, serious traumas, mental illness, or recurrent humiliation may make a life hard to endure, and it is understandable that people would focus their attention elsewhere. But if their lives are not grievously disturbed, people will have emotions about them.

Having emotions about one's life, however, is one thing; whether they are reasonable is quite another. In their origin, emotions are involuntary. They just happen. Strong ones assail us, weaker ones merely color our attitudes. They make us go up and down, influence our judgments, and affect how we regard our lives. Emotions tell us something that we may or may not welcome; strong ones do so insistently, weak ones softly. And if what they tell us is about our lives, then they intimate something important. But their intimations are often obscure and unreliable. This leads many thoughtful people to distrust emotions in general, and their own emotions in particular. They try to think of them as noise that is the by-product of the workings of their mental machinery. If this distrust were warranted, it would cast doubt also on the evaluations of which emotions are essential components. So we need to consider whether the distrust of emotions about one's life is reasonable.

The root of the distrust is that since emotions are involuntary, there does not seem to be a way of controlling them. To know that one ought to have a certain emotion will not produce it, and to know that one ought not to have it will not dissipate it. Fear of things going wrong, enthusiasm about a project, guilt at not having tried hard enough, joy at success, shame at failure either come to one or not, but they cannot be summoned up. We cannot practice to have them. They can certainly be faked by pretending to have them, but the pretense is for others; we cannot make ourselves feel the fear, enthusiasm, guilt, joy, or shame that we do not feel. What we should therefore do instead of trying to control the uncontrollable, skeptics say, is to concentrate on acting as we ought, regardless of whether emotions aid or hinder the effort.

This tendency to denigrate an essential component of the evaluation of one's life is at once futile and unwarranted. Even if emotions do not lend themselves to direct control, it is possible to control them indirectly. There may be little that can be done about having or not having particular emotions, but there is much that can be done to correct them by strengthening reasonable and weakening unreasonable ones. Such corrections are made possible by collateral beliefs. Reasonable emotions toward one's life are reactions to beliefs that are taken to be true: that one is loved; that one's project is the object of scorn; that a goal is within one's reach; that one has failed through lack of sufficient effort; that one has or lacks a necessary talent; that one's friend is true; that now nothing can go wrong; and so on. Then one feels joyous, angry, hopeful, ashamed, confident, or secure about one's life. Any of these beliefs may turn out to be false, and the realization of this is bound to affect the emotion, if it is a reasonable reaction to the false belief. The joy at being loved or the shame at failure cannot reasonably survive for long after the discovery that the love was simulated or that the apparent failure was in fact a success.

Emotions, of course, may not be reasonable. Thinking of them as reactions to particular collateral beliefs may just be a rationalization, not a reason. Their true sources are then hidden or disguised because they are too precious to be exposed, too threatening to face, or too shocking to admit. In that case, the realization that the collateral belief is false will not dispel the emotion. If the distrust of an emotion about one's life is based on the suspicion that the emotion is unreasonable in this way, then the distrust may be well founded. But the suspicion must itself be based on some reason, and that reason must be better than that what is suspected is an emotion. There is as little to be said for a global skepticism about emotions as there is for a global skepticism about beliefs or perceptions. They are all fallible, but only some of them are mistaken. If there is a reason to suspect that an emotion is unreasonable, then the very reason points to the way in which the suspicion may be confirmed or laid to rest, and thus the emotion may be brought under control. On the other hand, if there is no reason to suspect its reasonableness, then there is no reason to distrust it.

The distrust of emotions about one's life, however, may be based not on their supposed imperviousness to reason but on the frequency with which they turn out to be unreasonable. People tend to have false beliefs and unreasonable emotions about their lives because it is often easier to nurture them than to face the truth they disguise. This is lamentable but true. That, however, shows only that the reasonable evaluation of one's life is difficult, not that it is impossible. And that is not exactly news.

The third component of the evaluation of one's life is the motivational one. The beliefs and emotions about one's life, as well as external circumstances, prompt motives and move one toward action. In the simplest cases, finding one's life bad motivates one to make it better, and finding it good motivates one to continue to do whatever one has been doing. Such evaluations move one toward actions, and the actions aim to keep one's life good or make it better. If the motives result in actions, they typically have both immediate and more remote consequences. The immediate ones concern how to do some particular thing or what particular thing to do. The more remote ones concern the effect of what is done or how it is done on the development of one's character. Actions form patterns, the patterns solidify into character traits, and character traits make one's character what it is. Both kinds of consequence have a bearing on the evaluation of actions.

The connection between motive and action is often broken. This may happen for internal reasons: one may have more than a single motive, motives may conflict with each other, and only one of them can result in action. Or it may be the result of external obstacles found in one's circumstances that make it too costly or too risky to act as the motive prompts. Resolving internal conflicts and judging the seriousness of external obstacles is best done by appealing to the goal of the action for evaluating which of the conflicting motives is more important for the achievement of the goal, or whether the goal is important enough to make the risk involved in surmounting some obstacle worth taking.

The result of such evaluations may not be a decision to perform or not to perform a particular action, but a decision to question the importance of the goal for the sake of which the action might be done. That question can also be answered by appealing to one's most important goal, namely, to live a good life, which may be thought of as the ultimate standard with reference to which questions of importance about one's actions may be answered. Not to have such a standard—which, I repeat, need not be a conscious, articulate one—is to lack a conception of how one wishes to live. And that means lacking a sense of what is important or unimportant to oneself. People without that sense still have to make decisions and act, but their decisions and actions over time will lack coherence. They will be adrift in life, slaves to their momentary urges, and blind to their own interests.

In sum, the components of evaluations are cognitive, emotive, and motivational: beliefs, emotions, and motives. The beliefs concern the facts and their importance in one's life. The emotions express how one feels about the life as a whole. And the motives, prompted by beliefs and emotions, move one toward actions. The evaluation as a whole may or may not be reasonable, depending on whether the component beliefs, emotions, and motives are reasonable. Each can go wrong as a result of internal or external causes. Each can be corrected, although whether it should be corrected depends on whether the correction would be preferable to living with the mistake.

This finally allows me to return to the point of considering evaluations of one's life: a life is integrated if the relevant beliefs, emotions, and motives are congruous. This requires more than consistency. Beliefs, emotions, and motives are consistent if they are not incompatible, but they could be compatible and disjointed. They could constitute largely disparate and only marginally overlapping areas of one's life. The chief preoccupation of the beliefs may center on one's professional involvement with weather prediction; the focus of one's emotions may be a torrid love affair; and one's motives may concentrate on making a great deal of money. Such beliefs, emotions, and motives are consistent but not congruous. Congruity requires that there be a large area in which they overlap. Many of the beliefs, emotions, and motives should have the same object, so that actions flow from motives, motives reflect strongly felt emotions and reasonably held beliefs, and these beliefs make the strongly felt emotions reasonable. If it is added that the shared object of these beliefs, emotions, and motives is one's life in the light of one's conception of what a good life for oneself would be, then it is possible to see why an integrated life, in which the beliefs, emotions, and motives are congruous, is a condition of fulfillment. But it is not a sufficient condition because a well-integrated life may not be fulfilling as a result of external obstacles.

The fact is, however, that the lives of many people are not integrated but fragmented because their beliefs, emotions, and motives centering on their lives are incongruous. Such lives are full of serious conflicts because what people believe, feel, and are motivated to do about their lives move them in different directions. This is just what happened to Strether, and this is the reason why he lacked fulfillment.

Strether was born and raised in the morality of Woollett, and he lived his life in it. He was an exemplary member of that society. He accepted the obligations that set limits to what he might do, and he responsibly discharged his obligations. But he did all this at the great cost to himself of having to suppress much of what he really wanted to do. His character did not fit the morality that guided his actions. He resolved their incompatibility by ignoring the large part of his character that did not fit. This is why he was right to see that "I'm not in real harmony with what surrounds me" (2:320), that he is in a "false position" (1:xiii), and that "I seem to have a life only for other people" (1:269). The ignored part of his character, however, resisted suppression, and when the opportunity came, it skipped the control Strether imposed on it, reasserted itself, and gave Strether much surprise and pleasure. It opened up for him the joys of seeing, of letting his imagination explore the possibilities of life. His past and his allegiance to the morality of Woollett, however, doomed him to passivity because to follow where his imagination led would have been to violate the part of his character that was formed by Woollett. He was thus left with no reasonable choice but to live with the morality that has become his own, give as free a scope to his imagination as possible, but keep it firmly in control by not acting on the possibilities he so perceptively saw. He thereby doomed himself to live out his life in passivity because of the conflict that fragmented his life.

Lives can be fragmented in various ways. Beliefs may conflict with emotions, as in people who desperately feel that only religion can endow their lives with meaning but find religious beliefs utterly implausible. Or emotions may conflict with motives, when, for instance, people feel deeply that their country is immoral yet cannot make themselves act against it. Or motives may conflicts with beliefs, like those of parents who keep helping their children although they rightly believe that their help is wasted and undeserved. Strether's fragmentation, however, was more radical than any of these. For those of his beliefs, emotions, and motives that were formed by Woollett conflicted with the beliefs, emotions, and motives that sprang from the part of his character that was incompatible with the morality of Woollett. The result of his fragmented life was that however he acted amounted to a denial of part of himself. No wonder he opted for passivity, since that was the least destructive of his possibilities.

7.5 An Honorable Failure

Strether, then, was an honorable failure: failure because he was unfulfilled, honorable because he was responsible. His drama is that he was unfulfilled *because* he was responsible. And if he had been fulfilled, it

would have been at the cost of becoming irresponsible. But as I mentioned earlier, that was his drama, not his tragedy. His life would have
been tragic only if through no fault of his own he could have done nothing to avoid the choice between fulfillment and responsibility. But there
was. He could have used his imagination to understand himself, not just
others. The imagination I have in mind is not of the possibilities that may
or may not be open to him for exploration. Strether performed admirably
in that respect. The imagination he lacked or failed to use (James leaves
open which) is what might have enabled him to see why he made the mistake in the past that he acknowledges in such elegiac tones. If he had used
his imagination to look backward to his past, he might have asked himself
what it was in him, his circumstances, or the combination of both that led
him to suppress a valued part of himself rather than withdraw his allegiance from the morality that required the suppression. He might, then,
have asked why he stayed in Woollett and be maimed rather than leave for
a less confining life.

James does not say enough about Strether's past to make a confident answer possible. The likely answer, however, is that Strether was not strong
enough to leave the security of Woollett. Perhaps what he lacked was
courage and self-confidence; or perhaps he was too fond of security or insufficiently energetic to face the hardships of adjusting to new circumstances; or perhaps he was timid, cowed by the authorities of Woollett, and
not willing or able to think independently. These are speculations. But it is
not a speculation that Strether did not ask why he made the mistake that
deprived him of fulfillment. I am not saying that if he had asked, he would
have been able to correct the mistake. The fact remains, however, that by
not asking he made correction impossible; he was in effect resigning himself to living with the consequences of his mistake. Asking about its cause
would have opened up the possibility of correction, even if the realization
of that possibility was unlikely because of his age and circumstances.

The reason for stressing what Strether might have done is not to indict
poor Strether, who had enough trouble without it, but to call attention to
another condition of having a fulfilling life. Dissatisfaction with one's life
cannot be overcome by exploratory imagination alone; it needs to be supplemented by the corrective imagination. I concluded at the end of part
two that the imaginative understanding of one's past mistakes must be
combined with the pursuit of imaginatively explored future possibilities if
it is to lead to a fulfilling life. Just so, we can now see, the imaginative exploration of future possibilities must go hand in hand with the correction
of those aspects of one's character that are obstacles to the realization of
possibilities and thus to a fulfilling life.

Although Strether's imagination was not good enough for a fulfilling life, it nevertheless enabled him to avoid the pitfalls of both Promethean and aesthetic romanticism. Unlike Promethean romantics, he recognized that an active life in which the will was the dominant motivational force needs to be controlled by reason and responsibility. And unlike aesthetic romantics, he recognized that the same is true of a life in which the dominant forces are emotion and imagination. He recognized, that is, that a good life cannot just be fulfilling, that it must also be responsible. He achieved this recognition by reflective self-evaluation, and it was his exemplary reflective self-evaluation that led him to renounce a fulfilling life that would have involved the violation of what he accepted as his responsibility. Strether's life thus shows that the voluntarist ideal of reflective self-evaluation in combination with fortunate circumstances is inadequate as an account of a good life. For that ideal, even in such fortunate circumstances as Strether's, may lead a responsible person to renounce fulfillment and thus a good life. The next chapter is about someone who successfully combines both forms of the moral imagination and lives a good life that is both responsible and fulfilling.

CHAPTER 8

An Integral Part of Life

> I have painted my inward self with colors clearer than my
> original ones. I have no more made my book than my book has
> made me—a book consubstantial with its author, concerned with
> my own self, an integral part of my life.
>
> —MICHEL DE MONTAIGNE, "Of Giving the Lie," *Essays*

8.1 Self-Transformation

All the real or literary characters I have so far discussed fell short of a good life because their reflective self-evaluation was faulty. The fault lay with the extent or the manner in which the protagonists used their moral imagination. They had an impoverished understanding of the possibilities of life open to them; they were mistaken about what it would be like to live according to some possibility; they failed to recognize that observing the limits reason and morality set to the pursuit of possibilities is also among the conditions of a good life. These faults of their moral imagination were traceable to their character defects, which in turn caused them to be dissatisfied with their lives. Their dissatisfactions, therefore, are the result of their own deficiencies: narrow-mindedness, weakness, self-deception, self-absorption, or some combination of these and other vices. The remedy, of course, would have been to transform their character by correcting its defects. But this they could not do because the shortcomings of their moral imagination prevented them from seeing their defects as defects. They sought what they really cared about, their actions expressed their intentions, they were guided by their will, and thus they acted in conformity to the voluntarist ideal of reflective self-evaluation. Yet the satisfactions they hoped for eluded them. The voluntarist ideal, therefore, is mistaken because it fails to deliver what it promises. And it fails because it does not recognize the importance of self-transformation.

It is not enough for a good life to be clear about what one truly wants and then go after it. It must be recognized that what one truly wants may be incompatible with fulfillment or responsibility. It is an essential part of reflective self-evaluation to examine one's wants in the light of reason and morality and to transform oneself and one's wants accordingly. The point of the cases I have discussed up to now is partly to show in concrete detail some of the various ways in which the voluntarist ideal fails to recognize this and partly to identify the respects in which the balanced ideal must go beyond the voluntarist one.

The topic of the present chapter is a life that succeeds in being good and exemplifies the balanced ideal. The life is that of Michel de Montaigne, who lived a fulfilling and responsible life by creating an extraordinary instrument for the disciplined use of his imagination. It enabled him to look backward first to re-create the sources of his past mistakes and then to correct them, as well as forward to explore his personal possibilities. This instrument was the celebrated *Essays* he wrote and revised between the age of thirty-seven and his death at sixty.[1] There is much to be learned from Montaigne's life, even by those who do not follow him in creating their own literary instrument of self-transformation. I begin with a general account of the self-transformation by means of moral imagination that the balanced ideal requires, and then make this account concrete by discussing Montaigne's exemplification of it.

The object of self-transformation is one's character, composed of enduring patterns of motivation and action.[2] To act characteristically is to act in ways that are normal and predictable for a particular person in particular circumstances. The actions are characteristic because they are the means whereby people use their capacities to satisfy their desires in accordance with their values. If this happens repeatedly in similar situations, a pattern is formed of their particular desires, capacities, values, and actions, and it becomes a constituent of their character. But not all enduring patterns qualify as constituents. Routine conventional behavior (driving to work), trivial habits (the brand of soap one uses), and physiologically connected action patterns (eating an apple a day) may be enduring patterns in a life, but they are not important enough to be constitutive of character. A biography would not be incomplete if it failed to mention them. This suggests that an enduring pattern must be significant to qualify as a constituent. Although enormous variations in individual desires, capacities, values, actions, and situations make it impossible to specify in advance what particular pattern might qualify, the general rule is that a pattern is a constituent of character if the goodness or badness of a person's life depends on it and maintaining it requires individual effort directed at overcoming external or internal obstacles. Speaking one's mother tongue, recognizing familiar faces, and digesting food do not qualify because normally every adult is capable of them. The constituents of character, therefore, are not just statable facts about people but also evaluations that influence how their character should be regarded.

Character, then, is constituted of the enduring patterns of desires, capacities, values, and actions that acquire significance because of their contribution to living a good or a bad life. There are surely very few adults who do not have a character in this sense. What needs explanation is its lack rather than its possession. The explanation may be that people's desires, capacities, values, and actions are so fickle as to form no enduring patterns, or they do not aspire to a good life because they have no idea what it would be, or they are beset by lifelong adversity, or they are incapable or unwilling to make the required effort. But these are exceptional cases. Most of us can be assumed to have a character.

The extent to which we control the character we have, however, is quite varied. At one extreme, we are largely passive possessors of the enduring patterns that rule our lives. The patterns in such cases are the results of unchosen influences. The meager efforts we make consist in no more than continuing to conduct ourselves in our accustomed manner. The character we have, then, is not of our own making but the product of genetic inheritance and postnatal conditioning. I will call such characters *contingent*. At the opposite extreme, we are fully in control of our character. The enduring patterns of our conduct are then shaped not merely by influences to which we are subject but also by our evaluations of them. Such evaluations require considerable effort because they prompt us to make it a regular practice to encourage or discourage the satisfaction of particular desires, the exercise of particular capacities, the realization of particular values, or the performance of particular actions. I will call characters formed by such control *deliberate*.

Characters, then, can be arranged on a continuum ranging from contingent to deliberate. The more deliberate our character is, the greater is our control over the desires, capacities, values, and actions that provide patterns with substantive content. Since good lives partly depend on these patterns, the more control we have over them, the more control we have over the goodness of our lives. One important way of increasing the control we have is thus to make our character less contingent and more deliberate. And this is what I mean by self-transformation.

Moral imagination is one of the ways in which self-transformation can occur. Its corrective, exploratory, and disciplined forms are all involved in self-transformation, in increasing the control we have over our lives. One reason why people wish to transform themselves and to increase their control is that they are dissatisfied with the present patterns of their character. They come to see that some of their desires, capacities, or values do not receive adequate scope because some of the enduring patterns of their lives are malformed. Once they see that, it is natural for them to want to correct what has gone wrong. For this they need to use their corrective imagination in ways I have described. As we have seen, however, while this use of moral imagination can overcome mistakes that have been made in the past, it cannot evaluate the possibilities that might replace the mistakes. The task of the exploratory imagination is to form a reasonable view of the possible patterns that might come to constitute a deliberately formed character. Without corrective imagination self-transformation lacks reasonable motivation, and without exploratory imagination self-transformation lacks reasonable direction.

Self-transformation requires not merely the use of both kinds of imagination, however, but also a close connection between them. The corrections aim to free one's character from handicaps that prevented the exploration of satisfactory possibilities in the past. Similarly, the explorations aim to replace unsatisfactory past possibilities with satisfactory future ones. If the corrective and exploratory uses are reciprocally motivating in this manner, then they jointly form what I mean by the disciplined use of moral imagination. The disciplined imagination is self-transforming because it makes some patterns of one's character less contingent and more deliberate. By doing that, it makes one's life better—more fulfilling and more responsible.

8.2 A Book Consubstantial with Its Author

Montaigne's life exemplifies how the disciplined use of moral imagination leads to a successful process of self-transformation. But it does more because Montaigne was conscious of what he was doing and articulate about what it involved. His *Essays* simultaneously record his motivation and conduct and his lifelong reflections on them, and impart the significance for others what he had learned about his own life.

Montaigne was born in 1533 into a Gascon Catholic family of lesser nobility, residing not far from the city of Bordeaux.[3] He was educated first at home, where he learned Latin before French, and later at one of the best schools in France. He was trained in the law, and at the age of twenty-four he became a councillor in the Parlement of Bordeaux, where his duties required him to participate in legislation and to act as something like a magistrate. During this period he married, had six children, all but one of whom died in infancy, and formed the most significant relationship of his life: a friendship with La Boétie, who died from a painful illness four years later. In 1570, after thirteen years of service, Montaigne retired to his estate, "long weary of the servitude of the court and of public employments . . . where in . . . freedom, tranquillity, and leisure" (ix–x) he intended to read and reflect, and he began to record his thoughts in a form that eventually resulted in the *Essays*. But two years later he was called out of retirement to act as a mediator between the warring Catholics and Protestants of France. As a moderate Catholic and experienced negotiator, he was acceptable to both parties. He was intermittently engaged in this task for four years. In 1580, when he was forty-seven, the first edition of the *Essays*, containing books I and II, appeared. It was well received. Montaigne then traveled for almost two years in Switzerland, Germany, and Italy. In his absence, he was elected mayor of Bordeaux, a prestigious office he did not seek and was reluctant to accept. But he was prevailed upon, and when his two-year term came to an end, he was given the rare honor of a second term. Then he once again took up residence on his estate, finished book III of the *Essays*, and kept revising the first two books. The three books were first published together in 1588, when he was fifty-five years old. He continued revising them until the end. He died in 1592, a few months before his sixtieth birthday. He was generally regarded as a wise and learned man, an eminent scholar, and a distinguished public servant.

One of the most interesting aspects of Montaigne's life is its relation to the *Essays*. Montaigne consciously intended the *Essays* to be the instruments of his own self-transformation. They were meant as replacements of conversations with his dead friend; vehicles for articulating and reflecting on his attitudes; records of changes in his thought and sensibility; ventures in trying out arguments, thinking through various complicated matters, expressing scorn and admiration; and they formed "a book consubstantial with its author" (504). As Montaigne says: "I have no more made my book than my book has made me. . . . [It is] concerned with my own self, an integral part of my life" (504). The *Essays* shaped Montaigne's life, not merely by creating a record of it but also by Montaigne's lifelong evaluation of what the record showed, by his efforts to transform himself to conform ever more closely to his evaluations, and by making these evaluations and efforts also part of the record. There was a seamless connection between his conduct of life, his reflection on it, and his recording both the conduct and the reflection. "In modeling this figure upon myself, I have had to fashion and compose myself so often to bring myself out, that the model itself has to some extent grown firm and taken shape" (504). The *Essays* were thus both causes and effects, symptoms and diagnoses. They were efforts to take stock of how things were with himself, to firm up his resolve to transform himself in certain ways, and to plan how to make the transformations.

Montaigne's instrument of self-transformation was his moral imagination. He says in one of his first essays, "I am one of those who are very much influenced by the imagination. . . . Its impression on me is piercing" (68). And speaking of the imagination in his last essay, he says, "In my opinion that faculty is all-important, at least more important than any other" (833). Its importance is that "in the study that I am making of our behavior and motives . . . [it exemplifies] some human potentiality. . . . There are authors whose end is to tell what has happened. Mine, if I could attain it, would be to talk about what can happen" (75). Again and again in the *Essays* Montaigne says of himself, "I believe in and conceive a thousand ways of life" and "I . . . insinuate myself by imagination into their place" (169); and, when reflecting on another person, "I put myself in his place, I try to fit my mind to his bias" (179). It is imagination that enables him to keep his ideal of a good life in front of himself: "keep ever in your mind . . . [those] in whose presence even fools would hide their faults; make them controllers of all your intentions; if these intentions get off the track, your reverence for these men will set them right again" (183). And it is imagination again that makes vivid the possibilities of life: "we may strengthen and enlighten our judgment by reflecting upon this continual variation in human beings" (216). And it is imagination that inspires him because "I imagine numberless natures loftier and better regulated than mine" (617).

Yet Montaigne's attitude to the imagination is equivocal. He recognizes that "a strong imagination creates the event" (68) and that "the principal credit of miracles, visions, enchantments, and such extraordinary occurrences comes from the power of imagination" (70). He says that "it is by vanity of . . . imagination that he [i.e., man] . . . attributes to himself divine characteristics, picks himself out and separates himself from the horde of other creatures, carves out their shares to his fellows . . . and distributes among them such portions of faculties and powers as he sees fit" (330), and it is this "vainglory, which is an over-good opinion we form of our worth . . . which represents us to ourselves as other than we are" (478). He now distrusts examples of excellence he earlier appears to have praised: "These times are fit for improving us only backward, by disagreement more than by agreement, by difference more than similarity. Being little taught by good examples, I make use of bad ones. . . . I was setting myself unattainable standards" (703–704).

Contrary to appearances, however, Montaigne's attitude to the imagination is consistent. He is on to something important about the roles it might play in different lives. He says that "virtue is something other and nobler than inclinations toward goodness that are born in us" (306). The latter is expressed as "natural mildness and easygoingness," but "virtue presupposes difficulty and contrast, and it cannot be exercised without opposition" (307). In some people there is "so perfect a habituation to virtue that it has passed into their nature. It is no longer laborious virtue . . . it is the very essence of their soul, its natural and ordinary gait. They have made it so by a long exercise of the precepts of philosophy, coming upon a fine rich nature. The vicious passions that come to life in us can find nowhere to enter these men" (310). Montaigne thinks that Socrates and the younger Cato were such people.

These remarks of Montaigne suggest a threefold distinction between perfect virtue, laborious virtue, and natural inclination to goodness.[4] People like Socrates and Cato, who have perfect virtue, are no longer open to vice because they have achieved the necessary control over themselves. They naturally and effortlessly act for the good. Those with laborious virtue also act for the good, but it involves struggle because their self-control is imperfect. People with natural inclinations to goodness are like the virtuous ones in acting for the good, but they act so because their circumstances are fortunate and they have not been seriously enough challenged to have need for developing self-control.

Montaigne puts himself in the last group, which is, morally speaking, the lowest of the three. He says: "I am so far from having arrived at that first and most perfect degree of excellence whose virtue becomes a habit, that even of the second degree I have hardly given any proof. I have not put myself to great effort to curb the desires by which I have found myself pressed. My virtue is a virtue, or I should say an innocence, that is accidental and fortuitous. If I had been born with a more unruly disposition, I fear it would have gone pitifully with me" (311). The bearing of this on our present purpose is that moral imagination plays very different roles in the three contexts. If we understand their roles, the appearance of Montaigne's inconsistency disappears, and we can appreciate better what his self-transformation involves.

People with perfect virtue have successfully transformed themselves; consequently, they have no need of moral imagination. Living and acting according to their ideal of a good life is their second nature. They have overcome their past mistakes, so their corrective imagination lacks employment; and since they already are living according to possibilities that have passed the test of reflection, their exploratory imagination is rightly unemployed as well. Such people, of course, are extremely rare.

Those with laborious virtue are actively engaged in the difficult task of self-transformation. They need to use their exploratory imagination to make vivid for themselves the possibilities they are committed to realizing in their own lives. It is to such people that Montaigne says, "Keep in your mind [exemplary lives] . . . make them controllers of your intentions; if these intentions get off the track, your reverence for these men will set them right again" (183). Whether they also need to use their corrective imagination depends on how far their self-transformation has come. If they know the causes of their past mistakes, then they already know how they need to transform themselves, and their corrective imagination has done its job. If they are still prevented by psychological causes from living as they think they should, then their corrective imagination must still do its work.

The fortunate innocents, born with good inclinations, are in some ways similar and in other ways very different from those with perfect virtue. The innocents and the perfectly virtuous are alike because they can act spontaneously according to their good inclinations. They have nothing to correct or control, they are not called upon to make any effort, they need not transform themselves, and so they need not use their moral imagination either. This likeness, however, holds only until serious adversity challenges them. In the face of such challenges, the perfectly virtuous can continue to act spontaneously because they have achieved control over themselves in the past, but the fortunate innocents must become reflective because their naturally good inclinations are not sufficient for facing the complex problems, conflicts, and choices presented by serious adversity. For this reflection, they need moral imagination in order to direct their naturally good inclinations.

Montaigne puts himself among the spontaneous fortunate innocents, and this may well have sufficed during his early years. But sixteenth-century France was wracked by civil war; his beloved friend, his admired father, and five of his children died; he began to suffer from a dreaded and painful illness; he became a political figure with power over the life and death of many people; he had to protect his estate from marauding bandits; and he felt obliged to act as an intermediary between warring Catholic and Protestant factions. In these circumstances, he could not possibly have sustained his earlier spontaneity. He had to become reflective and to transform himself by learning to use his moral imagination. He started with trying to follow the exemplars of perfect virtue, but he soon saw "I was setting myself unattainable standards" (704). He was "little taught by good examples," so he made "use of bad ones" (703), meaning examples showing him how not to live. He thus began with the corrective use of imagination to avoid the mistakes he tended to make, and only later did he progress sufficiently to use his exploratory imagination for directing his naturally good inclinations. This was the process of his self-transformation. Let us now see how he did it.

Montaigne's life was complex, composed of many parts. He was a son, a friend, a husband, and a father; the lord of an estate and the master of his servants; a Catholic with a by no means uncritical attitude toward his church; an engaged political figure; a negotiator; a traveler; a constant reader, especially of classical authors; a physical man who paid attention to his body and welcomed the pleasures of sex, food, and good health; and, of course, a ceaselessly reflective person whose life was informed by the judgments he had formed. These parts of his life, and others, often came into conflict, and the need to resolve their conflicts gave a further reason to Montaigne to become reflective. Of the many conflicts in Montaigne's life I discuss three because they will be familiar to many people from their own lives and because it is instructive how Montaigne resolved them.

8.3 Innocence and Reflection

Retiring to his estate after long years of service as a councillor and magistrate in the government of Bordeaux, Montaigne intended to reflect and write. But he did not find this easy: "lately when I retired to my home, determined so far as possible to bother about nothing except spending the little life I have left in rest and seclusion, it seemed to me I could do my mind no greater favor than to let it entertain itself in full idleness. . . . But I find . . . that . . . like a runaway horse, it . . . gives birth to . . . chimeras and fantastic monsters, one after another, without order and purpose" (21). He came to realize that "by getting rid of the court and the market place we do not get rid of the principal worries of our life" (175), and that "it is not enough to have gotten away from the crowd . . . we must sequester ourselves and repossess ourselves" (176). That realization, however, still left him with an unruly imagination filling his mind with chimeras and monsters and persistent worries.

He understood what caused this psychic garbage to fill his mind, but he also saw that unless he succeeds in disciplining his imagination, he cannot overcome these unwelcome obstacles to his tranquillity and enjoyment of his newfound freedom and leisure. He realized that if you "retire into yourself," you must "first prepare yourself to receive yourself there; it would be madness to trust in yourself if you do not know how to govern yourself. There are ways to fail in solitude as well as in company" (182–183). The way to avoid failure, to "have a soul that can be turned upon itself . . . [one that] can keep itself company" (177), is to "let true ideals be kept before your mind . . . make them controllers of all your intentions. . . . They will keep you in a fair way to be content with yourself, to borrow nothing except from yourself" (183).

Montaigne in effect told himself and his readers that the transformation he sought from public to private life depended on the correction of his undesirable psychological tendencies and on the exploration of possible ways of life in order to find the one he can adopt for himself. Success in correction and exploration—in the disciplined use of imagination—will enable him to direct his intentions, impose "order and purpose on his mind," and "repossess" himself.

All these remarks, however, come from the early essays written shortly after his retirement. They represent only part of his reflection about private life. About fifteen years later, he added the following comment: "solitude seems to me more appropriate and reasonable for those who have given the world their most active and flourishing years" (178). Another part of his reflection is about what he did during his own "most active and flourishing years." Public service was a traditional and expected part of the life of nobility, and Montaigne had played that part with distinction. His view was that "I do not want a man to refuse, to the charges he takes on, attention, steps, words, and sweat and blood if need be" (770). Montaigne had acted accordingly, and he explained, partly no doubt to himself, why he did it.

He saw himself living in a "sick age." "I perceive . . . the strife that is tearing France to pieces and dividing us into factions" (760), and he felt that it was his duty to do what he could to make things less bad. But he found the laws he was administering unjust, the system corrupt, and the religious wars, with their massacres and cruelty, disgusting (759). "Consider the form of this justice that governs us: it is a true testimony to human imbecility, so full it is of contradiction and error. . . . How many condemnations I have seen more criminal than the crime!" (819–820). He also sees that "there is no hostility that excels Christian hostility. . . . Our religion is made to extirpate vices; it covers them, fosters them, incites them" (324).

Throughout his life, Montaigne felt the conflict between his desire to live a private life and his obligation to perform public service. The obligations of his social position, the admired examples of his father and his friend, La Boétie, the expectations of the court and his fellow noblemen all impelled him toward public service. The attractions of a tranquil life, the need to be reflective about how he lived, his fondness of rural life impelled him toward private life. His conception of a good life was connected with both the satisfaction of this desire and the discharge of this obligation. Some fortunate people, living in contexts less turbulent than those of sixteenth-century France, may have resolved this conflict by judiciously balancing the desire and the obligation, but Montaigne was not so fortunate. For him, public service conflicted with a private life. Montaigne saw this clearly and resolved the conflict in favor of private life. He extricated himself from public service as soon as he decently could and endeavored to transform himself from a public figure into a private person who lives the way he thinks he should. His clarity about his age and himself was made possible by the disciplined use of his imagination. The fact remains, however, that, on the basis of what Montaigne has said up to this point, the resolution of this conflict did not make his life good. He sought fulfillment by satisfying his desire for private life, and he strove to be responsible by discharging his obligation of public service. But seeking fulfillment seems to have led him to seek ideals outside himself, which is the very thing he thought he ought not to do, and acting responsibly seems to have involved him in immorality. The problem about the immorality of public service leads to the second conflict in Montaigne's life, and the problem about seeking ideals outside himself leads to the third one.

Montaigne's social position imposed on him the obligation to take a part in governing, and he accepted that as his responsibility. But he also saw that "in every government there are necessary offices which are . . . vicious. Vices find their place in it and are employed for sewing our society together. The public welfare requires that a man betray and lie" (600). This brought him face to face with what in our age is called the problem of dirty hands (the name comes from the English title and theme of one of Sartre's plays).

The obvious temptation of responsible people is not to dirty their hands. If political involvement is corrupting, then one should not be politically involved. But this is a naive view because if responsible people refuse to take a hand in politics, their place will be taken by irresponsible ones, and this will make matters even worse than before. Montaigne was anything but naive, and he resisted the temptation to keep his hands clean. Giving in to the temptation, he saw, would have meant betraying his responsibility both to himself and to others. What he did instead was to struggle with the conflict and find a resolution of enduring significance.

Reflecting on his tenure as mayor of Bordeaux, he wrote: "The mayor and Montaigne have always been two, with a very clear separation" (774). On one side of this separation, Montaigne said, "I once tried to employ in the service of public dealings ideas and rules . . . which I use . . . in private matters. . . . I found them inept and dangerous. . . . He who walks in the crowd must step aside, keep his elbows in, step back or advance, even leave the straight way, according to others, not according to what he proposes to himself, but according to what others propose to him, according to the time, according to the men, according to the business" (758). He added, "I perceive that in the strife that is tearing France to pieces and dividing us into factions, each man labors to defend his cause—but even the best of them resort to dissimulation and lying. . . . The justest party is still a member of a worm-eaten maggotty body. But in such a body the least diseased member is called healthy; and quite rightly, since our qualities have no titles except by comparison. Civic innocence is measured according to the places and times" (760). And he recognized that "an honest man is not accountable for the vice and stupidity of his trade, and should not therefore refuse to practice it: it is the custom of the country and there is profit in it. We must live in the world and make the most of it as we find it" (774).

On the other side of the separation, however, Montaigne said, "I have been able to take part in public office without departing one nail's head from myself, and give myself to others without taking myself from myself" (770). But how is this possible? How can we remain ourselves and engage in practices we recognize as stupid and vicious? Montaigne's answer was: by offering only "limited and conditional services. There is no remedy. I frankly tell them my limits" (603). He will dirty his hands up to a point, but not beyond it. "I do not . . . involve myself so deeply and so entirely" (774). The limits beyond which Montaigne will not go separate the deep core of his moral identity from the malleable surface of the public persona that he is prepared to adjust according to the time, the men, and the business. He is willing to perform public service, and thus both do his duty and participate in corrupt political arrangements, so long as they affect only the surface and do not compromise the deep core of his self. He does not depart one nail's head from himself because there is an area reserved for his private life, his "back shop," his "principal retreat," the object of his reflection when he withdraws into himself, into "real solitude."

The general significance of Montaigne's way of resolving this conflict is that since we live in a world that has not become appreciably purer since the sixteenth century, and since our responsibility is only to provide conditional services, we must learn to distinguish between the core of our self, where our deepest, identity-conferring commitments lie, and the outer layers, which we can compromise if we must. One central task of the moral imagination is to enable us to draw this distinction, and for this we need both its corrective and exploratory uses. By its corrective use, we overcome our past mistakes about the identification of what we really want out of life. By its exploratory use, we examine the possibilities of life open to us and adopt one among them as our ideal of what a good life would be, given our character and circumstances. And self-transformation, then, would involve changing our contingent character to the deliberate one that the balanced ideal of a good life calls for. This way of resolving the conflict, however, lands us in the middle of another conflict.

8.4 Growing Inward

On the one hand, Montaigne stresses the importance of individual judgment: you should "borrow nothing except from yourself" (183); we should "have a pattern established within us by which we test our actions, and according to this pattern, now pat ourselves on the back, now punish ourselves. I have my own laws and court to judge me, and I address myself to them more than anywhere else" (613); and we should follow the advice of the "god at Delphi: 'Look into yourself, know yourself, keep to yourself; bring back your mind and your will, which are spending themselves elsewhere; you are running out, you are scattering yourself; . . . you are being betrayed, dispersed, and stolen from yourself" (766).

On the other hand, Montaigne recommends learning from the lives and judgments of admirable people: "almost all the opinions we have are taken on authority and on credit. There is no harm in this" (792). He says that Socrates was "the man most worthy to be known and to be presented to the world as an example" (793). The *Essays* are chock-full of the ideals and examples of admirable classical figures eulogized by Plutarch, Cicero, Horace, Tacitus, and others. And he says, "Keep ever in your imagination Cato, Phocion, and Aristides, in whose presence even fools would hide their faults," for we get from them "the counsel of true and natural philosophy" (183). Should we then "borrow nothing" and rely on our own judgment, or should we listen to "the counsel of true . . . philosophy" and follow the judgments of admirable exemplars? Is Montaigne simply inconsistent?

The inconsistency is only apparent. The conflict is undoubtedly there, but so is its resolution. The key is to balance the requirements of moral conventions and individual judgment. Montaigne says that "it is the rule of rules, and the universal law of laws, that each man should observe those of the place he is in" (86). He recognizes that "our morals are extremely corrupt, and lean with a remarkable inclination toward the worse; of our laws and customs, many are barbarous and monstrous; however, because of the difficulty of improving our condition and the danger of everything crumbling into bits, if I could put a spoke in our wheel and stop it at this point, I would do it with all my heart" (497), because the alternative is "instability," which "is the worst thing I find in our state" (498). He sees that "it is very easy to accuse a government of imperfection, for all mortal things are full of it. It is very easy to engender in people contempt for their ancient observances. . . . But as for establishing a better state in place of the one they have ruined, many of those who have attempted it achieved nothing for their pains" (498). Well, then, what are we to do? Are we to acquiesce in what we recognize as immorality?

Montaigne's previous answer would have been to acquiesce in immorality that did not transgress the limits of our deep, identity-conferring commitments. In other words, we should base our individual judgment on our conscience. But the third conflict arises precisely because "the laws of conscience, which we say are born of nature, are born of custom" (83). If the prevailing moral conventions are corrupt, they will corrupt the conscience on which we base our judgment and from which we derive our deepest commitments. Montaigne saw that too: "the principal effect of the power of custom is to seize and ensnare us in such a way that it is hardly within our power to get ourselves back out of its grip and return ourselves to reflect and reason about its ordinances" (83). Notice, however, that crucial qualification: "hardly." It is not beyond our power to step back and reflect, it is only very difficult. So I return to the question: how can we do *that* if our conscientious judgments are in danger of being corrupted by the corrupt conventions of our society?

Montaigne's answer brings us to what is perhaps the most basic level of his thought. He said that "things in themselves may have their weights and measures and qualities; but once inside us, she [the soul] allots them their qualities as she sees fit.... Health, conscience, authority, knowledge, riches, beauty, and their opposite—all are stripped on entry and receive from the soul new clothing... which each individual soul chooses.... Wherefore let us no longer make the external qualities of things our excuse; it is up to us to reckon them as we will" (220). There are two centrally important points here.

First, being influenced by our moral conventions and relying on individual judgment are not inconsistent. We are unavoidably influenced by the conventions surrounding us. Among these influences are the social possibilities out of which we select some we recognize as our own. Conventional influences, therefore, are parts of the raw material with which moral imagination works. They make individual judgment possible in two crucial ways: by providing a stable and secure context in which we can concentrate on making good judgments about how we should live and by providing the possibilities of a good life that we evaluate by using our judgment. We must not think, then, that when Montaigne said "I turn my gaze inward, I fix it there and keep it busy" (499), he was retreating from the prevailing conventions in order to nurture the homegrown products of his individual judgment. What his judgment fixed on were the conventional possibilities by which he had been influenced. In his case, these possibilities were a rich mixture of what he had derived from Catholicism, Stoicism, and Pyrrhonism; the remembered conversations with his friend, La Boétie; the prevailing lifestyle of a country squire; his extensive readings of classical authors; his travels and conversations with other travelers;

his experience of public service; and so on. When he said "I have a soul all its own, accustomed to conducting itself in its own way" (487), what he had in mind was that he was accustomed to make judgments about the manifold conventional possibilities available to him. "The liberty of judgment" (500) that he valued so highly meant the liberty to evaluate the conventions by which he was influenced.

The second noteworthy point is that when we exercise our "liberty of judgment" to evaluate conventional influences, when we "reckon them as we will," we are engaged in what I have called self-transformation. Self-transformation essentially involves evaluation, but its objects are the conventional possibilities the disciplined imagination makes concrete and vivid to us. In self-transformation we change ourselves in accordance with the conventional possibilities we have chosen to try to realize on the basis of our judgments.

A distinction between creating and adopting possibilities will help to sharpen this point. We rarely create the possibilities we adopt as ideals. Possibilities are normally created by some classic work, like *The Republic*, *Nicomachean Ethics*, or the Bible; or by the exemplary life of a person, such as Socrates, Cato, or Jesus (whom Montaigne interestingly ignores); or by the expectations of a public office, which dictate that magistrates should be impartial, soldiers courageous, or statesmen judicious. Once created, they may become conventional ideals that individuals may adopt for themselves. One of the benefits of such conventions is that they represent generally accepted standards of excellence in a particular society. Self-transformation typically assumes its importance in the context of the adoption of conventional ideals, and only rarely and exceptionally in their creation. It usually involves the decision of individuals concerning whether they want to conduct some important aspect of their life in accordance with a conventional ideal. One reasonable way of making such decisions is by means of the disciplined imagination, which corrects mistaken evaluations and explores what it would be like to live according to some conventional ideal.

The conventional ideals of a society may or may not conform to the requirements of reason and morality. The irrationality or immorality of some ideals is obvious because they violate universal conditions of good life, as do slavery, burning heretics, killing political opponents, or prostituting children. The obvious, however, may be obscured from individuals by manipulation, indoctrination, self-deception, fear, greed, fanaticism, and so forth. In other cases, however, it is difficult to judge how reasonable or morally acceptable a conventional ideal is because the judgment rests on other prevailing ideals, and the credentials of these other ideals are also untested. This difficulty can be resolved only by the critical examination of the whole system of conventions prevailing in a society. Few people have the ability, training, determination, and opportunity to undertake such examination. Montaigne did so, and that is another reason for recognizing how exceptional a person he was.

Typically, however, self-transformation involves the attempt to improve one's character so as to approximate more closely some conventional ideal one has adopted. It may also involve—exceptionally—self-transformation according to an ideal one has created. This is what Montaigne did by using the *Essays* as a mirror, a sounding board, a standard, and a conversation with himself. He thus created and gave special form to an ideal that has become conventional: the ideal of reflective self-evaluation. In doing this, he had, of course, predecessors and he drew on the examples and suggestions of others, but his life and the *Essays* consubstantial with it constitute what was up to then the most systematic, deliberate attempt to transform himself by means of autobiographical writing. Augustine's *Confessions* may be cited as an earlier example of this genre. This, however, would not be quite accurate since Augustine's work records his self-transformation long after the fact and for the edification of others. Montaigne's work, on the other hand, is a means of his self-transformation, and he writes primarily for himself. He is right to say what Augustine could not, namely, that "I have no more made my book than my book has made me—a book . . . [that is an] integral part of my life" (504). Augustine would have been what he was even if he had never written the *Confessions*, but Montaigne could not have become what he became without the *Essays*.

For most people, however, self-transformation involves neither the critical examination of the whole system of conventional ideals of their society nor the creation of their own ideal, but the adoption of a conventional ideal. This, most emphatically, is not to say that the adoption of a conventional ideal stifles individuality or disregards reason. On the contrary: the expression of individuality and the employment of reason for evaluating a conventional ideal are indispensable to good lives conceived in this way, and the connection between these two processes is similarly indispensable. For people express their individuality by the conventional ideals they decide to adopt, and they employ reason for deciding which of the available conventional ideals is most likely to satisfy their desires and expectations. Nor is the adoption of an ideal a decision to follow a blueprint blindly. The ideals of public service or private life, for instance, can take countless different forms, depending both on the prevailing social conditions and on the character and personal circumstances of the person adopting the ideal. So the adoption of an ideal is a matter of trying to find a fit between a conventional ideal and individual aspirations. It proceeds by the reciprocal adjustments of the conventional ideal to oneself and oneself to the conventional ideal. This is just what Montaigne was doing with his *Essays*. The difference between him and most other people is that Montaigne had created the ideal he adopted whereas others typically adopt an ideal they find available in the context.

It will deepen this understanding of self-transformation to realize that the availability of conventional ideals themselves is connected with self-transformation. For such ideals derive from the accumulated experiences of many individuals who had succeeded in living a good life by following some not yet conventional ideal. In following it, they also had to engage in the same sorts of self-transforming evaluations as we do ourselves. And it is their evaluations and the examples of their good lives that made the ideals conventional. The favorable outcome of such experiments in living gives weight to a conventional ideal. For the experiments show that the ideals are reliable because they stand the test of time. There is nothing mysterious or arbitrary about the process by which ideals become conventional: they are repositories of favorable judgments tested by long experience from which reasonable people can benefit. Following conventional ideals and expressing one's individuality, therefore, are not incompatible but joint and interdependent conditions of good lives. This, I think, is the significance of Montaigne's closing words in the *Essays*: "there is no use mounting on stilts, for in stilts we must still walk on our own legs. And on the loftiest throne in the world we are still sitting on our own rump" (857).

8.5 Living Appropriately

Montaigne had to transform himself and become reflective because his spontaneous, prereflective inclinations—no matter how predisposed they were to goodness—were inadequate for resolving the conflicts he encountered. The turbulent context of his life would not, by itself, have caused these conflicts. They occurred because he himself was conflicted about how to respond to the surrounding unrest. His natural inclinations were incompatible and prompted mutually exclusive patterns of actions. He realized this, and he was compelled to reflect on what he really wanted, on which of his inclinations fit better with the life he hoped to have and with the character he wanted to develop. This reflection, provoked by the conjunction of his circumstances and prereflective inclinations, led to his self-transformation. In order to resolve his conflicts, he had to replace his contingent character, which gave rise to them, with a deliberately shaped one. This, in turn, compelled him to achieve clarity about his ideal of a good life.

We routinely find ourselves in contexts as unruly and complex as Montaigne's own. What he had to do was by no means unique or even exceptional. What is remarkable about Montaigne is how he did it and how well he succeeded. He did it, of course, by means of the *Essays*, which he used as a record of the stages of his reflection, as a means of clarifying his changing attitudes, and as the objective correlate of his inner states that enabled him to evaluate his inner states from the outside. By recording his thoughts he could evaluate them in the clear light of day, in cool moments, as if he were not the agent of but a witness to his self-transformation. The *Essays* were the bootstraps by which he lifted himself. But they were also more because they presented to their readers during the past five centuries a possibility of life that has permanently enriched the repertoire of human possibilities. This is what classic works do, this is their immeasurable value, and this is what the *Essays* are.

It is important to bear in mind, however, that Montaigne's life exemplifies merely one possible form a good life may take, and there are others. Equally important is that Montaigne's way of going about his self-transformation by means of the *Essays* is also only one way among others. There are many nonliterary ways in which people can reflect on their lives. They can meditate, undergo some kind of psychoanalysis, compare themselves to historical figures, try to emulate heroes, or follow philosophical recommendations, such as Plato's, Aristotle's, or Spinoza's. Furthermore, good lives are possible even without reflection for those whose circumstances are simple and fortunate or for those who live in a tightly structured context where conventions pervade many areas of life and the necessary reflection is left to resident authorities, who may be priests, sages, elders, heads of extended families, or chieftains of clans.

The particular form Montaigne's life took, however, was the cultivation of inwardness. He resolved each of the conflicts I have discussed by moving away from involvement with the affairs of the external world and moving toward attending to the personal concerns of his inner world. Montaigne knew that exclusive concentration on one or the other is virtually impossible. Nevertheless, choices favoring one or the other can often be made, and he made them by favoring private life over public service, moral limits over political stability, and personal judgment over following conventions. In making the choices he made, he recognized that public service, political stability, and conventions created conditions of good lives, but he thought that they were important merely as means to an end. The inwardness he cultivated, therefore, was not a subjectivity that ignored the external world, but the evaluation of facts, problems, and possibilities of the external world from the perspective of his individuality. As he said: "to compose our character is our duty, not to compose books, and to win, not battles and provinces, but order and tranquillity in our conduct. Our great and glorious masterpiece is to live appropriately. All other things, ruling, hoarding, building, are only little appendages and props, at most" (850–851).

But what is it to live appropriately? And did he succeed in creating a great and glorious masterpiece? To live appropriately is to live a responsible and fulfilling life. Montaigne lived responsibly because the extent and excellence of his public service—as councillor, magistrate, mayor, negotiator—were well beyond the call of duty. And we have his own words about having found his life fulfilling: "my conscience is content with itself" (612), and "if I had to live over again, I would live as I have lived" (620). I would say, therefore, that he succeeded in living a good life, a life that is a great and glorious masterpiece of the realization of one human possibility.

8.6 Overview

The cases I have so far considered illustrate how we make life worse than it might be and point to ways in which the rightly directed imagination might make life better. From these cases I derived a critical and a constructive argument: the first against the voluntarist ideal, the second for the balanced ideal. The problem with the voluntarist ideal is its inadequate account of reflective self-evaluation. The balanced ideal is better because it recognizes the crucial role of disciplined imagination in reflective self-evaluation.

Bentham and Verver show the grotesquely narrow view of the possibilities of life, the gross insensitivity to other people, and the impoverished emotional and imaginative sensibility that result from moral obtuseness. The remedy is to develop disciplined imagination to enlarge one's possibilities by correcting psychological tendencies that stifle imagination and by exploring what life would be like with richer possibilities. This remedy is uselessly vague, however, unless one can tell when the enlargement of possibilities is adequate. The way to tell, I argued, is by distinguishing between social, personal, and recognized possibilities. The possibilities one recognizes tend to be fewer than the personal possibilities one has the capacity and opportunity to realize. And one's personal possibilities tend to be fewer than the generally available social possibilities. The adequacy of the enlargement depends on how far recognized possibilities fall short of personal possibilities. The closer the set of recognized possibilities approximates the set of personal possibilities, the more adequate is the enlargement. This is one of the aims the balanced ideal has and the voluntarist ideal lacks.

Another such condition becomes apparent if we reflect on the Prince and Charlotte. They conducted themselves just as the voluntarist ideal recommends. Their reflective self-evaluation led them to believe that they cared most about living a luxurious life. They did what was necessary to get it, which was to transform themselves to comply with the requirements of the marriages they wanted. They knew the costs and willingly paid them. According to the voluntarist ideal, they ought to have been fulfilled, but, of course, they were not. The problem this points to is that the voluntarist ideal pays insufficient attention to the possibility that one may really care about the wrong thing and waste much effort to get it.

The balanced ideal, by contrast, stresses that the aim of reflective self-evaluation is not merely to find out what one most deeply cares about, but also to ascertain whether it is reasonable to care about it. This, once again, requires disciplined imagination in order to correct possible mistakes leading one to care about the wrong things and to explore alternative possibilities to care about. The imagination of the Prince and Charlotte was not disciplined enough and that is why they made a mess of their lives. Their frustrations show that the voluntarist ideal needs to recognize, as the balanced ideal does, that a disciplined imagination is necessary for reasonable reflective self-evaluation.

Countess Olenska and Archer are interesting partly because reflective self-evaluation prevented them from seeking fulfillment by way of enlarging their possibilities. They identified themselves with the conventional morality of their context and accepted and lived up to the responsibilities it dictated. Since the consummation of their love was contrary to what they regarded as their responsibilities, they knowingly doomed themselves to an unfulfilled life. Their failure suggests that both requirements of a good life—fulfillment and responsibility—ought to be as reasonable and balanced as possible. Reasonable responsibilities make fulfillment in general possible, and fulfillment is reasonable if it aims to realize possibilities that do not violate responsibilities. If Countess Olenska and Archer had been better reflective self-evaluators, they would have realized that their conventional morality imposed unreasonable responsibilities on them and that it was for the sake of these responsibilities that they sacrificed reasonable fulfillment. They were unfulfilled because they stopped short of questioning what they accepted as their responsibilities.

Their lives show that the connection between fulfillment and reflective self-evaluation is much more complicated than the voluntarist ideal leads one to suppose. Finding out what one cares about and acting accordingly are not sufficient for fulfillment. For one may care most about responsibilities that are incompatible with fulfillment, and the supposed responsibilities may not be reasonable. The balanced ideal recognizes these complications. Fulfillment and responsibility often conflict, and adequate re-flective self-evaluation must consider whether their claims are reasonable. One may resolve such conflicts by accepting that reasonable responsibili-ties have a stronger claim on one than reasonable fulfillment. Although Countess Olenska and Archer were mistaken in reaching this conclusion, others may reach it reasonably. The balanced ideal recognizes the lamen-table fact that in unfortunate circumstances one must choose between deeply valued possibilities, and whatever one chooses, something essential for a good life will be lost. The voluntarist ideal concentrates on fulfill-ment and fails to recognize that one may care most deeply about possibili-ties that exclude fulfillment.

Maggie, like Countess Olenska and Archer, had to choose between ful-fillment and responsibility, but unlike them, she chose fulfillment. And as Countess Olenska and Archer were wrong about their responsibilities, so Maggie was wrong about her fulfillment. All three were prevented by char-acter defects from using their imagination to correct their mistakes. Hide-bound timidity stood in the way of Countess Olenska's and Archer's ques-tioning the unreasonable responsibilities they had accepted. And Maggie's self-absorption prevented her from seeing that the manipulation by which she hoped to get what she wanted would destroy the relation-ships she valued. She acted according to the voluntarist ideal, found out what she really cared about, and went after it. But the means she chose de-stroyed the end to which they were supposed to lead. Her case shows that the voluntarist ideal fails to acknowledge that fulfillment has an essential moral dimension that limits what may be done for the sake of fulfillment and what forms fulfillment may take. The balanced ideal, by contrast, rec-ognizes that if fulfillment and responsibility are reasonable, then short-changing either makes a good life impossible. For reasonable responsibil-ities are to maintaining conditions that make fulfillment possible, and seeking fulfillment that violates these conditions undermines social and personal relationships necessary for fulfillment. If Maggie's exploratory imagination had been better, she would have realized that the relation-ships she valued were incompatible with manipulation. And if her correc-tive imagination had been better, she would not have been blinded by self-absorption from forming a realistic view of what she was doing.

This brings us to Strether, whose imagination was disciplined and who honorably met his responsibilities. He, unlike Maggie, was not self-absorbed. He saw himself and others realistically. Nor was he like Countess Olenska and Archer in failing to see the faults of the conventional moral-ity that formed him and to which he remained committed. Strether was thus a better reflective self-evaluator than Maggie, Countess Olenska, and Archer. One would expect him to have found fulfillment since he did everything the voluntarist ideal calls for and also everything I have so far claimed as a requirement of the balanced ideal. As we know, however, this expectation is not met. Strether did not act on the understanding his reflective self-evaluation enabled him to reach. This points to another inadequacy in the voluntarist ideal and a further condition the balanced ideal must recognize.

The assumption built into the voluntarist ideal is that the conclusions reached by reflective self-evaluation will motivate one to act accordingly. Strether's case shows that this is not so. He knew that his fulfillment depended on an active life, but he resigned himself to a passive one because he knew also that he lacked the necessary strength and determination. The voluntarist ideal fails to recognize that even if reflective self-evaluation reveals what one most deeply cares about, this will not by itself motivate corresponding action. For one may be doubtful about having the capacity to live the life one most deeply cares about. Strether believed this, his belief was true, and it made his life sad.

The balanced ideal, therefore, is committed to the further condition that there must be a fit between the character one has, or could transform oneself to have, and the life one cares about living. The accuracy of beliefs about one's character depends on the corrective imagination, and the accuracy of beliefs about the life one cares about depends on the exploratory imagination. The disciplined imagination combines the two by specifying that the character one should have is one that fits the life one cares about and the life one cares about should fit the character one has. This is why the disciplined imagination must be recognized as part of the balanced ideal.

Mill, like Strether, was exemplary in meeting his responsibilities although lacking fulfillment. The difference between them is that they lacked fulfillment for very different reasons. Strether had not the will to embark on the active life he knew was necessary for fulfillment. Mill had the will but not the emotions that would have enabled him to care about anything. He knew what would have brought him fulfillment, and he desperately wanted it because life did not seem worth living without it. Yet the knowledge and the will could not give him the emotions without which fulfillment is impossible. Mill's predicament shows that the voluntarist ideal is inadequate in yet another way. It stresses the overriding importance of the will and overlooks that emotions are just as important. The problem is not that the voluntarist ideal attributes overriding importance to the wrong psychological state, but that it supposes that there is any psychological state whose importance always overrides the importance of all other psychological states.

The balanced ideal accepts the importance of the will, but not at the expense of true beliefs, reasonable emotions, and disciplined imagination. The balanced ideal includes and the voluntarist ideal ignores the further condition of a good life that the cognitive, emotive, volitional, and imaginative components of one's psychological makeup should be reasonable and integrated.

The voluntarist ideal leads to romanticism, which is a permanent threat to good lives precisely because it rejects integration. By favoring one psychological state at the expense of others, it misses the importance of the others. Promethean romantics favor the will, and aesthetic romantics favor emotion and imagination. This leads them to denigrate reason and to subordinate responsibility to fulfillment when they conflict. I have objected to romanticism by showing that reason in this context functions as an indispensable method for evaluating one's psychological states. Romantics fail to recognize this because they mistakenly regard reason as a rival source of motivation. As a result, they deprive themselves of the means for evaluating various sources of motivation. They view life as a quest motivated by the will, emotion, or imagination, but they cannot ascertain whether their aims are worth the quest.

The enduring significance of Oedipus is that in the face of great odds, unfortunate circumstances, and much suffering he finally overcame his youthful romanticism and achieved the balanced ideal that would have given him a responsible and fulfilling life, and then he died. Oedipus, like Moses, saw the promised land but could not enter it. He saw and corrected the defects of the contingent character with which he started out and transformed himself by developing a deliberate character that became his second nature. What prevented him from enjoying the good life for which he worked so hard and richly deserved were the brute physical limits that mark the end of all human lives. We learn by reflecting on his case that conformity to reason and responsibility do not guarantee fulfillment, although unreason and irresponsibility are all too likely to result in frustration. This does not make life tragic, but it makes us vulnerable. It shows that we are at risk, not that we are doomed. The most we can do in the light of this is to be as reasonable and responsible as we can be and thereby lower the risk that even our best efforts to live a good life will be frustrated.

The antidote to these dispiriting thoughts about the human condition is the cheerful life of Montaigne. He faced the risk in which we all stand, but he was undaunted by it, and he shows that the possibility of a good life can be realized. He was not merely favored by good fortune. He worked hard to transform himself into someone who could and would make use of it. And the use he made was to discipline his imagination and live according to the balanced ideal of reflective self-evaluation. In the next part of the book I discuss some specific ways in which this kind of self-transformation may progress toward the balanced ideal.

Part Four

THE DISCIPLINED
IMAGINATION

CHAPTER 9

Toward a Purified Mind

The bad (or mediocre) man is in a state of illusion, of which
egoism is the most general name. . . . Obsession, prejudice, envy,
anxiety, ignorance, greed, neurosis, and so on . . . *veil* reality. The
defeat of illusion requires moral effort. The instructed and
morally purified mind sees reality clearly.

—IRIS MURDOCH, *The Fire and the Sun*

9.1 Purity

In the three chapters of this part of the book I consider how the
disciplined imagination affects purity, shame, and reason. In each case, I
begin with a misconception and go on to correct it. The corrected versions exemplify the work of the disciplined imagination, which depends
on the joint efforts of the corrective and the exploratory imagination.
These efforts yield clarity about the causes of one's faulty decisions in the
past and mistaken evaluations of future possibilities, thus prompting self-
transformation and moral progress. The self is transformed by improved
decisions and evaluations, and moral progress is made by approximating
more closely the ideal of a good—responsible and fulfilling—life.

Purity, shame, and reason, in very different ways, are important in seeking fulfillment and acting responsibly. I consider them in order to illustrate in concrete detail how the disciplined imagination can do its work. I
might have considered instead courage, guilt, and benevolence, among
numerous other possibilities. In concentrating on purity, shame, and reason, I do not mean to deny that there are other important dispositions
whose transformation by the disciplined imagination might constitute
moral progress toward a better life.

The topic of this chapter is purity as a character trait, a quality primar-

159

ily of motives. A pure motive is untainted, free of diluting or admixing elements. It excludes ulterior purposes, hypocrisy, pretense, artifice, and double-mindedness. It is clear, simple, genuine, natural, spontaneous, and transparent because it is without contrary ingredients. What is on the surface of it is what it is all the way through. There is no difference between its appearance and reality.

Iris Murdoch's paean is representative of many similar passages in a great variety of writings by a great variety of authors. Purity, or innocence, as Murdoch calls it here, "has a radiance which enlightens and purifies and which is not to be dimmed by foolish talk about the worth of experience. . . . And what are the marks of innocence? Candour . . . truthfulness, simplicity, a quite involuntary bearing of witness. The image that occurs to me is . . . the image of a bell. A bell . . . rings out clearly . . . it cannot speak without seeming like a call, a summons. . . . Consider too its simplicity. There is no hidden mechanism. All that it is is plain and open; and if it is moved it must ring."[1]

It is purity too that according to Montaigne makes Socrates "the master of masters" (824).[2] Montaigne says that Socrates was "the man most worthy to be known and to be presented to the world as an example. . . . It is a great thing to have been able to impart such order to the pure and simple notions of a child that, without altering or stretching them, he produced from them the most beautiful achievements of the soul. He shows it as neither elevated nor rich; he shows it only as healthy, but assuredly with a very blithe and clear health. . . . By these ordinary and common ideas, without excitement and fuss, he constructed not only the best regulated but the loftiest and most vigorous beliefs, actions, and morals that ever were. It is he who brought human wisdom back down from heaven, where she was wasting her time, and restored her to man, with whom lies her most proper and laborious and useful business" (793).

This effusive praise should not lead one to suppose that Montaigne's attitude to Socrates was simple or unqualified. Like Kierkegaard and Nietzsche, Montaigne recognized Socrates as a pivotal ideal of purity, and like them, he questioned whether he does or should measure up to the high standard set by Socrates. I will argue that this ambivalence is warranted because the notion of purity is far from simple. It can be a vice, not just a virtue. It can make lives bad, not just good. Much clarification is required for a proper understanding of its undeniable moral force.

9.2 Two Kinds of Purity

Montaigne says, "What good I have in me I have . . . by the chance of my birth. I have gotten it neither from law, nor from precept, nor from

any other apprenticeship. The innocence that is in me is a childish innocence: little vigor and no art" (313). "Virtue," on the other hand, "is something other and nobler than the inclinations toward goodness that are
born in us. . . . Virtue presupposes difficulty and contrast, and . . . it cannot be exercised without opposition" (306–307). And he compares himself with Socrates: "I know his reason to be so powerful and so much the
master in him that it would never so much as let a vicious appetite be
born. I can put up nothing against a virtue as lofty as his" (308). He goes
on: "My virtue is a virtue, or I should say an innocence, that is accidental
and fortuitous. If I had been born with a more unruly disposition, I fear it
would have gone pitifully with me" (311). Socrates and others like him, by
contrast, have "so perfect a habituation to virtue that it has passed into
their nature. It is no longer a laborious virtue . . . it is the very essence of
their soul, its natural and ordinary gait. They have made it so by a long exercise . . . coming upon a fine rich nature" (310). Montaigne is pure by
luck of birth, Socrates by a long exercise. I will call the purity Montaigne
attributes to himself at this point (he qualifies it later) prereflective and
Socrates' purity reflective. Prereflective purity is akin to innocence; reflective purity is close to integrity.

The difference between these two kinds of purity has also been remarked on by Wittgenstein. Writing about G. E. Moore, he says in a letter:
"That Moore is in some ways extraordinarily childlike is obvious. . . .
There is also a *certain* innocence about Moore; he is, e.g. completely un-
vain. As to it's [*sic*] being to his '*credit*' to be childlike—I can't understand
that; unless it's also to a child's credit. For you aren't talking of the innocence a man has fought for, but of an innocence that comes from the natural absence of temptation."[3] The "natural absence of temptation" is prereflective purity. It is the prelapsarian state of Adam and Eve and, in a
much later allegory, Melville's Billy Budd. Reflective purity is what "a man
has fought for." I do not know which Moore had. My interest is in the distinction itself.

I will argue that the moral status of prereflective purity is dubious and
that one form of moral progress, one goal of self-transformation is toward
reflective purity. Living a good life in this world of ours often requires
those who are prereflectively pure to leave their state behind. Reflective
purity, however, is a fine ideal whose approximation is one way in which
life can be made good. Let us begin with understanding prereflective purity or innocence and then why doubts about it are warranted.

Kierkegaard's *Purity of Heart*[4] is an extended meditation on a biblical
passage: "Draw nigh to God and he will draw nigh to you. Cleanse your
hands, ye sinners; and purify your hearts, ye double minded."[5] Drawing
near to God is interpreted by Kierkegaard as drawing near to the good.

Being double-minded is an obstacle to this, and overcoming it depends on purifying one's heart. "Purity of heart is to will one thing" (53). "To will one thing, therefore, is to will the Good without considering the reward" (72). And "willing the Good only out of fear of punishment . . . is the same as to will the Good for the sake of reward, to the extent that avoiding an evil is an advantage of the same sort as that of attaining a benefit" (79). But why should we think that if we are not double-minded, if we really will only one thing, then we will the good? Why could there not be motiveless malignity, unalloyed rage, fanatical thirst for revenge, passionate envy, relentless selfishness, all without consideration of cost to oneself or others? Why could the one thing willed not be evil?

Kierkegaard's answer is that "genuinely to will one thing, a man must in truth will the Good" (121–122). Those who will anything but the good must mistake whatever they will for the good, for people do not will anything unless they believe that it is in some way or another good or at least better than the alternatives. They make that mistake because they are prevented from seeing clearly by the presence of some corrupting taint. "The person who wills one thing that is not the Good, he does not will one thing. . . . For in his innermost being he is, he is bound to be double-minded" (55). "Would it be possible," Kierkegaard asks, "that a man by willing the evil could will one thing, provided it was possible for a man so to harden himself as to will nothing but the evil?" And he answers with the rhetorical question: "Is not this evil, like evil persons, in disagreement with itself, divided against itself?" (66). If this were so, evil people could not will one thing and could not be pure in heart. This answer, however, follows from a deeper supposition of Kierkegaard.

He thinks that moral progress is from double-mindedness toward prereflective purity. If we progress in this way, we gradually free ourselves from all desires except the one for the good. But why should we accept this? Why should we believe that our innermost desires will be for the good, not for evil? Kierkegaard ignores the possibility that if we reach deep down into ourselves, we may discover what Kurtz has discovered at the end of Conrad's *Heart of Darkness*: "The horror! The horror!"[6] Purity is compatible with evil. If purity is to will one thing, then whether purity is good depends not just on willing one thing but also on the goodness of whatever is willed. Whether one wills the good is a question not just of the quality of the will but also of the quality of the object that is willed.

Kierkegaard, however, denies that there could be a separation between willing one thing and willing the good because he believes that everyone's innermost self is attuned to a cosmic order that is permeated with goodness. He sees evil as resulting from misunderstanding that order, not as a part of it. Evil desires really aim at the good but mistake its nature. Without mistakes obstructing their moral vision, people would desire the good. And the good is one because the cosmic order is one. Consequently, people with mistaken desires are bound to be double-minded because they are bound to have the double purpose of aiming both at the real good and at what they mistake for it.

This is not the place to consider the reasons for and against the existence of a good cosmic order. I merely note that it is a pivotal tenet of one strand of the Western moral tradition, in which Christianity occupies a prominent place. I will argue, however, that even if there were such a cosmic order, Kierkegaard's conclusion—that prereflective purity is good because it leads to goodness, and double-mindedness is bad because it leads away from it—would not follow.

To begin with: *the good*, as in a good life, is a convenient shorthand that must not be taken to imply that there is some one quality that makes all good lives good. Good lives may take many different forms: among numerous others, the life of artists, scientists, statesmen, parents of happy families, athletes, inventors, benefactors of the needy, teachers of children, or those with a gift for friendship. Moreover, these and other forms of good life are made good by the presence in them of many good things, such as love, courage, honesty, discipline, robust health, a sense of humor, success, security, self-confidence, talent, being respected, belonging to a free and just society, peace, tranquillity, prosperity, and so on and on.

Normal people in normal circumstances have to decide which form of good life they should aim at and which goods they should try to have. Each has advantages and disadvantages, benefits and burdens, and each may be more or less suitable to the character and circumstances of the decision maker. People need moral imagination and reflective self-evaluation to understand what it would be like to live in the possible ways open to them, to judge how much they would care about having one set of goods and forgoing the other sets as a result of the decision they might make; and they have to get clear about their priorities in order to resolve the inevitable conflicts within and among the forms of life and the goods they prize.

To say to people in the throes of such decisions—which we all have to make—that they should will the good is a singularly unhelpful piece of advice. Even if they were convinced that there was a good cosmic order and were committed to live in conformity to it, they would not know how the cosmic order applies to their character and context. Reasonable decisions about their possibilities and conflicts depend on the particular features of their situation, not on the generalities of a supposed cosmic order. Their problem is not to will the good, but to know what the good comes to in their situation and to know which of the goods available to them are better than the others. Some possibilities may be ruled out, but countless others remain because many forms of good life and many goods are allowed by the cosmic order. The "childish innocence" and the "natural absence of temptation" that Montaigne and Wittgenstein speak about fall very far short of what most people need for making reasonable decisions. Prereflective purity may predispose people to make morally right decisions, but the actual making of them requires precisely that disciplined imagination, reflective self-evaluation, and realism about their surroundings that the childish innocents lack.

Kierkegaard, or his defenders, may shrug off this difficulty and point at the great moral force that prereflectively pure people often have. Goodness simply shines through them. It is unthinkable that they would be hypocritical or corrupt. Like a bell, they ring, and ring always true. Saint Francis is said to have been such a person; Dostoevsky's Prince Myshkin and Alyosha Karamazov are meant to be like that; and so is Melville's Billy Budd. Spontaneously, naturally, without requiring reflection, their actions are good. The temptations of evil—selfishness, greed, envy, cruelty, and the like—have no foothold in their character. Decisions that others may reach after struggle and reflection appear to them simply as a foregone conclusion, a natural response, the only possible course of action. It must be admitted that there are such people and they embody a moral ideal. They are rare, but that enhances their moral force.

A crucial question in trying to understand the ideal they represent is how they became prereflectively pure. A possible answer is that they were exceptionally fortunate in their native endowments, upbringing, and the social context of their lives. They were born without predispositions to vices, their moral education fostered the development of their virtues, and they lived in a society that did not force them to choose between morally unacceptable alternatives. For such people

the moral life is a *habit of affection and behaviour,* not a habit of reflective *thought,* but a habit of *affection and conduct.* The current situations of a normal life are met, not by consciously applying to ourselves a rule of behaviour, nor by conduct recognized as the expression of a moral ideal, but by acting in accordance with a certain habit of behaviour. The moral life in this form does not spring from the consciousness of possible alternative ways of behaving and a choice, determined by an opinion, a rule or an ideal, from among these alternatives; conduct is as nearly as possible without reflection. And consequently, most of the current situations of life do not appear as occasions calling for judgment, or as problems requiring solutions; there is no weighing up of alternatives or reflection on consequences, no uncertainty, no battle of scruples. There is, on the occasion, nothing more than the unreflective following of a tradition of conduct.[7]

This is an attractive picture, but it is not a picture of our moral life as it now is or ever was. We may wish that the picture were true because we are tired of reflection, struggles, choices, and the ever-present need for judgment, but wishing the facts to be different will not make them so. Perhaps for a few exceptionally fortunate people moral life can be prereflectively pure, but the overwhelming majority of humanity has to struggle with contrary native dispositions, confused and confusing upbringing, and a social context in which injustice, insecurity, deep moral divisions, and far-reaching changes continually pose difficult problems coping with which demands reflection and judgment. Prereflective purity is a moral ideal, but it is not one that can be reasonably pursued by us whose predispositions and upbringing are morally ambivalent and whose social context is permeated with serious moral conflicts.

It must also be said that prereflectively pure people may not only be saints but also scourges of humanity. Robespierre, Saint-Just, and many other fanatics, ideologues, true believers, torturers, and terrorists may also be prereflectively pure but evil. Purity of heart, willing one thing, being utterly convinced of the goodness of one's heart and will and of the justice of one's cause count for very little. The moral tradition to which one is unreflectively true may be vicious. The supposed purity of one's heart is always suspect because ignorance of one's real motives, self-deception, the refusal to acknowledge unpleasant facts, and the comforts of self-serving illusions are ever-present dangers. And the one thing willed may be the result of indoctrination, stupidity, irrationality, or wickedness. The ideal of prereflective purity, therefore, is both impractical and dangerous for the vast majority of people, even if there are some few who, favored by good fortune, combine prereflective purity and goodness.

The moral imagination of prereflectively pure people is unawakened. They will one thing because they are unaware of other possibilities of life, both good and bad, than the one they happen to favor. They are also unaware of the countless possibilities of their own motives being tainted by selfishness, greed, cruelty, malevolence. Their motives thus remain incorrigible, and their pursuit of the one thing they will remains unexamined. That in some rare cases prereflective purity and goodness happen to go together is a matter of luck twice over—luck in having benign predispositions and in living in a social context that is conducive to their development. The overwhelming majority of humanity, however, is not lucky in even one of these ways. That is why the ideal of prereflective purity is impractical and dangerous for them. And that is one reason why people need moral imagination to correct their flawed motives and to explore the possibilities of life open to them.

If we now return to what Montaigne says about himself in contrast with

Socrates, it is clear that Montaigne was prereflectively pure only at the beginning of his life. A man who was a magistrate and a legislator for thirteen years and mayor of Bordeaux for four, who was a respected mediator between two sides in a brutal civil war, who was kidnapped by brigands and talked his way out of captivity, who survived the devastation of the plague, who traveled extensively, who managed his estate prudently and ruled over his subjects with much practical wisdom, who lost five of his children, his beloved father, and his best friend could not have been prereflective, childlike, innocent, and simple. He knew that "we must live in the world and make the most of it as we find it" (774), and he knew the world in which he lived. He was no doubt fortunate in his native endowments, but he required much more than benign predispositions to navigate successfully the turbulent waters of sixteenth-century France.

Reflecting on his life, he says, "A thousand different troubles assailed me," but "these were useful troubles" because they were "teaching me in good time to restrict my way of life and arrange it for a new state of things," because "a spirit so indocile [as his] needs some beatings," and because they taught him "the tragic play of human fortune" (799–800). He has learned "to mistrust my gait throughout, and I strive to regulate it" (822). And he remarks that "by training myself from youth to see my own life . . . I have acquired a studious bent on the subject" (824). "If each man," he says, "watched closely the effects and circumstances of the passions that dominate him, as I have done with the ones I have fallen prey to, he would see them coming and would check their impetuosity" (822–823). All in all, "judgment holds in me a magisterial seat" (823). These are not the observations of a man with childlike purity. If Montaigne was pure, it was a purity "a man has fought for."

Perhaps Montaigne admired Socrates because Socrates achieved what Montaigne had spent a lifetime fighting for. Montaigne certainly left behind prereflective purity but did not think he had achieved the reflective purity he attributes to Socrates. His attitude to himself, I think, is a sign of modesty. He would have agreed wholeheartedly with the Zen koan "You have not arrived if you think you have." We are, at any rate, left with two questions: how should one fight for reflective purity? and what makes it worth fighting for?

9.3 Transcendental Romanticism

Iris Murdoch attempts to answer the first question. She is not unsympathetic to Kierkegaard's approach, but she disagrees with it on several points. Kierkegaard's answer is religious, Murdoch's is forthrightly secular:

"human life has no external point" and "there is, in my view, no God in the traditional sense of that term" (77).[8] Kierkegaard is committed to the voluntarist ideal that assigns priority to the will, Murdoch thinks of it as almost always corrupt: "What I have called fantasy, the proliferation of blinding self-centred aims and images, is itself a powerful system of energy, and most of what is often called 'will' or 'willing' belongs to this system. . . . Freedom is not strictly the exercise of the will, but rather the experience of accurate vision which, when this becomes appropriate, occasions action. It is what is behind and in between actions and prompts them that is important, and it is this area which should be purified" (67). Kierkegaard's view involves a romantic falsification of moral life. Murdoch rejects romanticism in favor of what she calls realism: "the later work of Kierkegaard is a distinguished instance of Romantic self-indulgence" (82); "Kierkegaard makes a drama of what . . . is a matter of experience";[9] and "Kierkegaard speaks eloquently and with emotion about dread and sickness unto death, but is also a romantic writer . . . [who] romanticize[s] despair."[10]

I will argue that Murdoch replaces the Promethean romanticism of voluntarists with her own transcendental romanticism, which also fails to do justice to common moral experience; her justified doubts about the voluntarist ideal lead her to unjustifiably generalize these doubts and advocate "unselfing" as the key to reflective purity; and her view of "the Good" relies on a mystical version of Platonic metaphysics for which she provides no acceptable reason. These criticisms are worth making because they point toward the right way to reflective purity.

Murdoch takes the traditional sense of God to have been "*a single perfect transcendent non-representable and necessarily real object of attention.*" Although she rejects God in that sense, she also thinks that "moral philosophy should attempt to retain a central concept which has all these characteristics" (55). That concept, Murdoch thinks, is the Good. "The image of the Good as a transcendent magnetic centre seems to me the least corruptible and most realistic picture for us to use in our reflections on the moral life" (75). But "if someone says, 'Do you believe that the Idea of the Good exists?' I reply, 'No, not as people used to think that God existed'" (74). On the very same page, however, she says: "The background to morals is properly some sort of mysticism, if by this is meant a non-dogmatic essentially unformulated faith in the reality of the Good." She does not believe that the Good exists, yet she has faith in the reality of the Good. Talk about mysticism here is obfuscation that does nothing to avoid the plain inconsistency. Let us nevertheless be charitable and interpret Murdoch as claiming that the Good exists as an ideal, and not inquire too closely into how it can be a transcendent magnetic center and yet human life be without an external point. The important thing is that in Murdoch's view the moral life ought to aim at the Good. What, then, is this ideal of the Good that morality ought to aim at? Murdoch says that "it is a concept which is not easy to understand partly because it has so many false doubles . . . invented by human selfishness" (92). This, of course, makes it much the more important to know what the Good is since when we aim at it we may in fact be aiming at a false double. The help we get from Murdoch, however, is meager. She says that "a genuine mysteriousness attaches to the idea of goodness and the Good" (99), and she often speaks of "the indefinability of the Good" (e.g., 102). She says that the "Good is mysterious because of human frailty. . . . If there were angels they might be able to define good but we would not understand the definition" (99).

This does not mean, however, that we know nothing about the Good. According to Murdoch, we know that it is "a transcendent reality" (93). We also know that the Good is to be distinguished from particular goods, such as the various virtues (70) and "Freedom, Reason, Happiness, Courage, History" (102). And we know as well that the Good is the unity behind "the multifarious cases of good behaviour" (61). "It is always beyond, and it is from this beyond that it exercises its *authority*" (62) as the "magnetic transcendent center" (75) toward which all good conduct aims. Moreover, it naturally leads to the idea of perfection, the idea of absolute goodness, the highest degree of excellence (61). "The proper and serious use of the term [i.e., the Good] refers us to a perfection which is perhaps never exemplified in the world we know . . . and which carries with it the ideas of hierarchy and transcendence" (93).

Why should we accept these claims? Why should we see mystery rather than Murdoch's inability to adduce reasons for her views? Why should we accept the indefinability of the Good rather than the incoherence of Murdoch's ideas? Why should we think that particular goods are made good by their approximation of a mysterious and indefinable transcendent perfection rather than by readily observable qualities that help make human lives better? Murdoch does not say. What she does say is that her view is "of course not amenable even to a persuasive philosophical proof and can easily be challenged on all sorts of empirical grounds" (74). Is there nothing, then, that might be said in favor of her view? She answers: "All one can do is to appeal to certain areas of experience, pointing out certain features, and using suitable metaphors and inventing suitable concepts where necessary to make these features visible" (75). On that basis, she "sets up a picture . . . as an appeal to us all to see if we cannot find just this in our deepest experience."[11] But since the very point of the metaphors and concepts she has invented is to indicate what supposedly lies beyond our deepest experience—namely, transcendence, perfection, and the

Good—her picture cannot appeal to our deepest experience. Murdoch's view thus fails the very test by which she has proposed to validate it.

The attraction of the Good, the pull of this transcendent ideal of perfection, is only one part of Murdoch's moral psychology. If it were all, it would leave unexplained why everyone does not strive for perfection, why many people often chase false doubles. Murdoch explains it in terms of human frailty. She says that "the Platonic metaphor of the idea of the Good . . . must of course be joined [with] a realistic conception of natural psychology" (71). And that psychology leads her to understand human frailty largely as a result of selfishness. "In the moral life the enemy is the fat relentless ego" (52). "The chief enemy of excellence in morality . . . is the tissue of self-aggrandizing and consoling wishes and dreams which prevents one from seeing what is there outside of one" (59). "The psyche is . . . relentlessly looking after itself. . . . One of its main pastimes is daydreaming. It is reluctant to face unpleasant realities. Its consciousness is . . . a cloud of more or less fantastic reverie designed to protect the psyche from pain. It constantly seeks consolation either through imagined inflation of self or through fictions of a theological nature" (78–79). "We are anxiety-ridden animals. Our minds are continually active, fabricating an anxious, usually self-preoccupied often falsifying *veil* which partially conceals the world" (84). "We are . . . the slaves of relentlessly strong selfish forces the nature of which we scarcely comprehend" (99).

The remedy is "unselfing" (84). "Anything which alters consciousness in the direction of unselfishness . . . is to be connected with virtue" (84). "The direction of attention should properly be outward, away from self" (59). Goodness requires "the suppression of self" (66). "The self, the place where we live, is a place of illusion. Goodness is connected with the attempt to see the unself . . . to pierce the veil of selfish consciousness" (93). What we must do "is to keep the attention . . . from returning surreptitiously to the self with consolations of self-pity, resentment, fantasy and despair" (91). And we can pierce the veil of selfish concerns by directing our attention outward to nature, great art or literature, learning a foreign language, or, in rare instances, through unselfish love, to another person. "The soul must be saved entire by the redirection of its energy away from selfish fantasy toward reality."[12] "The good artist helps us see the place of necessity in human life, what must be endured, what makes and breaks, and to purify our imagination . . . usually veiled by anxiety and fantasy."[13]

Murdoch thinks of this process of unselfing that removes selfish obstacles from the way of seeing the Good as the process of purification. "One of the main problems of moral philosophy," she says, is to find "techniques for the purification and reorientation of an energy which is naturally self-ish" (54). The way to the Good is the development of "an increasing awareness of goods and the attempt (usually only partially successful) to attend to them purely, without self" (70). "The purification and reorientation [of the soul] . . . must be the task of morals" (71). And "when we try perfectly to love what is imperfect our love goes to its object *via* the Good to be thus purified and made unselfish" (103).

By putting together the two parts of Murdoch's moral psychology—the Good and unselfing—we can evaluate the ideal of purity that emerges from them. That idea is best embodied by the humble man. "Humility," rightly understood, "is not a peculiar habit of self-effacement, rather like having an inaudible voice, it is selfless respect for reality and of the most difficult and central of all virtues" (95). "The good man is humble. . . . Humility is a rare virtue and an unfashionable one. . . . Only rarely does one meet somebody in whom it positively shines, in whom one appre-hends with amazement the absence of the anxious avaricious tentacles of the self. . . . The humble man, because he sees himself as nothing, can see other things as they are. . . . Although he is not by definition the good man perhaps he is the kind of man who is most likely to become good" (103–104). He is open to the disinterested love of the Good, to a "quality of at-tachment" that is "the energy and passion of the soul in its search for Good," which is "the magnetic centre towards which love naturally moves" (102–103).

The first thing that must be said about this ideal of purity is that it is not a rejection of romanticism but an overblown expression of it. Its hero is the humble man who is on a quest, is moved by passionate love, encoun-ters daunting obstacles that defeat most people, struggles with the obsta-cles and is enabled to prevail against them in the face of great odds by self-denial and the inspiration of true yet unattainable love. He is Murdoch's "verray parfit gentil knight" who, armed with love, conquers the most for-midable of all enemies: himself. His life is a drama in which the hero achieves his beloved ideal by making the supreme sacrifice. This is Mur-doch's version of *Liebestod*, which she rightly diagnoses elsewhere as a symptom of romantic self-indulgence (82). Those who are not swept off their feet by Murdoch's impassioned rhetoric will see her knight as on a pilgrimage from one unacceptable metaphor to another. Both unselfing and the Good involve serious misrepresentations of the very moral life to which Murdoch intends them to be true.

Let us take unselfing first. Murdoch is right to emphasize the endless guises through which self-deception, fantasy, and selfishness prevent us from seeing ourselves and others realistically. Nor is there any doubt that living a good life frequently depends on purifying ourselves by overcoming these corrupting tendencies. But this does not mean that we should repudiate our very self. The self has virtues, not just vices; strengths, not just weaknesses; realistic tendencies, not just illusions. One moral task is to rid ourselves not of the self but of dispositions that stand in the way of living a good life. If, per impossibile, we got rid of our selves, we would have gotten rid of the very possibility of living a good life, since the self is the agent who would be living such a life. Unselfing would kill the self in order to cure its disease.

Murdoch is also right in seeing that the voluntarist ideal is mistaken in assigning priority to the will. The will is as liable to corruption as beliefs, feelings, or any other psychological processes. We must guard against their corruption, but we cannot do that by surrendering our will, or anything else, to an external ideal. For that surrender is liable to the same corruption as the one we try to avoid by our surrender. The remedy must be to guard against corruption by trying as well as we can to correct our tendencies to go wrong and to explore reasonably the alternatives we have. That is what the disciplined imagination helps us do. Murdoch's remedy, however, is not the commonsense one of trying to purify our corrupt self, but the suicidal aspiration of abandoning it as if it were excess luggage in our pilgrimage toward the Good.

Consider the Good next. A realistic look at moral life reveals that people may desire many different goods: a good job, a good marriage, a good friend, a good character, a good society to live in, and so forth. For the sake of these goods they are sometimes willing to try to develop suitable character traits, control contrary desires, and establish priorities. They may succeed or fail, but either outcome is typically partial, a matter of degree. If the attraction of the particular good they are after is strong, it inspires them to try harder. Their task is difficult, the external and internal obstacles are many, and the contingencies of life may frustrate even their best efforts. But no one desires the Good apart from particular goods. What makes particular goods good is that they help one live a fulfilling and responsible life. Reflective people can often explain what makes or would make their job, marriage, character, friendship, or society good. The explanation, however, will always be in terms of specific qualities that a particular good has, not in terms of approximating the ideal of the Good, especially since the nature of that ideal, according to Murdoch, is a mystery and the object of the ideal does not exist.

It might be said that the Good is perfection, and that is what people desire when they desire the Good. But this does not help at all. For the desired perfection must be of some specific quality or activity and not of others, since presumably the perfection of a crime, an act of revenge, or an insult is not what morality enjoins us to seek. If the quality or activity is specified, then it must be explained wherein its perfection consists. To say that it consists in its exemplification of a mysterious transcendental ideal is no explanation at all. And if one were to succeed in the daunting task of explaining what particular qualities or activities would make a job, a marriage, a friend, a character, or a society perfect, the explanation could not be generalized because their perfection varies with the temperaments, expectations, strengths and weaknesses, historical circumstances, and social and economic conditions of the participants.

It must be added that it is just false to suppose that most people desire either general or particular perfection. They certainly often desire to have a better job, marriage, friendship, and so forth, but "better" means the removal of some defects of what they have, not the exemplification of an ideal with unknown content. They desire the better because they are dissatisfied with some particular aspect of their existing arrangements, and their desire would be satisfied if their dissatisfaction were removed. The desire for perfection is not part of common moral experience. Although people sometimes do say of others or of themselves that they are perfectionists, what they mean is that they desire to be or to have or to produce a faultless instantiation of the object they desire. But that has nothing to do with nurturing a passionate love for a mysterious transcendental object whose magnetic force attracts them.

There is an undeniable kernel of truth in both parts of Murdoch's moral psychology, but she inflates and dramatizes its importance in order to support a Platonic metaphysics. She tries to close the enormous gap between the kernel of truth and the full-blown metaphysics by inventing metaphors, appealing to emotions, invoking portentous mysteries. In this attempt she is aided by her considerable novelistic skill, heartfelt rhetoric, and desire to salvage as much as possible of traditional religious belief. Her enterprise, however, is a failure because closing the gap depends on reasons, and she has not provided them. We are thus left with a small kernel of truth, a large dose of overwrought romanticism, an oxymoronic secular mysticism, and a metaphysics unsupported by reasons.

The truth in unselfing is that we are often and easily led to falsify the facts of moral life by selfish fears, illusions, and hopes. Living a good life requires the correction of these falsifications. The truth in the Good is that a life is made good partly by the realization of possibilities that exist outside us and a good life requires the exploration of these possibilities. Both these truths and their interdependence are recognized by the disciplined imagination. We correct our falsifications in order to be able to explore our possibilities realistically. And the desire to realize possibilities we value motivates us to correct our falsifications. For this, however, we do not need to fall in love with a transcendental ideal, turn to metaphysics, or pursue perfection. We need to develop reflective purity, to which I now turn.

9.4 Reflective Purity

Reflective purity is a way of being and acting that few people achieve. It is, like prereflective purity, spontaneous, transparent, and truthful, and it excludes artifice and double-mindedness. But it is also different because it is the outcome of much reflection. Prereflectively pure people do not reflect because they are unaware of the complexities they may face. Those who have achieved reflective purity do not reflect either, but this is because they have no need for it, having reflected deeply and sufficiently in the past. They know where they stand and what they must do, they know the limits they will not transgress and the possibilities whose realization makes their life worth living. They know all this because their disciplined imagination has done its work. It has taught them to correct the tendencies that have led them to go wrong in the past, to explore their available possibilities, and to opt for those whose realization would make their life good. Thus enabled, they live their lives responsibly and find them fulfilling. This is obviously not a childlike state of innocence but a mature one for which they had to fight.

The answers, then, to the questions I asked earlier (at the end of 9.2) are, first, that reflective purity is worth fighting for because it is a way in which we can make our life good, and second, that the way to fight for it is to discipline our imagination and use it well. But these answers are too skeletal and general to be satisfactory. I will flesh them out and make them concrete by considering how Sir Thomas More lived and died. More did not achieve reflective purity, but he came as close to it in difficult circumstances as it is perhaps reasonable to hope for such fallible and vulnerable creatures as we are.

More's years were 1478–1535. His main work—*Utopia*—was published in 1516. After many years of distinguished service to the throne, in 1529 he was appointed lord chancellor, a position from which he resigned in 1532. Two years later he was imprisoned in the Tower of London, and in 1535 he was indicted of high treason and executed. More went to his death because he would not obey his king, Henry VIII, who required More to confer legal and moral legitimacy on the king's wish to divorce his wife and marry Anne Boleyn, with whom the king was besotted.

The larger issues in the background were the struggle between religious and political authority for supremacy and between the Catholic church and the Reformation as it played out in England. More, like Sophocles'

Antigone, believed that the requirements of religion were fundamental. The king, like Sophocles' Creon, held that political considerations could override religious ones. More, after having ingeniously temporized for a long time, finally ran out of evasions, and he was forced to take a stand. He then refused to do what the king had demanded, and that was the reason for his imprisonment, indictment, and execution.

In the introduction to a justly celebrated play, Robert Bolt writes that More was "a man with an adamantine sense of his own self. He knew where he began and left off, what area of himself he could yield to the encroachments of his enemies, and what to the encroachments of those he loved. It was a substantial area in both cases, for he had a proper sense of fear and was a busy lover. Since he was a clever man and a great lawyer, he was able to retire from these areas in wonderfully good order, but at length he was asked to retreat from that final area where he located his self. And there this supple, humorous, unassuming and sophisticated man set like metal, was overtaken by an absolutely primitive rigor, and could no more be budged than a cliff."[14] We might notice, to begin with, that More's approximation of reflective purity depended on his "adamantine sense of his own self," which would have been destroyed by unselfing. Furthermore, innocence and humility are conspicuously absent from More's character. What we find instead is an unshakable integrity.

More had a deep commitment to the priority of his religious beliefs over everything else, and he was unwilling to take an action, not even for the sake of saving his life or protecting those he loved, that would have involved violating this commitment. More had other commitments as well, and from these he retreated, when pressed, in "wonderfully good order." Some of his commitments mattered more to him than others, but his deep commitment mattered most.

During his fifteen months of imprisonment More was engaged in two significant activities. One was writing letters and shorter works in which he more or less indirectly reflects on his plight and on what he ought to do, and explains the reasons for the resolve he finally arrived at to go to his death rather than violate his deep commitment. The other was listening to a number of visitors—his daughter, various ecclesiastical authorities, and the king's representatives—who attempted to persuade him that his resolve was an act of inexpediency, stubbornness, pride, and disloyalty to his family, king, and country. His prison writings show him laying to rest his own doubts and answering his visitors.

To the pleas of his visitors he replies—as Job might have done—that they constitute a temptation that "spreads gradually and imperceptibly while those persons who despise it at first, afterwards can stand to hear it and respond to it with less than full scorn, then come to tolerate wicked discussions, and afterwards are carried away in error, until like cancer . . . the creeping disease finally takes over" (14:359).[15] He rejects "the soft speeches . . . [that] cajole him into leaving the way of truth" (14:543). Yet he wonders about himself whether "will not weaklings who are . . . cowardly and afraid take heart so as not to yield under the stress of persecution even though they feel great sadness welling up within them, and fear and weariness and horror at the prospect of a ghastly death?" (14:247). He tells his tempters: "I have ere I came here [the Tower] not left unbethought nor unconsidered the very worst and the uttermost that can by possibility fall. And albeit I know my frailty full well and the natural faintness of mine own heart, yet if I had not trusted that God should give me strength rather to endure all things, than offend him by swearing ungodly against mine own conscience, you may be very sure I would not have come here."[16]

These words express More's deep commitment. He would not swear the oath his king demanded of him because "in my conscience this was one of the cases in which I was not bounden that I should obey my prince." And he will "stand still in this scruple of his conscience . . . [even if] all his friends that seem most able to do him good either shall finally forsake him, or peradventure not be able indeed to do him any good at all." And, he says, "all the causes that I perceive move other men to the contrary, seem not such unto me as in my conscience make any change."[17] Deep commitments are the most serious convictions we have. They define our limits: what we feel we must not do, no matter what; what we regard as outrageous and horrible. They are fundamental conditions of being ourselves. Deep commitments are not universal, for they vary with individuals. Nor are they categorical, for we may violate them. But if through fear, coercion, weakness, accident, or stupidity we do so, we inflict grave psychological damage on ourselves. This is what the younger Oedipus and Conrad's Lord Jim have done to themselves.

More died rather than violate his deep commitment. Most of us are made of softer stuff, but the violation of deep commitments is no less damaging to weaker people. There is a crisis, we do something contrary to such a commitment, and we realize that we cannot come to terms with what we have done. If we were as we conceived ourselves to be, we would not have done that. So we are brought to the realization that we are not what we took ourselves to be. An abyss opens up at the center of our being: we disintegrate, go mad, or carry on in a desultory way looking in vain for a chance to undo the horrible thing we have done.

Many people have no deep commitments. Since having them renders one vulnerable, we may well wonder why we should be like More and create in ourselves the potential either to be driven to this state of "absolutely primitive rigor" or to fall apart. If we take nothing so terribly seriously, we are less open to lasting psychological damage. We cultivate greater suppleness and thus become better able to withstand the inevitable buffeting we suffer in navigating life's treacherous waters. A contrast between deep and formative commitments will show why this stratagem is inadvisable.

Formative commitments are the stuff of everyday life. They guide our intimate relationships, impersonal encounters with others, and the various forms that our personal projects may take. The way we raise our children, how we respond to friends, our attitude to the work we do, the direction in which ambition takes us, the fears we fend off, and the hopes that sustain us are all guided by formative commitments. They are defeasible because they could be reasonably overridden if sufficiently strong considerations are found against them. One difference between formative and deep commitments is that nothing we recognize as a good reason would override the latter because our judgments of what reasons are good and how strongly they weigh are dictated by our deep commitments. They are the standards by which we measure, and unless we abandon the yardstick, there could be no reason adduced that would incline us to reject conclusions that have been properly derived from our deep commitments.

More loved his wife and children. Yet his commitment to marriage and parenthood was formative because his religious commitment took precedence over it. When it came to the point, More honored his deep religious commitment and went to his death, leaving his wife and children to fend for themselves as well as they could. Others in More's position might have obeyed the king because they had no deep commitment at all, or had it to marriage and parenthood, not to religion. Yet that could only have been done by other people. More was what he was because his deep religious commitment took precedence over his other commitments.

It is possible to live a good life just by living according to formative commitments. Lucky circumstances, phlegmatic temperament, much savvy, intellect not given to reflection and self-analysis, the absence of political upheavals and glaring injustice, the enjoyment of robust health, a busy life, a happy family, and many good friends may make it possible for a few fortunate people not to have to ask themselves the kind of fundamental questions that, if asked at all, lead to their deep commitments. For most of us, however, these questions do arise because our formative commitments may conflict, because our lives may make it impossible or hard to live according to them, because we may waver in our allegiance to them, and because we come to see the attractions of other ways of life. These typically unavoidable questions force most of us to ask ourselves what we most fundamentally care about. And that question leads directly to our deep commitments, if we have any.

The cost of not having deep commitments is not being able to answer these questions about how we should live. This inability may handicap us in different ways. One is through the lack of a character in which beliefs, emotions, and motives form a coherent pattern. To have a coherent character is to have made deep commitments. The conflicts and difficulties of our formative commitments, and our doubts about them, are the result of discrepancies between our beliefs, emotions, and motives. We are pulled in different directions by the tensions inherent in our characters and circumstances. Deep commitments are constitutive of our moral identity, whereas formative commitments may leave us uncertain when conflicts, difficulties, and doubts become complex enough to raise the question of whether a formative commitment should be honored. In the absence of a coherent character, we face such complex situations with uncertainty and doubt. The psychological space left empty by the absence of deep commitments is thus filled with the sort of fantasy, fear, anxiety, and overcompensation which Murdoch talks about and which color and mislead our responses.

The lack of deep commitments may also handicap us through the resulting incapacity to resolve conflicting interpretations of complex situations suggested by our various formative commitments. In the absence of deep commitments, we lack a standard for deciding what would count for or against honoring a formative commitment. And if honoring it is difficult, as it usually is in complex situations, then, human nature being what it is, we shall be tempted to count the difficulty itself as a reason against honoring the commitment. If we have only formative commitments, it becomes impossible to decide between good and bad, and strong and weak reasons for violating them.

Peripheral commitments are the social aspects of our characters. Hume called them "a kind of lesser morality," and Jane Austen referred to them as "the civilities, the lesser duties of life."[18] Their objects are the manners and mores of one's society, the rules and customs of politeness, tact, and hygiene; the face one presents to the world; styles of clothing, furnishing, eating, socializing, and exercising; the rituals and ceremonies of everyday life; and so forth. More was a patriotic man who had a formative commitment to England. The form his patriotism took was fealty to his king. But for More this was a peripheral commitment. The author of *Utopia* understood that the forms of patriotism are historically and socially conditioned.

Peripheral commitments are comparable to aesthetic style: the way in which creative artists present their works and performing artists render their interpretations. If style is to be more than mannerism, it should be a vehicle suitable for the communication of substance. Analogously for people: their deep and formative commitments often must be expressed in social actions, so there must be peripheral commitments giving form to their expressions. But some forms are more suitable than others. When there were titles and honorifics, it was easier to express respect; before oaths and curses had become hackneyed vulgarities, they were reliable indicators of serious resolve and enmity; when kisses and embraces were not indiscriminately bestowed on pets, children, and casual acquaintances, they were meaningful signs of love.

Adherence to peripheral commitments is not a particularly praiseworthy moral achievement. Nevertheless, there need not be only a superficial connection between the forms peripheral commitments take and the substance that is constituted of deep and formative commitments. Ours is not a ceremonious age, and we are given to suspecting that attention to form is prompted by hypocritical attempts to disguise lack of substance. But in societies more homogeneous and less mobile than ours, there may be a seamless continuity from deep to formative to peripheral commitments. In such contexts, forms may have a natural affinity with substance. There is not much point in regretting that our society is not like that. But even the most earnest scourge of hypocrisy must recognize that it is easier to live good lives when there are generally recognized and available forms that they might take.

Reflection on More's life suggests the importance of a sharp separation between the center and the periphery of our character and not allowing the compromises in the periphery to affect the center. The way to effect and to maintain this separation is by distinguishing between our deep, formative, and peripheral commitments. Deep commitments constitute the center; peripheral commitments belong to the outer layer; and formative commitments, depending on their strength, range on a continuum between the core and the periphery. One main task of the disciplined imagination is to discover what our commitments are, whether they are deep, formative, or peripheral, and whether we have good reasons for holding them. And another of its main tasks is to form a coherent pattern of our beliefs, emotions, and motives which reflects the structure of our commitments. The life of More is admirable partly because he succeeded at both these tasks in very difficult circumstances.

Reflective purity or integrity is to know what one's deep commitments are and to remain true to them even when it is hard to do so. The reason for doing this hard thing is that this is one way of living a fulfilling and responsible life. Working toward being true in this way is reasonable and admirable, and one way in which we can transform ourselves for the better and make moral progress.

There remains a difficult question that should be asked about reflective purity. What if a deep commitment is based on false beliefs that one mistakenly holds as true? More may be a case in point, for it may be that his deep commitment was to false religious beliefs. Assume that this was so. Does that make More less reasonable and admirable? The answer depends on how he came to hold his false beliefs. One possibility is that he had good reasons to hold them and no reason to doubt them. Suppose they gave meaning to his life, everyone around him shared them, theological and philosophical authorities have provided arguments for them, More was convinced by these arguments, and he was not acquainted with convincing arguments against them. He, then, held false beliefs reasonably, and remains admirable. If, however, he had reasons to doubt his false beliefs but ignored the reasons, or if there were readily available and convincing arguments against his beliefs but he was too lazy, stubborn, dogmatic, or fearful to consider them, then he would have been unreasonable and consequently less admirable. This, I believe, is the right approach to answering this difficult question, but it depends on a deeper explanation of what makes a belief reasonable than I have hitherto given. I will provide that explanation in chapter 11.

Such difficulties, however, do not beset Montaigne's Socrates, who did not merely approximate but actually achieved reflective purity. He spent a lifetime examining the beliefs on which he had acted and the commitments he had made. He had good reasons for regarding them as true and the actions based on them as good. He, unlike More, did not have to do a great deal of soul searching in choosing to die rather than violate them. And he, unlike Montaigne, had found convincing reasons against skeptical doubts about truth and goodness. That is why Montaigne was right to regard Socrates as the master of masters and himself as falling short of that high standard.

9.5 Reflective Purity and the Balanced Ideal

We have seen how reflective purity depends on clarity about the respective importance of one's commitments and how the achievement of clarity contributes to the transformation of one's character from being at the mercy of contingency toward being more deliberately formed. The reason for aiming at a deliberately formed character is to make oneself the kind of person who could live a fulfilling and responsible life, that is, a good life. Good lives may take many different forms, depending, in part, on the realization of many different possibilities. But the form of good life I have been discussing is the balanced ideal. The ideal is to achieve two kinds of balance.

One kind depends on recognizing the importance of the cognitive, emotive, and motivational components of one's character; not allowing one component to enslave the others; and achieving a substantial amount of congruity among them so that they will not move one in incompatible directions. This requires that one's commitments should reflect one's beliefs, emotions, and desires. The second involves balancing the need for correcting the character defects that led to one's mistaken decisions in the past and the need for the exploration of possibilities that are appropriate to one's character and circumstances. This requires avoiding both insufficient and excessive concentration on one's past or future. The aim is correction that makes realistic exploration possible and exploration that makes realistic correction worthwhile. This depends on the work of the disciplined imagination having been done well.

If both kinds of balance are successfully maintained, the balanced ideal is achieved. One sign of that is reflective purity: clarity about one's commitments, realism about one's possibilities, and success in the transformation of one's character. Those who achieve this ideal are in as much control of their lives as it is possible for us to be.

CHAPTER 10

The Self's Judgment of the Self

The proximate cause of shame is the self's judgement of the self.
—DOUGLAS L. CAIRNS, *Aidos*

10.1 The Standard View

In the preceding chapter I aimed to show how the disciplined imagination may lead to reflective purity and thereby transform the self in a way that constitutes moral progress. In this chapter I aim to show how the disciplined imagination may make moral progress possible from more to less destructive experiences of shame and finally away from shame altogether toward the approximation of the balanced ideal.

The standard view of shame consists of an analysis and an evaluation. I have doubts about both. The analysis is faulty and leaves crucial questions unanswered. The problem with the evaluation has been succinctly stated by Aristotle: "if shamelessness . . . is bad, that does not make it good to be ashamed."[1] I start with the analysis, show its inadequacies, propose a revised view and a better analysis, then turn to the evaluation and argue that the disciplined imagination leads to better responses to moral failure than shame.

The best account I know of the standard view of shame is given by Gabriele Taylor.[2] Her overall account is widely accepted, although disagreements with details of it persist.[3] According to Taylor, "if someone has self-respect then under certain specifiable conditions he will be feeling shame. A person has no self-respect if he regards no circumstances as shame-producing. Loss of self-respect and loss of the capacity for feeling shame go hand in hand. The close connection between the two makes it clear why shame is often thought to be so valuable. It is, firstly, that a sense of value is necessary for self-respect and so for shame, so that whatever else may be wrong about the person feeling shame he will at least have retained a sense of value. And secondly, it is a sense of value which protects the self from what in the agent's eye is corruption and ultimately extinction. . . . Shame is the emotion of self-protection" (80–81).

It would be desirable to have at this point a definition of shame, but Taylor does not give it and I doubt that it could be given. The reasons for this have been plausibly set out by Douglas Cairns in *Aidos*.[4] Shame is certainly a negative, painful emotion, but many cases of it are indistinguishable from embarrassment, humiliation, chagrin, guilt, dishonor, regret, remorse, prudishness, disgrace, and so on. The search for necessary and sufficient conditions needed for a sharp definition is bound to result in simplifying these complex emotions and drawing arbitrary distinctions. We need to tell what is and is not shame, but a general description rather than a precise definition will suffice for this purpose.

Shame, then, is an emotion directed toward oneself: its subject and object are the same. It is a bad, unpleasant, disturbing emotion, for it involves seeing oneself in an unfavorable light. Shame is thus an emotion of self-evaluation because when we feel ashamed we recognize that there is some value of which we have fallen short. Commitment to that value is essential to feeling shame, for otherwise we would not feel bad about falling short of it. That something about us is regarded as shameful by others is not enough to make us feel ashamed, since we may be indifferent to or reject the value to which others appeal. All the same, few people are so totally at odds with their society as to be utterly indifferent to the values held by others in it. We often feel shame about something others would also regard as shameful. Understanding shame nevertheless depends on understanding the *feeling* of shame we may have, not the experience of *being shamed* by others. The two may go together, or they may not.

There is general agreement among defenders of the standard view that the reflective self-evaluation involved in shame—Taylor calls it self-assessment—depends on there being a certain distance between what we do or fail to do and our evaluation of it. This distance is essential to shame, to all forms of reflective self-evaluation, and to having some control over our actions. For in its absence our actions would be reflex-like responses to stimuli and we could not even consider choosing among possible alternative responses we might make. Imagination can have scope when the distance exists and we can evaluate our possibilities. And imagination is disciplined if it involves both the correction of defective tendencies that lead to mistaken evaluations and the exploration of available possibilities in order to form a realistic view of what would be involved in acting on them. Feeling shame indicates that our evaluation has gone wrong because our imagination was not disciplined enough. We failed to correct some misguiding tendency of ours or we failed to be realistic in the exploration of our possibilities. The causes of such failures are many, but self-deception, fantasy, excessive or insufficient self-confidence are prominent among them. If our imagination had been disciplined enough, we would have had no cause to be ashamed. We can thus see that the disciplined use of imagination and shame are contrary moral forces. The first increases the control we have over our actions; the second condemns us for misusing the control we had.

In feeling ashamed, then, we see a failure in ourselves as others might see it—or often as others do see it—and we accept this detached evaluation because we are committed to the value to which we have failed to live up. Perhaps the commitment is the result of outside social influences; what matters, however, is not its origin, but that the value is now ours. This is missed by several defenders of the standard account who insist that we feel shame because there is an actual or imagined observer who judges us adversely. Rawls, for instance, holds that "shame implies an especially intimate connection . . . with those upon whom we depend to confirm the sense of our own worth," and part of the explanation of shame is that a person "has been found unworthy of his associates upon whom he depends to confirm his sense of his own worth."[5] The general mistake this view exemplifies is the supposition that feeling ashamed requires an audience.[6] No doubt, shame is often felt when others judge us adversely, but there are many occasions when we are ashamed about failures only we regard as such: not achieving our intended personal best, falling short of a supererogatory commitment, or being insufficiently diligent in pursuing a purely personal project.

Taylor's observation about this is absolutely right: "There is, then, this point to the metaphors of an audience and being seen: they reflect the structural features of the agent's becoming aware of the discrepancy between her assumptions about her state or action and a possible detached observer-description of this state or action, and of her further being aware that she ought not to be in a position where she could be so seen. . . . In particular cases of shame an actual or imagined observer may or may not be required. . . . Whether or not there is, or is imagined to be, such an observer is a contingent matter" (66).

Shame, then, is the result of a detached comparison we make between some aspect of ourselves and a value we want to live up to, and the result is that we find that we have failed. In such cases, shame assails us as a sudden realization, a shock, a discovery. This dramatic aspect of shame, as Taylor aptly calls it, disrupts our previous equanimity. Prior to becoming ashamed we have not seriously evaluated the relevant aspect of ourselves or we have subsumed it under a neutral or even complimentary description. If we assess it at all, we say privately that we are, for instance, cautious, or just, or clever, and then something happens, the veil is lifted, and we realize that, in fact, we have been cowardly, cruel, or dishonest. Self-deception, lethargy, fear, and stupidity have great scope here. But the salient point is that when shame occurs, we suddenly see some aspect of ourselves in a new and unfavorable light. We see what has been there, but we see it for the first time differently from the way we used to. Shame essentially involves self-evaluation, and what provokes it is some episode, criticism, or comparison we ourselves or others make and whose significance dawns on us, as it dawned on Adam and Eve after eating the apple of knowledge that they were naked.

The evaluation involved in shame has a moral aspect. To acknowledge this is to question the sharp distinction, drawn for instance by Rawls,[7] between natural and moral shame. According to it, we may feel natural but not moral shame because we feel ugly, stupid, deformed, or incompetent. These may detract from our self-respect, but they do not violate moral values. They are unfortunate but not blameworthy. Or people may invade our privacy, observe our intimate frolics, rituals, or lovemaking, and make us feel ashamed by violating our dignity, even though we have done nothing morally censurable. Moral shame, by contrast, is supposedly caused by a moral deficiency. Acting in a cowardly way, betraying a friend, being caught in a lie, carelessly hurting someone we love are blameworthy matters that may make moral shame appropriate. Both natural and moral shame are said to depend on damage to our self-respect, but one is and the other is not supposed to be a moral damage.

If, however, we take a sufficiently broad view of morality to accommodate a wide enough range of moral experiences, we will reject a sharp distinction between natural and moral shame because it rests on the voluntarist assumption that morality and the domain of choice coincide. Since the objects of natural shame are not chosen, natural shame is placed outside morality. But morality is wider than the domain of choice. It is concerned with living a good life, and there are many constituents of good lives about which we often have no choice. A secure society hospitable to our endeavors, the possession of native endowments that could be developed, the absence of paralyzing personal handicaps are as necessary for good lives as morally praiseworthy choices. If we are committed to a certain ideal of a good life but find that we have failed, our self-respect may suffer, and we may come to feel shame even though we have not made wrong choices. What matters to shame, according to the standard view, is not that we have made morally blameworthy choices but that we suffer damage to our self-respect. Rawls himself seems to recognize this, although inconsistently: "we should say that given our plan of life, we tend to be ashamed of those defects in our person and failures in our actions that indicate a loss or absence of excellences essential to carrying out our more important associative aims."[8]

It is essential to living a good life that we should not feel badly about ourselves. Self-respect depends on the sense that we are living up to our values. Shame occurs when we realize that we have fallen short of them. Shame is thus the experience of failure, but it may or may not be culpable failure. Once again, Taylor gets this right: "Shame can be seen as a moral emotion, then, not because sometimes or even often it is felt when the person believes himself to have done something morally wrong, but rather because the capacity for feeling shame is so closely related to the possession of self-respect and thereby to the agent's values" (84).

Whether we feel shame, then, depends on whether we have violated some value of ours, and not on whether the violation was the effect of chosen or unchosen, innate or acquired, voluntary or involuntary, accidental or cultivated causes. Consequently, there is a kind of harsh judgment associated with shame. It understands only success and failure. If we feel ashamed, appeal to extenuating factors rarely brings relief. For shame painfully brings home to us the brute fact that we have committed ourselves to be and to act in a certain way and we failed. Since our reason for making the commitment was that we regarded being and acting that way good, having failed, we feel bad about the way we are and act. Shame is this primitive, inexorable emotion. Like grief or unrequited love, it is contingent on an unarguable fact. In the case of shame, the fact is that we find some aspect of our life deficient. Shame is a moral emotion because morality has to do with living a good life. This completes the outline of what I take to be the standard view of shame.

10.2 Doubts about the Standard View

Defenders of the standard view follow Taylor in accepting that "shame is the emotion of self-protection" (81). They may differ about how shame protects the self, but they agree that the central role of shame is to do that. John Deigh says that "shame inhibits one from doing things that would tarnish one's worth . . . thus protecting one from appearing to be an unworthy creature." According to J. David Velleman, "threats to your standing as a self-presenting creature are thus a source of deep anxiety, and anxiety about the threatened loss of the standing is, in my view, what constitutes the emotion of shame." Bernard Williams writes that "the root of shame lies . . . in being at a disadvantage: in . . . a loss of power. The sense of shame is a reaction of the subject to the consciousness of this loss: in Gabriele Taylor's phrase . . . it is 'the emotion of self-protection'."[9] But if shame involves "the loss of self-respect" (Taylor, 81); if it "tarnish[es] one's worth" (Deigh); if its source is the loss of standing as a self-presenting creature (Velleman); if it is consciousness of the loss of one's power (Williams),[10] then it cannot possibly be the emotion of self-protection. It is, on the contrary, an emotion felt when the protection of the self has failed. That is precisely why shame is a painful indication of failure. Shame cannot be both the emotion that protects the self from suffering a certain sort of damage and a reaction to having suffered that damage. The standard view that holds that shame is both is plainly inconsistent.

It is not hard to see, however, what defenders of the standard view mean, even if they put it badly. They mean that the *fear* of shame is the emotion of self-protection. Putting it this way avoids the inconsistency, but only at the cost of a confusion that dooms the standard view as much as the inconsistency. The confusion becomes apparent if we ask what exactly is feared in the fear of shame. The answer is that it is the loss of self-respect that results from the violation of some value to which we are committed. But if our commitment is genuine, we care about its violation because we prize the value, not because we would have bad feelings as a result of its violation. If we really value justice and have acted unjustly, what we mind is our unjust action, not that we feel badly about it. Of course we might feel badly as well, but that is hardly the point. The point is that we have done what we believe we ought not to do. The key to protecting self-respect is to do what we believe we ought to do, not to avoid bad feelings on account of having failed to protect our self-respect.

If the standard view concentrates on the motivational importance of the fear of shame, then it concentrates on the wrong thing. What ought to motivate us when we do what we ought to do is commitment to some value. If we were motivated by fear of shame, we would already have violated the commitment because even if we end up doing what we ought to do, we would do it for the wrong reason of protecting our self-respect, not for the right reason of its being what we ought to do. We would, then, care more about how we feel than about the value we prize.

Human motivation, of course, is rarely simple, and we could have two reasons for doing something: because it is right and because we would feel badly if we did not do it. But if our commitment is genuine, we feel badly because we did not do what is right, so doing what is right is basic, and how we feel about it is derivative. The confusion involved in substituting fear of shame for shame as the emotion of self-protection is to mistake the derivative for the basic. If defenders of the standard view avoid this confusion and do not substitute fear of shame for shame, then they fall back into the inconsistency that the substitution was meant to avoid.

This is a major but by no means the only reason for doubting the standard view. Another reason is that explaining shame as an emotional reaction to the violation of one's values cannot possibly be a full explanation since we may come to be ashamed of the values we hold. I do not mean that commitment to one of our values may make commitment to another of our values shameful. I mean that we may come to be ashamed of the whole system of values to which we have committed ourselves. It is possible that when Communists, Nazis, terrorists, and holy warriors of all stripes are brought face to face with the ghastly consequences of acting according to their commitments, with the mangled, tortured, starved, bloodied, brutalized bodies of innocent people, then it may dawn on them that they have been led by their values to do dreadful things, and they feel ashamed for having those values. This is a possible experience, even if the blinding force of ideologies makes it infrequent. But if shame were felt only for the violation of one's values, then this experience would be impossible. The standard view fails to recognize that one may be ashamed for *having* the values one has, not for violating them.[11] A full explanation of shame, therefore, must go beyond commitment to values and recognize the possibility that commitments may be mistaken and that people may become ashamed of having made them.

A further reason for doubting the standard view emerges from an illuminating distinction drawn by Michael Stocker between global and local shame.[12] Global shame affects the self as a whole; local shame is on account of some specific deficiency that may have little effect on one's attitude to one's self. To feel ashamed at being a coward, a traitor, or a systematic loser is to feel global shame, whereas shame felt about one's tactless question, social gaffe, or poor French is local. Global shame is general; local shame is specific. The first permeates the self; the second is episodic and may reflect on one's self only superficially.

Defenders of the standard view treat shame as if it were always global, affecting one's whole self. Taylor says that "the self-directed adverse judgment in shame is always the same: that he is a lesser person than he should be" (77) and that shame is felt about "something which the agent thinks of great importance, of great value to himself and to the life he envisages himself as leading" (80). Deigh thinks that "shame . . . is felt upon discovery of shortcomings in oneself that falsify the worth one thought one had, [it] includes a sense that one lacks worth." Velleman claims that "the realm of privacy is the central arena for shame . . . because it is the central arena for threats to your standing as a social agent." And Williams writes that "in the experience of shame one's whole being seems diminished or lessened."[13] But these inflated claims do not fit feeling shame for forgetting one's mother's birthday or being bored by Proust.

Defenders of the standard view may respond by saying that local shame is really only embarrassment and that shame proper is always global. This strikes me as an attempt to save the standard view by arbitrarily rejecting counterexamples as illegitimate. The fact is that shame shades into embarrassment and it is often impossible to distinguish between them. The standard view should recognize that some experiences of shame are much more serious, much more degrading and self-diminishing than others.

One reason for doubting the standard view, then, is that it lacks the resources to distinguish between wrenching shame that destroys self-respect, less serious shame that has a lesser effect on self-respect, and shame that is just inappropriate. How could it be decided on the standard view whether it is appropriate to feel ashamed for inherited wealth, for falling short of desired perfection, for unintentionally harming someone, for nonculpably failing to discharge a significant obligation, or for lacking a skill that would have made an important moral difference in an emergency? The standard view offers no principled way of deciding when the feeling of shame is appropriate and when it is not, or of deciding whether the strength of appropriately felt shame is excessive, just right, or insufficient.

The standard view of shame as the emotion of self-protection is thus mistaken and, apart from that, too blunt a tool. It leaves unasked such surely important questions as whether part or the whole of the self needs protection; whether the self, or part of it, deserves protection; whether shame is the best way of protecting it; whether it is reasonable to be committed to the value whose violation causes shame; and whether there is a reasonable way of gauging how much, how strong, and how lasting shame is warranted. I am not saying that these questions cannot be answered, only that defenders of the standard view have not answered them. I now turn to a revised view that answers them and counters the other doubts about the standard view.

10.3 The Revised View

One of the remarkable stories Herodotus tells concerns Candaules, king of Lydia, his wife, the queen, and Gyges, the king's friend and adviser.[14] The king was so besotted by his wife's charms that he could not keep his great good fortune to himself. He bragged to Gyges about his marital bliss and bullied him to hide in their bedroom so that Gyges could have direct evidence of the queen's superior graces. Gyges was horrified:

"What an improper suggestion!" he said. But the king persisted: " 'off with her skirt, off with her shame'—you know what they say about women." Gyges pleaded: "Do not ask me to behave like a criminal." Kings have a way of prevailing, however, and Gyges finally did as he was told and hid in the bedroom. "Unluckily the queen saw him. At once she realized what her husband had done. But she did not betray the shame she felt by screaming, or even let it appear that she had noticed anything. Instead she silently resolved to have her revenge. For with the Lydians . . . it is thought highly indecent even for a man to be seen naked." Next day the queen summoned Gyges and said to him: "There are two courses open to you, and you may take your choice between them. Kill Candaules and seize the throne, with me as your wife; or die yourself on the spot, so that never again may your blind obedience to the king tempt you to see what you have no right to see. One of you must die: either my husband, the author of this wicked plot; or you who have outraged propriety by seeing me naked." Gyges chose to live; the next night he hid once again in the bedroom, but this time at the queen's behest, and killed Candaules. He succeeded him, married the queen, and reigned for thirty-eight years.

This story could be told from the point of view of each participant, and in each version shame would figure prominently. King Candaules was shameless; Gyges had a sense of shame, but he was not strong enough to act on it; and the queen, whose strength matched her charm, was moved by shame. I will concentrate on the queen's perspective. Her outrage was violent, majestic, and inexorable. But to understand why it was so extreme we need to understand its moral context. Viewed from our moral context, arranging the murder of her husband appears to be a disproportionately violent reaction to his vulgar sophomoric plot. She was certainly badly used, but not so badly as to call for blood. We can understand that Lydians are touchy about being seen naked, the queen was so seen, she was ashamed, and it would be proper for her to resent her husband, but that should be the end of it. Candaules certainly deserves censure, but in having him murdered, the queen greatly overreacted.

The inadequacy of this response results from a much too simple view of shame and of the queen's shame. It assumes that shame is caused by the violation of what I have called (in 9.4) peripheral commitments to such superficial values as propriety, seemliness, and good manners. This kind of shame—I will refer to it as *propriety-shame*—is rightly regarded as having only marginal moral importance. Propriety matters, but not very much. It belongs to a class of minor graces of which cheerfulness, amiability, and tact are other members. Good and evil, virtue and vice, right and wrong are too weighty to be brought to bear on propriety-shame. According to the simple view of shame, the queen's mistake was to inflate the importance of the relatively unimportant value of propriety. If she had a better sense of proportion, she would not have been driven by her justified propriety-shame to unjustified murder.

The queen's reaction will seem less excessive, however, if we understand that her moral context was not ours but the Lydians' and it led her to make a formative commitment (see 9.4) to propriety. She was not a superficial person who cared too much about appearances; rather, she saw living and acting with propriety as essential to her honor. Her dignity, status, and self-respect all depended on conformity to Lydian morality, which she had internalized so completely as to make it her personal morality. This does not mean that she conflated the public and the private. On the contrary, her honor was inseparably connected with maintaining their distinctness. In Lydian morality, there were activities proper to each sphere, and her formative commitment required that she should play the proper role and perform the proper actions in both spheres. The language of play, role, and performance should not lead to the suspicion that she was hypocritical or insincere. She was through and through—in public and in private—what it was proper for her to be and to act according to Lydian morality. That was the object of her formative commitment.

If her husband's plot is understood in terms of this moral context, it will be seen no longer as a violation of the queen's inflated sense of propriety, but as a serious attack on her honor, causing her indignity, loss of status, and self-respect. For it forced a situation on her in which the distinction between the private and the public was destroyed and she was doomed to violate her formative commitment. Candaules deliberately put her in that situation and caused her to be dishonored in her own eyes. I will call her shame, resulting from the violation of her formative commitment, *honor-shame*. It is a deeper and more significant emotion than propriety-shame.

But this is not all. The queen did not merely feel honor-shame. She also realized that her husband, by coercing her in this way, did not respect her, did not see how important it was to her to be true to her formative commitment to distinguishing what was proper in private and in public and to act according to propriety in both contexts. Her honor-shame and the resulting resentment at her husband for having caused it—remember his "off with her skirt, off with her shame"—jointly explain her outraged reaction. It will no longer seem excessive, then, especially not if we realize that it is cast in the heroic mold familiar to us from the literature of ancient Greece. The reactions of Achilles, Oedipus, Ajax, and Medea come from the same mold. Each was dishonored, felt the burn of honor-shame, and reacted with rage. The expression of honor-shame in dramatic action does not remove the shame, but it makes it easier to bear by dissipating the pent-up passion.

Our response to the queen's action, however, may still remain even if we understand all this and see the queen as acting in the Lydian moral context. We may continue to hold that there is something very wrong with Lydian morality since it turns propriety into a matter of honor and countenances murder for its violation. The queen ought to have seen the wrongness of that and ought not to have accepted Lydian morality as her personal morality. This response makes good sense to us, but it would not have made any sense to the queen. For it assumes that a distinction between personal morality and the morality of one's society has been drawn and that it is possible to evaluate social morality from the perspective of personal morality. We can certainly do that because we draw that distinction, but the queen could not. She had no morally acceptable option but to make Lydian social morality her personal morality, and this deprived her of the possibility of evaluating either from the perspective of the other. This is why the reaction that is available to us was not available to her.

It was not the queen's fault that she knew only one morality. In her moral context one either endeavored to act morally or not. The first required acting according to Lydian morality; the second led to immorality and ostracism from the society in terms of which its members conceived of a good life. In a sense this gave a choice to Lydians, but in another sense they had no choice at all since one alternative contained all that was valuable and the other involved forsaking it all. A consequence of living in such a moral context was that it left little scope for the development and use of disciplined imagination because the imaginable possibilities were extremely limited. This placed Lydians in a position similar to the one in which the queen placed Gyges. They could choose between the possibility of a good life and physical, or perhaps only social, death. The result was that they had little control over their lives and actions because many of their choices were among alternatives forced on them by the only morality they knew. If they were condemned by that morality, they could not reject or be indifferent to the condemnation because there was no other morality providing other possibilities of life that disciplined imagination might lead them to prefer to the one that condemned them.

Now contrast the queen's predicament with what Nietzsche says about Mirabeau, "who had no memory for insults and vile actions done to him and was unable to forgive simply because he—forgot. Such a man shakes off with a *single* shrug many vermin that eat deep into others. . . . That is the sign of strong, full natures in whom there is an excess of power to form, to recuperate and to forget."[15] Part of the limitation of the queen's formative commitment to Lydian social morality was that it left her no scope to develop and exercise a disciplined imagination through which she might have found a morally acceptable way of purging herself from the vermin in her soul. Her inability reflected the social morality of her society, which attributed a very high value to propriety, made honor depend on it, and lacked alternative values and alternative evaluations. The queen accepted this morality, but that very acceptance made it impossible for her to question it. For if one's personal morality is the prevailing social morality, then there is no moral basis for questioning the social morality.

The consequence of such a moral outlook is the impoverishment of life by the foreclosure of important possibilities. Questioning the prevailing morality becomes a sign of moral failure. For by questioning it one attacks the only available system of moral values. There is, therefore, no possibility of protesting against the moral status quo from the point of view of another moral outlook, for there is no other moral outlook available. There may be other outlooks, of course, but they either conform to the prevailing morality or, if they deviate from it, are unavoidably seen as immoral. Individuals in such a context must see their own dissatisfactions with the prevailing morality as a moral failure. Shame is symptomatic of the perception of that failure, and there is nowhere for the shame to go. Like vermin, it eats deeper and deeper into the soul. The moral reform that might remove the failure is inexpressible in morally acceptable terms. The self-destructive emotion of shame just sits there poisoning one's inner life and then suddenly explodes in some spectacular action, like the queen's revenge, Oedipus's self-blinding, Achilles' rage, Medea's murder of her children, or Ajax's crazed flagellation of cattle.

My claim is not that in such a context moral criticism of the prevailing morality is impossible. It was impossible for the queen and others, but it was not for Socrates, Plato, and Sophocles. It required exceptionally reflective people with exceptional intellectual and moral resources. If there were no such people, deep criticism of the moral outlook of a society would not be possible. But most people lack what exceptional ones have, and it would be a mistake to suppose that what is possible for a few is possible for many.

For the unexceptional ones, like the queen, the impoverishment that followed from their identification of personal and social morality meant that no room was left for a certain kind of excuse for failure. It made no difference to the queen's honor-shame that she had in no way contributed to the impropriety of being seen naked. The only thing that mattered was that she was so seen; her contrary intention was irrelevant. What counted was conformity to the recognized values; the reasons for failure to conform were beside the point. When well-trained moral agents fell short, they felt properly ashamed. They could not articulate, could not give moral weight to the fact that they were the victims of circumstances or of other people's plots and had no share in bringing about their failure. Once again, therefore, understandable frustration and bitterness were bound to pervade their lives and they were left with no morally acceptable way of coping with them.

Nietzsche's Mirabeau, by contrast, had such a way available to him. He could shrug off the insults that would have moved the queen to seek bloody revenge because he was able to draw the distinction between the social morality surrounding him and his personal morality. It was not so much that the distinction was based on his invention of values that were not present in the prevailing social morality. Few people can invent the values to which they commit themselves. What they can do, however, and what Nietzsche praises Mirabeau for having done, is to impose their own hierarchical ranking on the values they take over from their social morality and to which they commit themselves. Their morality is personal, then, because they make it so by the disciplined use of their imagination, through which they assign their own hierarchy of importance to some subset of the ambient social values. They can reflect on and decide which of their commitments are peripheral, formative, and deep. Their deep commitments are to values they prize above all others and from which they derive their sense of worth and self-respect. Their formative commitments are to the prevailing legal, political, aesthetic, professional, role- or employment-related, and similar other values in terms of which they relate to others and participate in the affairs of their society. And their peripheral commitments are to the more or less superficial customs, manners, and mores that help to make smooth the casual interactions of people living together in a society. Their commitments form a hierarchy that enables them to judge the respective importance of the values they hold and explain why one value is more or less important to them than another.

This hierarchy of commitments formed by the right use of disciplined imagination makes it possible for those who have them to juxtapose their personal evaluations to those that prevail in the surrounding social morality. They can say that the social morality is faulty because it attributes too much or too little importance to certain values; they can live and act according to an ideal of a good life that differs from those of others in their social context; and they can ignore insults, criticisms, and adverse evaluations that reflect a system of values they do not hold and therefore do not touch their self-respect. Through disciplined imagination Mirabeau had a moral possibility available to him that the queen lacked: to derive his self-respect from living and acting according to his personal morality, which he juxtaposed to the prevailing social morality. The queen could not do that because her personal morality was the social morality and her imagination was impoverished by the lack of possibilities. If she had rejected her social morality, she would have rejected morality, and she could not have derived her self-respect from another source because none was available to her.

This, of course, does not mean that Mirabeau and people in his position are immune to shame. He and they are just as vulnerable to it as the queen was, but the shame was neither propriety-shame nor honor-shame but what I will call *worth-shame*. Mirabeau could say that his social morality attributes much too great an importance to propriety, and he could refuse to see his honor in terms of the status, role, obligations, and privileges that the prevailing social morality assigned to him. His sense of worth was made possible by the work of his disciplined imagination, which led to the hierarchical structure of his commitments that constituted his personal morality. Whether he felt good or bad about his worth depended on whether he lived and acted in conformity to his structure of commitments. Self-respect followed from conforming to it, and worth-shame was a consequence of its violation.

Mirabeau had another possibility available to him that the queen lacked. If he could truthfully say that he had done what he could to conform to his commitments and he failed only because circumstances or other people prevented him, then he could excuse his failure and not allow it to affect his self-respect. What made this possible was that his worth depended on his own evaluations and not on those of others. He was in a position to know what others could not, namely, that he has been true to his commitments and it was not his fault that he failed to act according to them. The queen, once again, lacked this possibility because her truthful evaluations could not differ from those of others since they derived from the only available source: their shared social morality.

We are now in a position to understand why the revised view is an improvement over the standard view. By distinguishing among three kinds of shame and by correlating propriety-shame with peripheral commitments, honor-shame with formative commitments, and worth-shame with deep commitments, we can answer the questions to which the standard view gave unsatisfactory answers as well as those it left unanswered, or, indeed, unasked.

To begin with, shame is not the emotion of self-protection but the emotion of self-condemnation for having violated one's commitment. It is right to fear shame, not in order to protect one's self but to strengthen one's commitments to prized values. It is doubtful, however, whether the fear of shame is needed for this, because, as I will argue shortly, really prizing a value is enough to maintain a strong commitment to it, and that obviates the need to fear shame, and if one does not really prize a value, then one is unlikely to fear shame for violating it.

Next, the revised view makes it readily explainable why the emotion of shame varies in strength and how strong a shame is warranted for the violation of particular commitments. The appropriate strength of shame depends on the importance of the commitment whose violation causes the shame. As commitments become more important the closer connection they have to one's sense of worth, so the strength of shame for the violation of commitments increases.

The revised view also makes it possible to explain why feeling shame for the violation of a commitment may be inappropriate in some cases. People's commitments often conflict, and the conflict can often be resolved only by violating one of the conflicting commitments. If one violates a peripheral commitment because only that way can one honor a formative commitment, or if one violates a formative commitment in order to remain true to a deep commitment, then the violation is justified and feeling ashamed because of it is inappropriate. It is not shameful to be impolite to a pedophile or to abandon a political cause if continued adherence to it is incompatible with one's deepest values.

Nor is it difficult, given the revised view, to account for the fact that some experiences of shame are global and others local. The less important a violated commitment is, the more localized the shame caused by its violation is likely to be. Propriety-shame resulting from tactlessness, bad manners, or faux pas is unlikely to threaten one's honor, and honor-shame following from the violation of political, legal, aesthetic, or similar values is unlikely to threaten one's sense of worth if the violation is prompted by the belief that conformity would damage one's sense of worth. Only the violation of deep commitments will make the resulting worth-shame a global condemnation of one's self rather than condemnation of a localized aspect of it.

I conclude that the revised view offers a better analysis than the standard view. It is an advantage of this better analysis that it shows how reflective self-evaluation may lead to the self-transformation involved in moving from liability to superficial propriety-shame to vulnerability to a deeper worth-shame. This takes us from the periphery toward the core of our commitments, toward understanding what is more and what is less important to living a good life. Disciplined imagination is the means by which we work toward this deepening understanding. It helps us to correct the deceptions, illusions, and fantasies that prevent us from seeing what we might and perhaps ought to be and helps us to explore realistically what possibilities leading to a good life may be open to us given our character and circumstances.

10.4 Doubts about the Revised View

From the analysis of shame I now turn to its evaluation. There is widespread agreement that shame is a positive moral force. Taylor thinks that it "protects the self from . . . corruption and ultimately extinction" (81); Deigh believes that shame "protects one from appearing to be an unworthy creature"; Helen Merrell Lynd claims that "if experiences of shame can be fully faced, if we allow ourselves to realize their import, they can inform the self, and become a revelation of oneself, of one's society, and of the human situation"; Herbert Morris says that "shame leads to creativity"; Williams writes that "shame continues to work for us, as it worked for the Greeks, in essential ways by giving through the emotions a sense of who one is and of what one hopes to be."[16] The thought behind these favorable evaluations is that shame is an emotion that forcibly brings to our attention the values we hold and motivates us to avoid violating them in the future. As Taylor says, "if someone has self-respect then under specifiable conditions he will be feeling shame. . . . The close connection between these makes it clear why shame is often thought to be valuable" (80).

These favorable evaluations of shame are mistaken. There is a close connection between self-respect and shame, but it is like the connection between the heart and heart attacks. Having a heart makes one vulnerable to heart attacks; that, however, hardly warrants a favorable evaluation of heart attacks. Shame is a painful, disturbing emotion of self-condemnation that results from the realization that we have violated a commitment to a prized value. It thus inflicts on us the moral equivalent of double jeopardy. It is bad enough to realize that we have acted deplorably; shame, however, makes it worse by adding a second bad feeling to the one we already have. I do not see how this second feeling could be valuable. It might be valuable if it brought home to us the fact that we have acted badly. But we must already know that, since otherwise we would not feel ashamed. The second bad feeling, therefore, merely makes an already bad situation worse.

Defenders of shame might respond by pointing at the self-transformation and moral progress that shame might produce. This is perhaps the central issue in the evaluation of shame, and it is crucial to be clear about it. My view is that defenders of shame are right in stressing the importance of the self-transformation and moral progress that may follow from the realization of moral failure, but they are wrong to suppose that shame is a good means to them.

Consider first what defenders and critics of shame may agree about. In propriety-shame we care about appearances; in honor-shame we care about appearing as we are; in worth-shame we care about being in a certain way and we do not care about appearances. The movement is from caring about how we seem to caring about how we are. Since our control over the private sphere is always greater than over the public one, a moral orientation that concentrates on the private sphere is more likely to lead to good lives than others. The movement from propriety-shame to honor-shame to worth-shame is toward greater concentration on the private. This increases the area of our control, improves our chances of living a good life, and thus constitutes moral progress. None of this is meant to suggest that things cannot go wrong. We can misuse the control we have or progress toward a misguided ideal of a good life. Good lives depend on many things: one is having sufficient control over our commitments; another is having morally acceptable and fulfilling commitments. Normally, both are necessary and neither is sufficient.

Defenders and critics of shame as an important moral force can agree, I think, about this internal evaluation of different kinds of shame. But I now go on to an external evaluation of shame itself, and here defenders and critics part company. My claim is that the reasons for regarding the movement from propriety-shame to worth-shame as moral progress are also reasons for regarding the movement away from all kinds of shame as moral progress.

There was a time when the prevailing wisdom in one dominant school of medicine was to treat illness by administering mild doses of poison as antidotes. It was thought that judiciously selected poisons would counteract the poisons that caused the illness and thus cure it. This worked for some illnesses, but it was eventually found that the treatment considerably weakened patients and left a residue of poisons with which they had to contend in a weakened state.[17] My doubts about shame are analogous: it weakens us when we have already been weakened by the realization of our moral failure, and it leaves a residue that worsens the sense of failure with which we have to contend. But why does shame weaken us?

To begin with the obvious: shame is a bad feeling. It is not just painful; the pain it makes us feel is on account of our own deficiencies and undermines our self-respect. It may be thought, as Taylor does, that the pain of shame is morally good: "if someone has self-respect then under specifiable conditions he will be feeling shame. . . . Loss of self-respect and loss of the capacity to feel shame go hand in hand. . . . A sense of value is necessary for self-respect and so for shame, so that whatever else may be wrong about the person feeling shame he will at least have retained a sense of value. . . . [It] protects the self from what in the agent's own eyes is corruption and ultimately extinction" (80–81). There are several reasons for doubting these claims.

First, it is true that shamelessness is bad and self-respect is good, but shame is not the only alternative to shamelessness. Being angry at ourselves, resolving to improve, desiring to make amends, trying to understand why we failed, reaffirming our commitment to the value we have violated are some other possible reactions. Just because we do not feel shame at our acknowledged moral failure does not mean that we are bound to lack self-respect. We may sustain self-respect in other ways.

Second, the protection against the corruption and the extinction of the self that shame allegedly provides may be forward- or backward-looking. If it is forward-looking, it is supposed to protect us from acting shamefully in the future. But it cannot be shame that protects us, since the wrong act is in the future and we cannot be ashamed of it before it happens. The best that can be said is that the protection is provided by the fear of shame, not shame itself. But why should fear be necessary at all, and if it is fear, why should it be of shame? We can be deterred from future wrongdoing by self-respect itself, by understanding the consequences of wrong actions for others, or by pride, vanity, kindness, decency, and so on. And if we have fear as a deterrent, then fear of punishment, fear of loss of love, respect, or status may serve just as well as fear of shame.

If the alleged protection provided by shame is backward-looking, concerning the wrong we have already done, then, once again, it cannot protect the self from corruption and extinction. For such corruption as there is has already set in, as shown by the wrong we have done. We may acknowledge the wrong, but there is no reason to suppose that unless the acknowledgment elicits shame, we will be incapable of limiting or remedying the corruption. Not to acknowledge corruption is certainly worse than acknowledging it, but the acknowledgment may prompt many morally acceptable reactions other than shame.

As for the extinction of the self, it would seem that shame makes it more, not less, likely. Recall how Mirabeau's capacity for shame was an improvement over the queen's, as well as over Oedipus's, Achilles', Medea's, and Ajax's. Their honor-shame had no outlet, they had no way to undo the dishonor, regardless of whether they were to blame. When a likely target appeared in the form of someone they may have had some reason to resent, they reacted to their hapless target with inhuman rage, as the queen did in murdering her husband, Oedipus in blinding himself, Achilles in humiliating Hector, Medea in murdering her children, and Ajax in flogging cattle. Mirabeau would have been in a somewhat better position because his shame would have been worth-shame and he could have disregarded what others thought if he knew he was blameless. But if he had violated his values and felt worth-shame, he would have been as badly off as the queen and the others. All forms of shame involve personal failure. Those who feel it have been counted and found, in their own eyes, wanting. The causes of their shame may be different, but their feelings are the same: diminished self-respect, self-condemnation, and distrust of their own motives and judgments. The stronger shame is, the more it threatens the self. Taylor says that shame protects the self from extinction because it shows that its subjects have retained a sense of values. But since in feeling ashamed we use the retained values for self-condemnation, shame undermines, rather than protects, the self.

If we are to live a good life, we must have a robust self capable of living it. We must be able to make more or less detached decisions, withstand adversity, and have strength, confidence, and integrity. Shame undermines all this and weakens the self, and that is why self-transformation and moral progress consist not merely in developing from propriety-shame through honor-shame to worth-shame, and thereby growing in independence and control, but also in moving beyond worth-shame to less destructive responses to the recognition of our moral failure.

This is missed by defenders of a favorable evaluation of shame. Morris, for instance, thinks that in "feeling shame because of what we have done, we actually see ourselves as shameful persons and the steps that are appropriate to relieve shame are becoming a person that is not shameful. Shame leads to creativity."[18] But why would it lead to creativity rather than to self-loathing? How could we take the appropriate steps to relieve shame when it is the nature of shame to make us doubt, suspect, and denigrate our self, the only agency capable of taking those steps? Where do the energy, the confidence, the moral aspiration come from when it is the consequence of shame to sap them? Our moral economy is such that the more intensely we feel shame, the less capable we are likely to be of the effort required for reform.

I want to guard against a possible way of misunderstanding the case I have been making against shame. There is no doubt that those who are incapable of feeling shame are morally deficient. If we have self-respect, then we must mind violating it. Shame is a primitive, elemental reaction to our moral failure. If we truly love someone, have deeply identified with a cause, have made a basic commitment to truth, justice, or loyalty, and realize that we have betrayed it, blaming ourselves is an inexorable consequence. Shame is the name for this self-blame. What I have been saying is that our reaction to moral failure need not be primitive. We can interpose reflection between our failure and our reaction to it. The point of this kind of reflection is not to lessen our sense of the wrong we have done but to consider whether there might not be a better response to it than shame.

Through reflection we might recognize that the world has not come to an end; we have other responsibilities; life must go on; and we need to have enough strength to go on. Inflicting on ourselves the psychological equivalent of flogging will sap our remaining strength. If reflection makes it possible to distance ourselves from what we have done, to look at it as dispassionately as we can manage under the circumstances, then we will be able to see that there are reasonable reactions other than shame to our acknowledged failure. If through reflection we come to this recognition, then we will try to cultivate other reactions that do not weaken even further our already sapped strength.

I have been making a case for the availability of these other and better reactions. I readily acknowledge that my recommended alternatives make moral sense only in the case of those who have a capacity for shame. I am not denying or minimizing the importance of recognizing the wrong one has done. I am recommending for those who have a capacity for shame the cultivation of a less self-destructive capacity as a substitute response to their moral failure. I say a little more below about how that substitute response may be cultivated.

It may be thought that arguments for or against shame are pointless because feelings of shame are not under voluntary control. Shame may or may not assail us, but in either case there is nothing we can do about it. This is not so. It is true that we do not have direct control over shame because we cannot decide to have it or not to have it. But we do have indirect control over it because once we have it we can decide to cultivate or minimize it, strengthen or weaken it, and attribute more or less importance to it. I turn now to how this can and should be done.

10.5 Shame and the Balanced Ideal

The approximation of the balanced ideal depends on maintaining two kinds of balance. One is between backward- and forward-looking requirements of self-transformation: between correcting one's tendencies that have caused the misinterpretation of past possibilities and exploring realistically future possibilities for a fulfilling and responsible life. The correction makes realistic exploration possible, and the exploration makes correction highly desirable. The other is between the cognitive, emotive, and motivational components of the psychological states and processes that constitute the self. The balance aims at a substantial degree of coherence among these components, thereby preventing any one of them from regularly dominating the others. If the disciplined imagination works well, both kinds of balance are maintained and the reflective purity I discussed in the preceding chapter follows. Shame upsets both kinds of balance, and that is the basic reason for the doubts I have expressed about its favorable evaluation. Seeing why shame leads to these imbalances will readily point to a better response to one's moral failure.

Shame upsets the first kind of balance by dwelling on the past at the expense of the future. It forces our attention on having violated a commitment to a prized value, and it relegates to the periphery the desirability of the value. It makes us focus on our deficiency, at the expense of the reasons for overcoming it; on the failure in the past, at the expense of a promise for the future; on regretting a loss, at the expense of working for a gain. Shame upsets the second kind of balance because its emotive component overwhelms its cognitive and motivational components. It wallows in the feeling of self-condemnation and squelches beliefs and motives about the possibility of rectification and improvement. Shame is thus an obstacle to self-transformation and the disciplined use of the imagination that might improve our lives. But what better response is there to moral failure, and do the imbalances caused by shame point to it?

It is essential to shame that we compare how we are to how we are committed to being and find that we have fallen short. Once we have accepted this, we can direct our attention away from the failure toward another object. We can refuse to dwell on the feeling, relegate it to the background, and deliberately hold this other object in the focus of our attention. Shame is an insistent feeling, however, so this other object on which we might focus in preference to shame must have sufficient importance to counteract the pressure of shame to reclaim center stage. The object that is bound to have that importance is the value to which we have committed ourselves and failed to achieve. The intensity of shame partly depends on how much we mind our failure; the more intense the shame is, the more important we must find the value we have failed to achieve. Shame, therefore, always points toward a better, less self-destructive response to failure. The better response is to remind ourselves of the importance we believe the failed value has. By focusing on that belief, we move away from dwelling on the failure and motivate ourselves to do what we can to prevent failure in the future. We thus redress the imbalance by stressing the importance of the mooted future and of previously overwhelmed cognitive and motivational considerations. As we succeed, so we bring shame under control and enable ourselves to find a better response to our moral failure.

Achieving this control is difficult. It requires a great conscious effort to distance ourselves from a usually intense feeling. Whether we succeed depends on many things particular to our character and circumstances. But there are two general considerations I want to mention in closing. One is that the feeling from which we need to distance ourselves is bad, and few of us would not want to free ourselves from it if we could. But if the arguments I have given are correct, then we can do that in the case of shame by remembering the importance of the value we have violated. So a response better than shame is always available.

The other general consideration is that we are all influenced by the moral outlook prevailing in our society. Whether we respond to moral fail-

ure by feeling shame or by redoubling the effort to be true to our commitment to the value we have failed depends partly on how shame is regarded
in our society. Part of moral education is to inculcate responses to failure.
It is an implication of the revised view of shame I have been defending
that the morality of a society is better if it lays little stress on shame, which
undermines the self, and great stress on the desirability of the values to
which we have committed ourselves. For societies, as for individuals, part
of moral progress is to rely less on blame, in one form or another, and
more on the hope for a better future. This is not to recommend shamelessness but to recognize that shamelessness being bad does not make
shame good.

CHAPTER 11

The Hardest Service

At every step one has to wrestle for truth; one has to surrender
for it almost everything to which the heart, to which our love,
our trust in life, cling otherwise. That requires greatness of soul:
the service of truth is the hardest service. What does it mean,
after all, to have *integrity* in matters of the spirit? That one is
severe against one's heart, that one despises "beautiful
sentiments," that one makes of every Yes and No a matter of
conscience.

—FRIEDRICH NIETZSCHE, *The Antichrist*

11.1 Reason and Reflective Self-Evaluation

The service of truth is the hardest because it requires severity
about the promptings of the heart. There are, of course, truths in many
areas where the heart is involved only negligibly, if at all. Truths often can
and ought to be pursued impersonally, dispassionately, disinterestedly, but
truths about oneself neither can nor ought to be. The heart is unavoidably
involved because we have hopes, fears, illusions, and a need to think well
of and feel good about ourselves. We have to be severe about the promptings of our hearts because we have a vested interest in not facing unpleasant truths that shatter the comforting stories we tell ourselves about ourselves. But if we do not want to perpetuate past mistakes and misjudge
future possibilities, it is also in our interest to face such unpleasant truths
and construct stories based on facts, not on what we wish were facts.

We normally have, therefore, both incentives and disincentives to undertake this hardest of services. The disincentives may be stronger if the
external or internal conditions of life are precarious and facing unpleasant truths makes them worse. But facing them may also make life better

because the precariousness of conditions is often the effect of just those unpleasant truths that we are not severe enough to face. Judging the respective weight of these incentives and disincentives, forming a realistic view of the conditions of our lives, evaluating the reliability of our relevant decisions are difficult and the results are fallible. And even if the incentives prove stronger, the pursuit of truths that subvert our comforting view of ourselves remains difficult, as we have seen in the various cases discussed up to now. Nevertheless, we cannot overcome dissatisfactions with our lives if we do not acquire and face the truths about their causes. We can do this by making use of a particular conception of reason. I have appealed to this conception throughout the argument, but I have left its substantive content implicit. The aim of this chapter is to make it explicit.

The first step toward this end is to make clear how reason is connected with what I have been saying about reflective self-evaluation, disciplined imagination, and the balanced ideal. Through reflective self-evaluation we increase control over our lives and decrease the extent to which we are at the mercy of contingency. This makes life better by making it more responsible and more fulfilling. Living responsibly involves protecting the minimum conditions of all good lives. Reason obviously favors this since the good lives thus enabled include our own and the lives of those we care about.

The key to a fulfilling life is to correct our past mistakes and explore future possibilities. Corrective imagination aims at the first, exploratory imagination aims at the second, and disciplined imagination combines the two. Disciplined imagination thus enlarges life by leading to a more realistic view of our limits and possibilities. If done well, disciplined imagination brings the possibilities we recognize closer to what is personally and socially possible for us in the context formed of our character and circumstances. The connection between a fulfilling life and reason is that it is by following reason that the disciplined imagination leads to a more realistic view of what we can and cannot do to make our lives better.

The possibility of making progress toward a more realistic view also connects reason and the balanced ideal. The balanced ideal is to have an integrated self. This requires a substantial degree of coherence among the beliefs, emotions, and desires involved in important decisions about how we live. A fragmented self is incoherent because its beliefs, emotions, and desires prompt different, often inconsistent, actions. The inevitable consequence is that one or another aspect of the self dominates over the others and the dominated ones are frustrated. A fragmented self, therefore, leads us to act in ways contrary to our beliefs or emotions or desires, and thus dooms to frustration some essential aspect of our self. Reason aims to prevent this from happening by balancing the beliefs, emotions, and desires that have an important bearing on how we live. The common defect of the Promethean, aesthetic, and transcendental forms of romanticism I have been criticizing is that they are alike in advocating that one aspect of the self should dominate the others. Regardless of what that aspect is, fragmentation of the self follows. Reason and romanticism thus lead in opposite directions: reason to the balanced ideal, romanticism to incoherence produced by imbalance.

Reason is connected also with what I have been saying about moral progress in the two immediately preceding chapters. The discussion of purity was intended as a concrete illustration of how disciplined imagination can lead to moral progress. I argued that it involves the transformation of the contingent self with which we all start out in life into a deliberate self constituted partly of the hierarchy of our commitments. Coming to know these commitments and their respective importance leads us from prereflective to reflective purity, from the innocence of an unexamined first nature to the integrity of a reflectively formed second nature. This self-transformation is one kind of moral progress, and it is made possible by the use of reason for evaluating our commitments.

Another concrete illustration of moral progress and the use of reason was the discussion of shame. It involved going from a bad response to increasingly better responses to our failure to live up to our commitments. Shame is a bad response because it weakens our chances to live a good life by weakening the self, which must be strong to achieve the life we want. Reason moves societies and individuals toward the better response of reaffirming the attractions of the life we want to but failed to achieve. The movement from denigrating the self toward strengthening its commitments constitutes another form of moral progress that reason makes possible.

The task before us now is to make explicit the conception of reason that makes it reasonable to perform the hardest service of facing unpleasant truths about ourselves, forming a more realistic view of our limits and possibilities, developing a better integrated self, and progressing toward the balanced ideal.

11.2 The Uses of Reason

Reason has many uses and I doubt that it is desirable or possible to list all of them. Even if one constructed a very long list including many uses, it could not be shown that the list was complete. In any case, my purpose is not to draw up such a list but to discuss only four pairs of contrasting uses. This will be sufficient for making explicit the substantive content of the conception of reason that so far has been only implicit.

There are, to begin with, theoretical and practical uses of reason. Its theoretical use aims at true beliefs; its practical use aims at successful actions. The two overlap but also diverge. They overlap because successful actions often depend on true beliefs, and forming true beliefs often depends on successful action. But these two uses also diverge because there are many true beliefs (for example, about the codes spies used in the Napoleonic Wars or the mating habits of seagulls) that normally have no implication for successful action. And successful actions often involve no beliefs (such as waking up at the usual time or forming sentences in one's native language) or even false beliefs (as did Columbus's discovery of America or buying the winning lottery ticket because, since the drawing fell on his birthday, the buyer was certain he will win).

Reason also has universal and particular uses. Its universal use aims at beliefs that are true and actions that are successful in all contexts. It is a universally true belief that all human beings will die or that water is composed of hydrogen and oxygen, regardless of who holds it in what circumstances. And prolonged fasting will always lead to weight loss for everyone regardless of the prevailing religious, political, or economic conditions. The particular use of reason, on the other hand, aims at beliefs or actions whose truth or success depends on the context. The truth of the belief that chastity is prudent depends on whether it was held before or after effective contraception became easily available. And whether marriage will succeed in making the partners happier depends, among other things, on their personal histories, their compatibility, and the strength of their reciprocal affection, all of which vary with couples.

A third pair is the genetic and justifying uses of reason. The genetic use is to form beliefs as the outcome of certain processes—such as thinking, calculating, experimenting, judging, analyzing—that may collectively be called reasoning, and not as the outcome of emotion, intuition, inspiration, faith, fantasy, and the like. The justifying use has to do with accepting beliefs only if they pass certain tests: conform to logic, take account of all relevant facts, withstand criticism, and so forth. The genetic use is concerned with the formation of beliefs, the justifying use with their testing. The first concentrates on what is done before beliefs are formed, the second on what is done afterward. These two uses also overlap and diverge. Beliefs arrived at by reasoning are more likely to be justified by the tests than beliefs formed on the basis of other processes. Consequently, the genetic and the justifying uses may yield the same result. Or they may not because even excellent reasoning may lead to beliefs that fail the tests of justification, as we know from the fate of Ptolemaic astronomy and Newtonian physics. And beliefs may pass the tests even if they are the outcome of emotions (such as trusting someone because of love even though reasoning points in the other direction) or of hunches, sudden insights, or lucky guesses (as were many important scientific discoveries).

The last contrasting pair is the requiring and the permitting uses of reason. There are many beliefs and actions that those committed to reason must hold or violate their commitment. Beliefs vouchsafed by logic (modus ponens), mathematics ($a \times b = b \times a$), extensive experimental confirmation (germ theory of disease), or universal human experience (having a head) are required by reason. The same holds for some actions. One must breathe and eat in order to live, use signs of some sort to communicate with others, sleep from time to time, and so forth. It is unreasonable always, everywhere, for everyone to deny the truth of such beliefs or the necessity of such actions. Or, to put it differently, reason forbids denying them. There are also many beliefs and actions that reason neither requires nor forbids. Such beliefs and actions are permitted by reason. Reason permits believing that human beings are basically good, or bad, or ambivalent; that politics drives economics, or vice versa; or that there is or there is not intelligent life elsewhere in the universe. Reason also permits actions that conform to or violate the Ten Commandments; involve or refrain from taking risks, like cigarette smoking, sunbathing, or soldiering; or participate in or shun commercial activities, such as shopping, advertising, or bargaining. The only alternative to believing or doing what reason requires is to be unreasonable, but there are many alternative beliefs and actions that are permitted by reason. Not to hold a belief or perform an action that reason permits need not be unreasonable, but it is unreasonable not to hold or perform it if reason requires it.

All these uses of reason are legitimate, as I hope the examples show. They are also all fallible because the users are human beings who can and often do make mistakes. The causes of such mistakes are even more numerous than the uses of reason because there are more ways of failing than of succeeding. The process by which beliefs are formed may be misused, the tests by which beliefs are justified may be misapplied, what are taken to be relevant facts may not be relevant or facts, and so forth. The same holds for actions. The goals they succeed in achieving may be unreasonable, the cost of success may be too high, the importance attributed to succeeding in some particular way may be too great or too small, and so on. Defenders of reason should acknowledge all this. The strength of their position is that regardless of the fallibility of the uses of reason, reason is more likely to lead to true beliefs and successful actions than anything else. The human effort to cope with the world has so far found no more reliable means and many less reliable ones. This much, I think, is true.

It is unfortunately also true that when reason is actually put to work, only some of its many uses are regarded as legitimate. It would be instructive to examine the works of great defenders of reason by asking which uses of it they were defending and which they were denigrating. Although this is a digression from my present task, an example might help to show what I have in mind. It is widely believed that reason is valuable only if it is put to theoretical, universal, and requiring uses. Reason, then, will yield true beliefs that everyone must accept or be unreasonable. And, of course, the paradigm of such uses of reason is science. Now the trouble with this is not that these uses of reason are not important and valuable. Of course they are both. The trouble is that such uses are regarded as the ideal of which other uses fall so far short as to be recognizable only as pathetically inept attempts to approximate the ideal. The practical, particular, permitting uses of reason, then, are thought to lead to beliefs whose truth is questionable or insignificant and to actions whose success is doubtful or unimportant. From which the absurdity follows that human activities such as poetry, drama, music, morality, politics, and history, in which reason is used in these supposedly pathetic ways, should either become much more scientific than they currently are or be seen as feeble attempts to provide true beliefs and successful actions that science can much more reliably deliver. This, to put it mildly, impoverishes human life by denigrating valuable parts of it whose importance is no less than that of science.

11.3 Reason in Reflective Self-Evaluation

My present concern, however, is not with the misuse of reason but with making explicit the conception of reason to which I have appealed throughout the book. This conception is constituted of the practical, particular, and permitting uses of reason, as well as both its genetic and justifying uses. This is the conception involved in the work of disciplined imagination by means of which reflective self-evaluation can be reasonably conducted and by means of which the integrated self of the balanced ideal can be reasonably pursued.

The use of reason in reflective self-evaluation is practical rather than theoretical because its aim is to discover what should be done to make life better. And that, as we have seen, involves the correction of past mistakes and the exploration of future possibilities by the disciplined imagination. The root cause of past mistakes is a self fragmented in some way, and their correction involves the transformation of the self to make it better integrated. The better integrated the self becomes, the closer it approximates the balanced ideal. The exploration of future possibilities aims at reducing the gap between the possibilities that are recognized and the possibilities that are in fact personally and socially available, given one's character and context. The less difference there is between the possibilities one thinks one has and the possibilities one actually has, the more realistic is the emerging view of what one might do to make life better.

To say that this use of reason is practical is not to deny that true beliefs about one's mistakes and possibilities are indispensable to it. It is to say, rather, that true beliefs are sought not for their own sake but for the sake of guiding what should be done to make life better. This use of reason is practical, therefore, because true beliefs are sought as means to actions that transform the self in the right way.

The use of reason in reflective self-evaluation is also particular rather than universal because different people must do very different things to make life better. Everyone has to correct past mistakes and explore future possibilities, but the mistakes and the possibilities vary from person to person. Even if we all make mistakes as a result of false beliefs, inappropriate emotions, or misdirected desires, or as a result of allowing the cognitive, emotive, or volitional aspect of the self to regularly override the others and thus fragment the self, we still differ about the specific mistakes we have made and the specific ways in which our self is fragmented. The same is true of the exploration of possibilities. There cannot be many people whose view of their possibilities is completely realistic. There is always a gap between what we think and what is possible for us. But the specific possibilities we think are open, those that actually are open, and the nature and size of the gap between them vary with individuals. There is, therefore, no universal answer to the question what can I do make my life better. There always are specific things that any of us can do, but what that is differs from person to person.

That this use of reason must be particular does not mean that its universal use is irrelevant to reflective self-evaluation and disciplined imagination. It means rather that its universal use can provide, at best, only minimal guidance about what we can do. It is universally reasonable for all human beings to correct their mistakes and explore their possibilities realistically, but this says very little unless it is combined with the identification of specific mistakes and possibilities, and for that the particular use of reason is needed. It is also universally reasonable to believe that reflective self-evaluation depends on such mundane matters as having enough to eat, being at least moderately intelligent, and not living in a state of terror, but these truisms provide very much less than what is needed to conduct reflective self-evaluation reasonably. The more that is needed can be provided only by the particular use of reason.

The third use of reason in reflective self-evaluation is the permitting, as opposed to the requiring, one. What this amounts to is perhaps best explained by the distinction between moral necessity and moral possibility (in 1.3). Moral necessity concerns limits that protect minimum conditions required by all forms of good life. The question I have been concerned with throughout the book is, assuming that the minimum conditions are met, what individuals can do to make their lives better, in the context of reflective self-evaluation and the domain of moral possibility. In this context individuals have numerous possibilities open to them, and their task is to decide which they should pursue. I have been examining reflective self-evaluation because it is perhaps the most widely accepted ideal in contemporary Western societies for making such decisions. The decisions, then, concern possible ways of living, each one of which is permitted by reason and none of which is required by it. Such decisions may be better or worse, and the permitting use of reason is concerned with making them better. This depends on forming a realistic view of what it would be like to live according to particular possibilities one recognizes as available; how satisfying it would be for one to live that way, given one's history, experiences, character, beliefs, emotions, and desires; and whether there is a sufficiently close fit between a particular recognized possibility and the overall view one has formed of oneself.

The decisions reached about such matters may be more or less reasonable. The work of disciplined imagination is to make them as reasonable as possible. This, as we have seen, depends on correcting mistakes one has made in the past and exploring possibilities that may be pursued in the future. Imagination is disciplined, however, not merely by performing these backward- and forward-looking activities, but by performing them so as to reciprocally reinforce each other and thus make the resulting decisions more realistic. This happens if the point of correction is to avoid repeating mistakes that would lead exploration astray and if the point of exploration is to live a more satisfying life than one has managed to live in the past.

It is obvious, I hope, that reasoning in this way is practical (because individuals have to decide which among their reasonable possibilities to *act* on), particular (because *individuals* have to decide which among their reasonable possibilities to act on), and permitting (because individuals have to decide which among their *reasonable possibilities* to act on). All this, however, leaves open the question of how such decisions could be made reasonably. I have been arguing that individuals should rely on their disciplined imagination to make them, but I have so far said little about how to distinguish better and worse results prompted by disciplined imagination. This brings us to the final component of the conception of reason I have been appealing to in discussing reflective self-evaluation: the genetic and justifying uses of reason.

11.4 Wrestling with Truth

I will argue that both the genetic and the justifying uses of reason are essential to reflective self-evaluation. The argument, however, needs to be made concrete, and I will make it so with the help of Arthur Koestler's novel *Arrival and Departure*.[1] The novel's central figure is Peter, a young man of twenty-two, who arrives in a country Koestler calls Neutralia during the darkest days of World War II, when the Nazis occupied much of Europe and only England stood against them, for America has not yet entered the war. Peter is a hero of the anti-Nazi resistance of his country, not because of what he did but because of what he did not do. What he did was to take part in an ineffective resistance group, distributing flyers that accomplished nothing. He was soon caught and tortured as severely as his captors knew how. What he did not do was to give away information that in any way compromised the resistance. He, unlike other victims of torture, remained silent and betrayed no one. He did not give in, although he understood that the resistance was useless and he was offered safe conduct out of the country in exchange for telling what he knew. His torturers were not really interested in the information he had since the resistance group was full of informers; what they cared about was breaking him and depriving the resistance movement of heroes. But Peter did not break. His torturers eventually gave up and jailed him, and he escaped to Neutralia with all this behind him.

Because he is in Neutralia illegally, he has to leave and face the question of where to go. There are two realistic possibilities: he can go to England and join the English forces fighting against the Nazis, or he can go to America, where financial support and the chance to continue his interrupted university education await him. (Those reminded of Sartre's young man facing a not too dissimilar choice should bear in mind that Koestler's book was published several years before Sartre's.) Peter thinks he is quite clear that the choice he has to make is between a life of risk and hardship and a life of security and promise. He knows firsthand how evil Nazism is, but he knows as well that he has already done more than his duty in opposing it. It makes his choice even more acute that he and a young woman fall in love. She leaves for America and wants him to follow. But he also remembers vividly the evils of the transports taking Jews to their deaths (he is not Jewish), the murders and tortures he witnessed, and the viciousness of his interrogators and torturers. And so Peter agonizes over the choice he has to make. The horrors he lived through haunt him, he is sleepless because of recurrent nightmares, and, unsurprisingly, he falls ill. His illness is psychosomatic, a commonplace of psychopathology: it takes the symbolic form of losing the use of his legs. He cannot walk because he does not know which way to walk. This, in turn, precipitates a deep depression, and Peter has not the will to get out of it.

A sympathetic psychoanalyst takes charge and gets Peter to talk. Under her direction Peter works his way back through his recent to his more remote past. This is the first time he talks about it to anyone. He tries to understand himself, why he made the choices he made, why he joined the resistance, why he was able to withstand torture, and why he is now paralyzed in face of the choice he has to make. He is finally led back to a half-forgotten childhood accident in which he blinded and killed his younger brother, of whom he was jealous. He was not blamed—who indeed could blame a barely four-year-old child?—but he nevertheless felt guilty. The unassuaged guilt formed the unconscious undercurrent of his life. Unknown to himself, he wanted to be punished. This unconscious wish influenced his choices and made him take unnecessary risks, and when he was caught and tortured, he got his wish. He withstood torture because he felt he was getting what he deserved. The extreme pain was redeeming him by lifting the burden of guilt he had carried since the accident. Peter comes to understand that he was not the hero of the resistance but the actor in the melodrama of his life, in which the resistance was merely a stage prop enabling the action to unfold.

Although this is not the end of Peter's story, we might pause to note some points that have already emerged from it. We can see, to begin with, that the service of truth is indeed hard, for it is impossible not to sympathize with poor intrepid Peter. His search for truth led him to realize that his heroism under torture was motivated by a quixotic delusion. He came to see that he was deluded in both his conscious and unconscious processes. He was wrong to believe that loyalty to the resistance motivated him when in fact it was his supposed guilt. And he was wrong to feel guilty because a four-year-old child cannot be reasonably blamed for causing the accident, which really was just an accident. Peter has brought his pains upon himself. He suffered greatly but needlessly. The truth he found disclosed that he was a fool and acted foolishly. It is no doubt also true that although the truth he found was hard to bear, he is likely to have a better life in the future as a result of having found it. But since we may all find such hard truths about ourselves, countless people are reluctant to seek them too ardently. Their disinclination is not perverse, merely imprudent in the long run.

The second point that emerges from the story is that with the help of his psychoanalyst Peter found the truth through what I have called the genetic use of reason. This is the endeavor to establish whether one's beliefs, emotions, and desires are reasonable by understanding the process whose results they are. It is to ask and answer the question of why one has the beliefs, emotions, and desires one has rather than others one might have had. The motivation for the genetic use of reason is dissatisfaction with one's life, and the source of the dissatisfaction is often the fragmentation of one's beliefs, emotions, and desires. One does not know what to do because whatever one does will be contrary to one's beliefs or emotions or desires. One will have good reasons to act by following the promptings of any one of them, and one will have equally good reasons not to act on any of their promptings.

Peter's paralysis was an extreme consequence of the fragmentation of his self. The genetic use of reason enabled him to understand why the fragmentation occurred, and it pointed toward the means of correcting it. He understood that his desire for punishment was misguided, his feeling of guilt inappropriate, and many of his beliefs about himself false. And this understanding, of course, is just what the corrective imagination is meant to yield. We can thus see the intimate connection between the genetic use of reason and the corrective imagination.

Let us now return to the interrupted story. Having understood what led to his paralysis, Peter regains the use of his legs. He is no longer motivated by guilt, he no longer seeks punishment, and he decides to go to America and resume his happy love affair and university education. He embarks on the ship that is ready to sail, but in the last moment he realizes that he cannot carry out the decision he has made. He must go to England and fight the evils of Nazism, and he knows better than most the risks he will thereby take. And that is what he does. The story ends as Peter is on a plane preparing to parachute into the country from which he escaped to Neutralia and resume his work for the resistance there.

The second part of the story brings us to the justifying use of reason and the exploratory imagination. We are brought to them because the story shows that the genetic use of reason and corrective imagination, although necessary, are not sufficient for understanding the truth about oneself. If they were sufficient, Peter would go to America, but since he did not because he could not make himself, more needs to be said to understand why he could not.

The genetic use of reason, corrective imagination, and psychoanalytic help enabled Peter to understand that his motive for resisting the Nazi evil was misguided. This shows that Peter had been unreasonable, but it does not show that resisting the Nazi evil was unreasonable. There may have been good reasons for doing that even if Peter did not do it for those reasons. This is precisely the point at which the genetic and justifying uses of reason point in different directions and at which the corrective imagination needs to be supplemented by exploratory imagination.

The correction of one's false beliefs, inappropriate emotions, and misdirected desires helps one to avoid repeating one's past unreasonable decisions, but they do not enable one to make reasonable decisions in the future. For those decisions rest on having a realistic view of what possibilities are available to one and on understanding what it would be like to live according them. This is the work of the exploratory imagination, and this is the work Peter had done to reach the decision that he could not go to America.

Similarly, the genetic use of reason must be supplemented by its justifying use because actions can be justified even if the genetic use shows them to have been unreasonably motivated. Having unreasonable motives reflects adversely on those who have them, but it leaves open whether or not the resulting decisions were themselves unreasonable. If Peter had decided to go to America, he would have ignored the possibility that his past decision to resist Nazi evil was reasonable even though his motives for it were unreasonable. He would, then, have made another big mistake, but this time he caught it in time. It is perfectly understandable that having freed himself from unreasonable guilt and feeling the attractions of a normal life in America where his girl and university education awaited him, he would be tempted to go there rather than accept the hardship and grave risks that going to England meant. Another person might reasonably have made that decision, but Peter was not that person. His exploratory imagination led him to discover that about himself and prevented him from making another mistake.

Peter's discovery was that he had a deep commitment at the core of his self and that honoring that commitment was more important to him than any other possibility available to him. He used his exploratory imagination to envisage what it would be like to be a student again, make love to his girl and she to him, to live once again a normal life. But he found it impossible to opt for that possibility, no matter how attractive it was, when he juxtaposed it to the other possibility of not resisting Nazi evil when he could. The horrors he witnessed and experienced, the helplessness of innocent sufferers, the viciousness of the torturers and murderers, the futile and heartbreaking cries for help of the victims of barbaric outrages, the shattering of the very prohibitions that form the basis of civilized life were kept by his exploratory imagination vividly in his mind. He felt that since he can resist this evil in some small way, he must do so. The worst he could imagine was actually a common occurrence under Nazi rule, and it was so bad that the necessity of opposing it dwarfed the importance of the other possibility, attractive though it was, that was open to him. His discovery was that he could not live with himself if he failed to honor this deepest of his commitments.

For the first time in his life Peter overcame the fragmentation of his self. His beliefs, emotions, and desires prompting what he should do all pointed to going to England. Of course, he had contrary beliefs, emotions, and desires as well—it would have been amazing if he had not—but his deep commitment was to opposing Nazi evil, and this elevated the importance of the first set of motives far above the importance of the second. The decision Peter made is much like the decision Thomas More had made (see 9.4). And if Peter had decided wrongly and had gone to America, his resulting frame of mind would have been much like Oedipus's was when he discovered that he had violated his deep commitments (see 4.2–4.3). If Peter had done that, he would, once again, have been wracked by guilt, but this time reasonably because although a four-year-old child could not, the young man he became could justifiably blame himself for violating his deepest commitment when the possibility of honoring it was available. Peter's exploratory imagination made vivid to him both possibilities, and after some understandable hesitation he decided in favor of the one that seemed to him to be more reasonable than the other. And with this we have reached the question that must be asked.

Was Peter's decision really reasonable? He thought it was, but was he right? This time he was not wrong either about his motives or about his possibilities. He discovered his deep commitment and he acted on it. But was the decision that followed from his deep commitment reasonable? Given the conception of reason that I have been making explicit in this chapter, the answer is yes. His decision was reasonable provided we understand being reasonable as combining the practical, particular, permitting, genetic, and justifying uses of reason.

The practical use of reason is concerned with successful action. Peter's aim was to do what he could to oppose Nazi evil, and by going to England, from there back to his country to join the resistance, he achieved his aim. But was the aim itself reasonable? Well, Nazism certainly was evil, and opposing it is at the very least permitted by reason. Thus, so far as the practical use of reason goes, Peter's decision was reasonable.

In making that decision, Peter was also engaged in the particular use of reason. What he had to decide was whether *he* should oppose the Nazis, not anyone else. And packed into "he" are the character, circumstances, history, and available possibilities of Peter, not of anyone else. The decision he had to make was a decision for a person who had already taken part in the resistance, who was caught and tortured, who had been deluded about his motivation in a particular way, who escaped to Neutralia, who could go to America, who was in love with his girl, whose university education was interrupted, and so forth. There was only one person who had to make the decision in that context. Was his decision, then, reasonable, given his particular context? It was reasonable because Peter's deep commitment to opposing Nazi evil left him with no other reasonable possibility. If he had gone to America, he would have betrayed what was most important to him, destroyed his self-respect, and precipitated a worse psychological breakdown than the one from which he has just recovered.

If we ask whether Peter was reasonable in having that particular deep commitment, we come to the permitting use of reason. His deep commitment was certainly not required by reason: it would not have been irrational not to have a deep commitment to opposing Nazi evil. Many reasonable people outside Europe did not have it. And many reasonable people had it as a formative rather than a deep commitment. Nor is there anything in reason that would forbid having a deep commitment to opposing Nazi evil. Reason, therefore, does not require or forbid, but permits both having and not having that as a deep commitment. Peter had reasons for having it, as well as reasons against it, but the first outweighed the second because he had the experiences and character he had. Someone with different experiences and character might have judged the comparative weight of reasons differently, but reason permitted Peter to judge it as he did.

The same conclusion follows if we examine Peter's decision by the use of genetic reason. This time his motivation was not faulty because his corrective imagination had done its work. His relevant beliefs were true, his emotions were appropriate, and his desires were informed by his beliefs and emotions. The decision he made reflected his newly integrated self, and he was realistic about what he said yes and no to, what risks were involved, and what sacrifices he had to make. As we have seen, however, even if the genetic use of reason certifies a decision as reasonable, the justifying use of reason may still show that it was unreasonable because the deficiencies of the exploratory imagination led to an unrealistic view of one's possibilities. But Peter's decision cannot be faulted on this ground either. He had considered, indeed agonized over, what his life would be like if he decided to go to England or to America. In evaluating his possibilities, he made no mistakes in logic, he took account of the relevant facts, he asked himself again and again whether he might be making a mistake, but he found none, and he had reasons that weighed heavily with him for deciding to go to England and not to America. He has done, therefore, what the justifying use of reason requires of a reasonable decision.

It is justified to conclude, therefore, that given the conception of reason formed of its practical, particular, permitting, genetic, and justifying uses, Peter's decision was really reasonable, that is, he did not merely believe that it was reasonable, but he believed it on good grounds. The point of my discussion of Peter, of course, is not to judge the conduct of a fictional character but to make explicit the conception of reason I have been using throughout the book. The discussion of Peter's case enabled me to show in concrete terms what that conception of reason includes and what it excludes. It excludes the idea that it is impossible to be reasonable unless one puts reason to theoretical, universal, and either requiring or forbidding uses. I hope to have shown that it is possible to be reasonable in other ways, and that when reflective self-evaluation is reasonable, it is made so by these other uses of reason.

11.5 Overview

We have now reached the end of my account of the ideal of reflective self-evaluation and the place of moral imagination and reason in it. I hope it will not be thought that it is anywhere close to a complete account. If there are many and various possibilities and limits and many and various ways of being mistaken about one's past and future, then a complete account of reflective self-evaluation cannot be given. There is no blueprint for living a good life. The efforts toward that end are unavoidably practical and particular because what has to be done varies with individuals and contexts. We can be more or less reasonable and realistic in our actions, but what that comes to can be settled only by reference to the particularities of individuals and contexts. Reason and realism are the best guides to a responsible and fulfilling life, but there is no universal rule telling us how to be responsible and fulfilled. Universal rules may help us to avoid elementary mistakes like logical inconsistency, but beyond the obvious, such rules can yield only unhelpful homilies: take account of relevant facts, be open to reasonable criticism, allow for fallibility, and so on. These truisms are no doubt quite correct, but as soon as we ask, in the context of a particular person trying to live a particular kind of good life, which facts are relevant, which criticisms are reasonable, which beliefs or actions may be mistaken, the inevitable generality of universal rules must be replaced by precision and concreteness that only the practical and particular uses of reason can provide. This is not how it is in the context of science, but that is not the context of trying to live a good life.

This view of the place of reason in reflective self-evaluation is not relativism under another name. One task of reason in this context is to guide moral imagination. Relativists suppose that there are no objective grounds on which the deliverances of moral imagination could be criticized or justified. What seems to us to follow from the corrective and exploratory uses of imagination is the only basis for our subsequent judgments. If it seems to us that we have misinterpreted the facts on which we based important decisions in the past, then that is what we will want to correct. Likewise, if it seems to us that a particular possibility is attractive and worth pursuing, then that is what we will pursue. Relativists deny that there is anything else to which we could appeal to test how reasonable our judgments are about our past or future. I hope to have shown that this is not so, that we can use reason to test our judgments about our apparent misinterpretations in the past and about the choiceworthiness of our possibilities in the future. Showing this, as we have seen, depends on showing how particular individuals in particular circumstances could do it well or badly. This was precisely the reason for proceeding by way of reflection on literary works that make vivid individuals and circumstances in their concreteness and particularity.

Consider first how Mill, Oedipus, and Archer corrected their misinterpretations. Mill realized that the cognitive component of his self has expanded so far as to leave virtually no room for his emotions and desires. Oedipus saw that he mistook the object of the kind of control he needed: he came to understand that he had to control himself, not others. And Archer recognized that fulfillment eluded him because he had allowed his responsibility, which was dictated by restrictive moral conventions, to dominate his desires so completely as to squelch the desire for fulfillment. In each case, the protagonist grew dissatisfied with his life because his self was fragmented. He realized that the cause of his dissatisfaction with his life was the domination of one part of his self over the other parts. The direct consequence was the frustration of the dominated parts, and the indirect consequence was his dissatisfaction with his life.

Mill responded by changing how he lived; Oedipus was ready to change, but the proximity of death made it impossible; and Archer resigned himself to a misspent life. In all three cases, however, reflective self-evaluation did more than merely reveal their dissatisfaction: it led them to understand the cause of their dissatisfaction. Their resulting judgments, therefore, had a basis, namely, the truth about the fragmentation of their self. They discovered that truth by their corrective imagination guided by the genetic use of reason. Contrary to relativism, therefore, they did not just form a judgment; they had reasons for the judgment they have formed. And their reasons were good reasons because they explained the cause of their dissatisfaction and guided them to what they should do to remove it. Mill was successful in following the guidance of reason; Oedipus would have succeeded as well if death had not prevented him; and Archer could have succeeded if it had not been for his lassitude. The guidance of reason is thus to transform one's fragmented self into a better integrated one and thereby bring it closer to the balanced ideal.

Turning now to how reason can guide us to form a realistic view of our possibilities, let us recall that the balanced ideal is to maintain two kinds of balance: among our beliefs, emotions, and desires bearing on the possibilities and limits of a good life, and between the self taken as a whole, be it fragmented or integrated, and the possibilities of a good life we recognize as fitting our self and circumstances. Corrective imagination focuses on what causes the first kind of balance to fail; exploratory imagination aims to maintain the second kind of balance.

Finding a fit between the self and the possibilities whose realization might lead to a responsible and fulfilling life depends on two conditions. One is having a self that could be satisfied by the realization of some possibility. The other is having a realistic view of what possibilities are available that could be pursued with some prospect of success. The first condition is met if one's self is integrated, not fragmented. For a fragmented self could not be satisfied with the realization of any possibility because its beliefs, emotions, and desires prompt different, often incompatible, actions. The result is that whatever one ends up doing, parts of one's self will be frustrated. As we have just seen, the work of corrective imagination is to help to form an integrated self.

The second condition is to have a realistic view of one's possibilities. This is the work of the exploratory imagination. The first step toward forming a realistic view is distinguish between social possibilities available in the context of one's society; personal possibilities available to oneself, given one's strengths and weaknesses, abilities and inabilities, talents and deficiencies; and possibilities one recognizes as available to oneself. A completely realistic view is one that recognizes all and only possibilities that are personally and socially available to oneself. The next step is for individuals to use their exploratory imagination to understand what their lives would be like if they pursued these possibilities. And the third step is to choose the possibility that they find the most attractive and best fitting the self they believe themselves to have.

Montaigne's life exemplifies the enormous benefits of using reason to form a realistic view of oneself and one's possibilities and limits. One of the most interesting features of his life is his use of the *Essays* as instruments of reflective self-evaluation. They were at once the records of his reflection and the means for criticizing or justifying the judgments he was in the process of reaching. He used some of the essays to evaluate ideals he might employ to guide his self-transformation toward a more integrated self. In other essays, he assesses his character and struggles with formulating a view of what he can and cannot do, of where his possibilities and limits lie. He uses the essays to articulate his often unexpressed reasons for seeing himself and his possible actions as he does. He tests and probes these reasons again and again as he keeps revising the essays by adding to them or by commenting on the soundness of the reasons he had earlier given. His reasons, in turn, are revised as a result of his revision of the essays. He, in effect, conducts a Socratic dialogue with himself in which the two protagonists are the *Essays* and himself. Each is made more reasonable by this reciprocal questioning of the other.

The characters of James I have discussed illustrate, in contrast with Montaigne, some of the many ways in which reason can be used badly and the consequences that follow. The Prince and Charlotte subordinated everything in order to enjoy the benefits of a luxurious life. But they reasoned badly because they overlooked its costs. They ended up with a perpetually fragmented self because they could not act on their real beliefs, express how they really felt, and satisfy their genuine desires. By their unrealistic view of the possibility they opted for, they doomed themselves to a life of dissimulation and dissatisfaction.

Maggie found that responsibility and fulfillment pulled her in opposite directions. Reasoning badly, she chose to sacrifice responsibility to fulfillment. She failed to realize that she could have the fulfilling relationship she wanted with her husband and her father only if she honors her responsibilities to them, that the demands of responsibility and fulfillment need to be balanced, and that giving up either in favor of the other makes both, and consequently a good life, impossible. And she used reason badly because her fragmented self allowed her to feel the force of only one of her many reasons for action: her desire for her husband's affection. She thus used reason to serve, rather than to control, her passion.

Strether's imagination was disciplined, his reflective self-evaluation was accurate, his view of his possibilities and limits was realistic, and he used reason well in making his decision to return to America and to a life of dissatisfied passivity. Where he had gone wrong was that he began these admirable uses of imagination, self-evaluation, and reason too late. If he had used them well much earlier, before settling for the frustrations of Woollett, he could perhaps have achieved the self-transformation that he now rightly recognizes as belated. His misuse of reason had to do with timing: he came to using it well too late.

As these cases once again show, judgments about the particular possibilities individuals should choose to pursue can and should be guided by reason, contrary to what relativists claim. In this context, however, it is the justifying, not the genetic, use of reason that is required. Whether one's choice to pursue a particular possibility is reasonable, then, depends on whether one is justified in believing that it is socially and personally available and on whether one has reasons for preferring it to other personally and socially available possibilities. Reasonable judgments are based on justifying reasons of this kind, but the reasons, of course, are practical, particular, and permitting rather than theoretical, universal, and required.

Reasonable judgments are fallible because individuals can and do make mistakes both in their corrective imagination, which helps them move toward an integrated self, and in their exploratory imagination, which helps them choose one possibility among others. The disciplined imagination combines these two and provides a strong impetus for trying to avoid such mistakes. For the reason for correcting one's mistaken decisions in the past and transforming one's fragmented self into a more integrated one is to be able to pursue possibilities that would make one's life good. And the reason for exploring one's possibilities is to choose one that would enable the self one supposes to have to live responsibly and fulfillingly. It is in this way that the disciplined imagination and the balanced ideal of having an integrated self that pursues realistic possibilities are interdependent, reinforce each other, and explain what reflective self-evaluation requires one to do in pursuit of one form that a good life may take.

Notes

1. *Reflective Self-Evaluation*

    1. Outstanding histories of this process are Jerome B. Schneewind, *The Invention of Autonomy* (New York: Cambridge University Press, 1998), and Charles Taylor, *Sources of the Self* (Cambridge, Mass.: Harvard University Press, 1989). See also Charles Guignon, *On Being Authentic* (London: Routledge, 2004), and Bernard Williams, *Truth and Truthfulness* (Princeton, N.J.: Princeton University Press, 2002). A nonhistorical account of autonomy as it is understood in contemporary life is Gerald Dworkin, *The Theory and Practice of Autonomy* (Cambridge: Cambridge University Press, 1988).

    2. See Harry G. Frankfurt, *The Importance of What We Care About* (New York: Cambridge University Press, 1988), especially 1–8; *Necessity, Volition, and Love* (New York: Cambridge University Press, 1999); and *The Reasons of Love* (Princeton, N.J.: Princeton University Press, 2004); Stuart Hampshire, *Thought and Action* (London: Chatto and Windus, 1960); *Freedom of the Individual* (Princeton, N.J.: Princeton University Press, 1965; rev. ed., 1975); *Morality and Conflict* (Cambridge, Mass.: Harvard University Press, 1983); and *Innocence and Experience* (London: Allen Lane, 1989). Similar accounts are given by Alasdair MacIntyre, *After Virtue* (Notre Dame, Ind.: University of Notre Dame Press, 1981), especially chap. 15; Charles Taylor, *Human Agency and Language* (Cambridge: Cambridge University Press, 1985), especially essays 1, 2, and 4; and Richard Wollheim, *The Thread of Life* (Cambridge, Mass.: Harvard University Press, 1984).

    3. Schneewind, *Invention of Autonomy*, 5.

    4. Frankfurt, *Importance*, 16.

    5. Hampshire, *Thought and Action*, 177.

    6. Frankfurt, *Importance*, 24.

    7. Hampshire, *Thought and Action*, 177.

    8. John Stuart Mill, "Bentham" (1838), in *Essays on Literature and Society*, ed. Jerome B. Schneewind (New York: Collier-Macmillan, 1965), 258–260.

    9. Frankfurt, *Importance*, 81.

    10. Hampshire, *Thought and Action*, 177.

    11. Mill, "Bentham," 264.

    12. Ibid., 259.

    13. Ibid., 256.

    14. Ibid., 258–259.

    15. Bernard Williams, "Internal and External Reasons," in *Moral Luck* (Cambridge: Cambridge University Press, 1981), 104–105.

223

16. Ibid., 110.
17. John McDowell, "Are Moral Requirements Hypothetical Imperatives?" in *Mind, Value, and Reality* (Cambridge, Mass.: Harvard University Press, 1998), 85.
18. See, e.g., Eva Brann, *The World of Imagination* (Chicago: University of Chicago Press, 1986); Gregory Currie and Ian Ravenscroft, *Recreative Minds* (Oxford: Clarendon Press, 2002); John Livingston Lowes, *The Road to Xanadu* (1927; Princeton, N.J.: Princeton University Press, 1964); Mary Warnock, *Imagination* (London: Faber, 1976); and Alan R. White, *The Language of Imagination* (Oxford: Blackwell, 1990).
19. Peter F. Strawson, "Imagination and Perception," in *Freedom and Resentment* (1970; London: Methuen, 1974), 45.
20. Strawson, "Social Morality and Individual Ideal," in *Freedom and Resentment*, 26.
21. Strawson, "Imagination and Perception," 45.
22. Hide Ishiguro, "Imagination," in *British Analytical Philosophy*, ed. Bernard Williams and Alan Montefiore (London: Routledge, 1966), 176.

2. Moral Imagination

1. John Stuart Mill, *Utilitarianism* (1861; Indianapolis: Hackett, 1979), 3.
2. Immanuel Kant, *Groundwork of the Metaphysic of Morals* (1785), trans. H. J. Paton (New York: Harper, 1964), 60, 57.
3. Aristotle, *Nicomachean Ethics* (c. 330 BC), trans. Terence Irwin (Indianapolis: Hackett, 1985), 1103b29–30.
4. See Stuart Hampshire, *Innocence and Experience* (London: Allen Lane, 1989), 101.
5. Iris Murdoch, "Imagination," in *Metaphysics as a Guide to Morals* (London: Chatto and Windus, 1992), 323.
6. Charles Taylor, "Self-Interpreting Animals," in *Human Agency and Language* (Cambridge: Cambridge University Press, 1985), 62.
7. See Stuart Hampshire, *Morality and Conflict* (Cambridge, Mass.: Harvard University Press, 1983), 28–29.
8. Harry G. Frankfurt, *The Reasons of Love* (Princeton, N.J.: Princeton University Press, 2004), 23.
9. Hampshire, *Innocence and Experience*, 30–31.
10. Hampshire, *Morality and Conflict*, 155–156.
11. All quoted passages are from Murdoch, "Imagination," 321.
12. All quoted passages are from Murdoch, "Metaphysics: A Summary," in *Metaphysics as a Guide to Morals*, 507–508.
13. Peter F. Strawson, "Social Morality and Individual Ideal," in *Freedom and Resentment* (1970; London: Methuen, 1974), 26.
14. Iris Murdoch, "On 'God' and 'Good,' " in *Existentialists and Mystics* (New York: Allen Lane, 1998), 360.

3. Understanding Life Backward

1. John Stuart Mill, *Autobiography* (1873; Indianapolis: Bobbs-Merrill, 1957). References in the text are to the pages of this edition.
2. Harry G. Frankfurt, *The Importance of What We Care About* (New York: Cambridge University Press, 1988), 16, 80–81, 87–88.

3. Stuart Hampshire, *Morality and Conflict* (Cambridge, Mass.: Harvard University Press, 1983), 86–87.

4. See Iris Murdoch, "Against Dryness" and "The Idea of Perfection," in *Existentialists and Mystics* (London: Allen Lane, 1998).

5. Murdoch, *Existentialists and Mystics*, 288–289.

6. Ibid., 290–291.

7. Ibid., 293–294.

8. Lionel Trilling, *Sincerity and Authenticity* (Cambridge, Mass.: Harvard University Press, 1971), 1–2.

9. Edmund Burke, *Reflections on the Revolution in France* (1790; Harmondsworth, U.K.: Penguin, 1969), 171.

10. Matthew Arnold, "St. Paul and Protestantism" (1869), in *Dissent and Dogma*, ed. R. H. Super (Ann Arbor: University of Michigan Press, 1968), 51.

11. Frankfurt, *Importance*, 175, 163.

12. Stuart Hampshire, "Sincerity and Single-Mindedness," in *Freedom of Mind* (Oxford: Clarendon Press, 1972), 249, 244, 245.

13. George Bernard Shaw, *Man and Superman* (1903; New York: Heritage Press, 1962), act IV.

14. Jean-Paul Sartre, *Being and Nothingness* (1943), trans. Hazel E. Barnes (New York: Philosophical Library, 1956), 63, 65.

15. Arthur O. Lovejoy, "On the Discriminations of Romanticism," in *Essays in the History of Ideas* (Baltimore: Johns Hopkins University Press, 1948), 232. For general surveys, see Crane Brinton, "Romanticism," in *Encyclopedia of Philosophy*, ed. Paul Edwards (New York: Macmillan, 1967), and Franklin L. Baumer, "Romanticism," in *Dictionary of the History of Ideas*, ed. Philp. P. Wiener (New York: Scribner's, 1973). Illuminating philosophical discussions are Isaiah Berlin, "The Apotheosis of the Romantic Will," in *The Crooked Timber of Humanity*, ed. Henry Hardy (London: Murray, 1990), and *The Roots of Romanticism*, ed. Henry Hardy (Princeton, N.J.: Princeton University Press, 1999); and Edward Craig, *The Mind of God and the Works of Man* (Oxford: Clarendon Press, 1987), chap. 5.

16. Berlin, *Crooked Timber*, 185, 187, 192.

17. Hampshire, *Freedom of Mind*, 250.

18. Berlin, *Roots of Romanticism*, 140.

19. Wallace Stevens, "Chocorue to Its Neighbor," in *The Collected Poems* (New York: Vintage, 1982), 300.

4. From Hope and Fear Set Free

1. Plato, *Republic* (c. 370 BC), trans. Robin Waterfield (Oxford: Oxford University Press, 1993); references in the text are to the lines of this edition. Sophocles, *Oedipus the King* (c. 441 BC) and *Oedipus at Colonus* (c. 407 BC), both in *The Three Theban Plays*, trans. Robert Fagles (New York: Viking, 1982); references in the text are to the lines of this edition, *Oedipus the King* abbreviated K and *Oedipus at Colonus* abbreviated C.

2. See Sebastian Gardner, "Tragedy, Morality, and Metaphysics," in *Art and Morality*, ed. Jose Luis Bermudez and Sebastian Gardner (London: Routledge, 2003).

3. William Wordsworth, "The Prelude" (1850), in *Poetical Works* (Oxford: Oxford University Press, 1969), book XI, 3–7.

4. Georg W. F. Hegel, *Reason in History* (1837), trans. Robert S. Hartman (New York: Liberal Arts, 1953), 26–27.

5. Thomas Nagel, *The View from Nowhere* (New York: Oxford University Press, 1986), 208.

6. Thomas Nagel, *Mortal Questions* (Cambridge: Cambridge University Press, 1979), 25.

7. Leo Tolstoy, *The Death of Ivan Ilych* (1886), trans. A. Maude (New York: Signet, 1960), 121–122.

5. All Passion Spent

1. Edith Wharton, *The Age of Innocence* (1920; New York: Library of America, 1985). Since the novel has many editions and short chapters, I indicate the location of the quotations by chapter number.

6. Registers of Consciousness

1. Henry James, *The Golden Bowl* (1904; Harmondsworth, U.K.: Penguin, 1966). Parenthetical references in the text are to the pages of this edition.

2. Dorothea Krook, *The Ordeal of Consciousness in Henry James* (Cambridge: Cambridge University Press, 1967), 236.

3. R. W. B. Lewis, *The American Adam* (1955; Chicago: University of Chicago Press, 1971), 5.

4. Ibid., 154.

5. Krook, *Ordeal of Consciousness*, 269.

6. Richard Wollheim, "Flawed Crystals," *New Literary History* 15 (1983): 185–191; the quoted passage is on 189.

7. Martha Nussbaum, "Flawed Crystals: James's *The Golden Bowl* and Literature as Moral Philosophy" and " 'Finely Aware and Richly Responsible': Literature and the Moral Imagination," both in *Love's Knowledge* (New York: Oxford University Press, 1990).

8. Nussbaum, "Flawed Crystals," 133.

9. Ibid., 134.

10. Ibid., 134–135.

11. Ibid., 135.

12. Ibid., 140.

13. Ibid., 142.

14. Nussbaum, "Finely Aware," 152.

15. Ibid., 154.

16. Ibid., 156.

17. Ibid., 163.

18. Ibid., 155.

19. Ibid., 148.

20. In *The Art of Life* (Ithaca: Cornell University Press, 2002), part 2, I discuss and criticize aesthetic romanticism in much greater detail. An excellent historical account of it is Robert E. Norton, *The Beautiful Soul* (Ithaca: Cornell University Press, 1995).

21. Nussbaum, "Finely Aware," 163.

22. Ibid., 164.

23. Nussbaum, "Flawed Crystals," 134.

24. Ibid.

7. This Process of Vision

1. Henry James, *The Ambassadors*, 2 vols. (1902; New York: Scribner's, 1937). References in the text are to the volumes and pages of this edition.

2. Here I follow a suggestion by Joan Bennett in "The Art of Henry James: *The Ambassadors*," *Chicago Review* 9 (1956): 16–26.

3. John Maynard Keynes, *Two Memoirs* (New York: Augustus M. Kelley, 1949), 99, 103.

4. Iris Murdoch, *The Sovereignty of Good* (London: Routledge, 1970), 39–40.

5. Matthew Arnold, "Stanzas in Memory of the Author of 'Obermann,'" (1852), in *Arnold* (Harmondsworth, U.K.: Penguin, 1954), lines 101–104.

6. For a detailed discussion, see part 2 of my *The Art of Life* (Ithaca: Cornell University Press, 2002), especially chaps. 8–9.

7. Plato, *Apology* (c. 399 BC), in *The Collected Dialogues*, ed. Edith Hamilton and Huntington Cairns (Princeton, N.J.: Princeton University Press, 1989), 38a.

8. This discussion of emotions is indebted to Joel Kupperman, *Value . . . and What Follows* (New York: Oxford University Press, 1999), especially chap. 2, and to Richard Wollheim, *On the Emotions* (New Haven: Yale University Press, 1999).

8. An Integral Part of Life

1. Michel de Montaigne, *The Complete Works of Montaigne*, trans. Donald M. Frame (Stanford, Calif.: Stanford University Press, 1958). References in the text are to the pages of this edition.

2. This account of character is indebted to Joel Kupperman, *Character* (New York: Oxford University Press, 1991), especially chap. 1.

3. See Donald M. Frame, *Montaigne: A Biography* (San Francisco: North Point Press, 1984).

4. My discussion is indebted to Ann Hartle, *Michel de Montaigne: Accidental Philosopher* (Cambridge: Cambridge University Press, 2003), especially chap. 8, as well as to an unpublished manuscript of hers, "Montaigne's Marvelous Weakness."

9. Toward a Purified Mind

1. Iris Murdoch, *The Bell* (Harmondsworth, U.K.: Penguin, 1962), 135.

2. As in the preceding chapter, numbers in parentheses refer to the pages of Montaigne's *Essays*, in *The Complete Works of Montaigne*, trans. Donald M. Frame (Stanford, Calif.: Stanford University Press, 1958).

3. Norman Malcolm, *Ludwig Wittgenstein: A Memoir* (London: Oxford University Press, 1958), 80.

4. Søren Kierkegaard, *Purity of Heart* (1847), trans. Douglas V. Steere (New York: Harper and Row, 1938). References in the text are to the pages of this edition.

5. James 4:8, AV.

6. Joseph Conrad, *Heart of Darkness* (1902; Harmondsworth, U.K.: Penguin, 1999), 130.

7. Michael Oakeshott, "The Tower of Babel," in *Rationalism in Politics and Other Essays*, rev. ed., ed. Timothy Fuller (Indianapolis: Liberty Press, 1991), 467–468.

8. Iris Murdoch, *The Sovereignty of Good* (London: Routledge, 1970). References in the text are to the pages of this edition.

9. Iris Murdoch, *Metaphysics as a Guide to Morals* (London: Chatto and Windus, 1992), 355.

10. Ibid., 499.

11. Ibid., 507.

12. Iris Murdoch, *The Fire and the Sun* (Oxford: Clarendon Press, 1977), 38.

13. Ibid., 80.

14. Robert Bolt, *A Man for All Seasons* (New York: Random House, 1965), xiii. The historical accuracy of Bolt's portrayal of More has been seriously questioned by G. R. Elton, "The Real Thomas More?" in *Reformation Principle and Practice*, ed. Peter Newman Brooks (London: Scolar Press, 1980), 23–31, and by Richard Marius, *Thomas More* (New York: Knopf, 1984). But the doubts raised by these works have been laid to rest in Louis Martz, *Thomas More: The Search for the Inner Man* (New Haven: Yale University Press, 1990). My account follows and is indebted to Martz's interpretation of More's character.

15. *The Yale Edition of the Complete Works of St. Thomas More*, 14 vols., ed. R. S. Sylvester (New Haven: Yale University Press, 1963). References in the text are to the volumes and pages of this edition.

16. From More's letter to his daughter Margaret in *The Correspondence of Sir Thomas More*, ed. Elizabeth Frances Rogers (Princeton, N.J.: Princeton University Press, 1947), 514.

17. Ibid., 514–515.

18. David Hume, *Enquiries Concerning the Human Understanding and Concerning the Principles of Morals* (1777), ed. L. A. Selby-Bigge (Oxford: Clarendon Press, 1961), 209, and Jane Austen, *Sense and Sensibility* (1811; Harmondsworth, U.K.: Penguin, 1969), 338.

10. The Self's Judgment of the Self

1. Aristotle, *Nicomachean Ethics* (c. 330 BC), trans. W. D. Ross, rev. J. O. Urmson, in *The Complete Works of Aristotle*, ed. Jonathan Barnes (Princeton, N.J.: Princeton University Press, 1984), 1128b31–34.

2. Gabriele Taylor, *Pride, Shame, and Guilt* (Oxford: Clarendon Press, 1985). Quotations from this work are cited in the text by page number.

3. See, e.g., John Deigh, "Shame and Self-Esteem," in *Ethics and Personality*, ed. Deigh (1983; Chicago: University of Chicago Press, 1992); Helen Merrell Lynd, *On Shame and the Search for Identity* (New York: Harcourt Brace, 1958); Herbert Morris, "Guilt and Shame" and "Persons and Punishment," in *On Guilt and Innocence* (Berkeley: University of California Press, 1976); John Rawls, *A Theory of Justice* (Cambridge, Mass.: Harvard University Press, 1971), 442–446; John Sabini and Maury Silver, "In Defense of Shame," in *Emotion, Character, and Responsibility* (New York: Oxford University Press, 1998), which has a useful bibliography of the psychological literature; Michael Stocker, *Valuing Emotions* (New York: Cambridge University Press, 1996), 217–230; J. David Velleman, "The Genesis of Shame," *Philosophy and Public Affairs* 30 (2001): 27–52; and Bernard Williams, *Shame and Necessity* (Berkeley: University of California Press, 1993), chap. 4.

4. Douglas L. Cairns, *Aidos* (Oxford: Clarendon Press, 1993), 0.3 and 0.4, 14–47.

5. Rawls, *Theory of Justice*, 443, 445.

6. See, e.g., Jean-Paul Sartre, *Being and Nothingness* (1943), trans. Hazel E. Barnes (New York: Philosophical Library, 1956), part 3, chap. 1, sec. 4.

7. Rawls, *Theory of Justice*, 444–446.

8. Ibid., 444.

9. Deigh, "Shame and Self-Esteem," 151; Velleman, "Genesis of Shame," 37; Williams, *Shame and Necessity*, 221.

10. Deigh, "Shame and Self-Esteem," 151; Velleman, "Genesis of Shame," 37; Williams, *Shame and Necessity*, 221.

11. For a similar view, see Anthony O'Hear, "Guilt and Shame as Moral Concepts," *Proceedings of the Aristotelian Society* 77 (1976–77): 73–86.

12. Stocker, *Valuing Emotions*, 217–230.

13. Deigh, "Shame and Self-Esteem," 152; Velleman, "Genesis of Shame," 37; Williams, *Shame and Necessity*, 89.

14. Herodotus, *The Histories* (c. 430–424 BC), trans. A. de Selincourt, (Harmondsworth, U.K.: Penguin, 1954), book 1, 16–17.

15. Friedrich Nietzsche, *On the Genealogy of Morals* (1887), First Essay, sec. 11, in *Basic Writings of Nietzsche*, trans. Walter Kaufmann (New York: Modern Library, 1966), 475. I rearranged the order of the quoted sentences.

16. Deigh, "Shame and Self-Esteem," 151; Lynd, *On Shame*, 71; Morris, "Guilt and Shame," 62; Williams, *Shame and Necessity*, 102.

17. For a fascinating account, see Hugh Trevor-Roper, "The Paracelsian Movement," in *Renaissance Essays* (London: Secker and Warburg, 1985).

18. Morris, "Guilt and Shame," 62.

11. The Hardest Service

1. Arthur Koestler, *Arrival and Departure* (1943; London: Hutchinson, 1966).

Works Cited

Aristotle. *Nicomachean Ethics* (c. 330 BC). Translated by Terence Irwin. Indianapolis: Hackett, 1985.

———. *The Complete Works of Aristotle.* Edited by Jonathan Barnes. Princeton, N.J.: Princeton University Press, 1984.

Arnold, Matthew. "St. Paul and Protestantism" (1869). In *Dissent and Dogma*, edited by R. H. Super. Ann Arbor: University of Michigan Press, 1968.

———. "Stanzas in Memory of the Author of 'Obermann'" (1887). In *Arnold*. Harmondsworth, U.K.: Penguin, 1954.

Austen, Jane. *Sense and Sensibility* (1811). Harmondsworth, U.K.: Penguin, 1969.

Baumer, Franklin L. "Romanticism." In *Dictionary of the History of Ideas*, edited by Philp. P. Wiener. New York: Scribner's, 1973.

Bennett, Joan. "The Art of Henry James: *The Ambassadors.*" *Chicago Review* 9 (1956): 16–26.

Berlin, Isaiah. *The Crooked Timber of Humanity.* Edited by Henry Hardy. London: Murray, 1990.

———. *The Roots of Romanticism.* Edited by Henry Hardy. Princeton, N.J.: Princeton University Press, 1999.

Bermudez, Jose Luis, and Sebastian Gardner, eds. *Art and Morality.* London: Routledge, 2003.

Bolt, Robert. *A Man for All Seasons.* New York: Random House, 1965.

Brann, Eva. *The World of Imagination.* Chicago: University of Chicago Press, 1986.

Brinton, Crane. "Romanticism." In *Encyclopedia of Philosophy*, edited by Paul Edwards. New York: Macmillan, 1967.

Burke, Edmund. *Reflections on the Revolution in France* (1790). Harmondsworth, U.K.: Penguin, 1969.

Cairns, Douglas L. *Aidos.* Oxford: Clarendon Press, 1993.

Conrad, Joseph. *Heart of Darkness* (1902). Harmondsworth, U.K.: Penguin, 1999.

Craig, Edward. *The Mind of God and the Works of Man.* Oxford: Clarendon Press, 1987.

Currie, Gregory, and Ian Ravenscroft. *Recreative Minds.* Oxford: Clarendon Press, 2002.

Deigh, John. "Shame and Self-Esteem." In *Ethics and Personality*, edited by John Deigh. 1983; Chicago: University of Chicago Press, 1992.

Dworkin, Gerald. *The Theory and Practice of Autonomy.* Cambridge: Cambridge University Press, 1988.

Elton, G. R. "The Real Thomas More?" In *Reformation Principle and Practice*, edited by Peter Newman Brooks. London: Scolar Press, 1980.

Frame, Donald M. *Montaigne: A Biography*. San Francisco: North Point Press, 1984.

Frankfurt, Harry G. *The Importance of What We Care About*. New York: Cambridge University Press, 1988.

——. *Necessity, Volition, and Love*. New York: Cambridge University Press, 1999.

——. *The Reasons of Love*. Princeton, N.J.: Princeton University Press, 2004.

Gardner, Sebastian. "Tragedy, Morality, and Metaphysics." In *Art and Morality*, edited by Jose Luis Bermudez and Sebastian Gardner. London: Routledge, 2003.

Guignon, Charles. *On Being Authentic*. London: Routledge, 2004.

Hampshire, Stuart. *Freedom of Mind*. Oxford: Clarendon Press, 1972.

——. *Freedom of the Individual*. Rev. ed. Princeton, N.J.: Princeton University Press, 1975.

——. *Innocence and Experience*. London: Allen Lane, 1989.

——. *Morality and Conflict*. Cambridge, Mass.: Harvard University Press, 1983.

——. *Thought and Action*. London: Chatto and Windus, 1960.

Hartle, Ann. *Michel de Montaigne: Accidental Philosopher*. Cambridge: Cambridge University Press, 2003.

Hegel, Georg W. F. *Reason in History* (1837). Translated by Robert S. Hartman. New York: Liberal Arts, 1953.

Herodotus. *The Histories* (c. 430–424 BC). Translated by A. de Selincourt. Harmondsworth, U.K.: Penguin, 1954.

Hume, David. *Enquiries Concerning the Human Understanding and Concerning the Principles of Morals* (1777). Edited by L. A. Selby-Bigge. Oxford: Clarendon Press, 1961.

Ishiguro, Hide. "Imagination." In *British Analytical Philosophy*, edited by Bernard Williams and Alan Montefiore. London: Routledge, 1966.

James, Henry. *The Ambassadors* (1902). 2 vols. New York: Scribner's, 1937.

——. *The Golden Bowl* (1904). Harmondsworth, U.K.: Penguin, 1966.

Kant, Immanuel. *Groundwork of the Metaphysic of Morals* (1785). Translated by H. J. Paton. New York: Harper, 1964.

Kekes, John. *The Art of Life*. Ithaca: Cornell University Press, 2002.

Keynes, John Maynard. *Two Memoirs*. New York: Augustus M. Kelley, 1949.

Kierkegaard, Søren. *Purity of Heart* (1847). Translated by Douglas V. Steere. New York: Harper and Row, 1938.

Koestler, Arthur. *Arrival and Departure* (1943). London: Hutchinson, 1966.

Krook, Dorothea. *The Ordeal of Consciousness in Henry James*. Cambridge: Cambridge University Press, 1967.

Kupperman, Joel. *Character*. New York: Oxford University Press, 1991.

——. *Value . . . and What Follows*. New York: Oxford University Press, 1999.

Lewis, R. W. B. *The American Adam* (1955). Chicago: University of Chicago Press, 1971.

Lovejoy, Arthur O. "On the Discriminations of Romanticism." In *Essays in the History of Ideas*. Baltimore: Johns Hopkins University Press, 1948.

Lowes, John Livingston. *The Road to Xanadu* (1927). Princeton, N.J.: Princeton University Press, 1964.

Lynd, Helen Merrell. *On Shame and the Search for Identity*. New York: Harcourt Brace, 1958.

MacIntyre, Alasdair. *After Virtue*. Notre Dame, Ind.: University of Notre Dame Press, 1981.

Malcolm, Norman. *Ludwig Wittgenstein: A Memoir.* London: Oxford University Press, 1958.

Marius, Richard. *Thomas More.* New York: Knopf, 1984.

Martz, Louis. *Thomas More: The Search for the Inner Man.* New Haven, Conn.: Yale University Press, 1990.

McDowell, John. *Mind, Value, and Reality.* Cambridge, Mass.: Harvard University Press, 1998.

Mill, John Stuart. *Autobiography* (1873). Indianapolis: Bobbs-Merrill, 1957.

———. "Bentham" (1838). In *Essays on Literature and Society,* edited by Jerome B. Schneewind. New York: Collier-Macmillan, 1965.

———. *Utilitarianism* (1861). Indianapolis: Hackett, 1979.

Montaigne, Michel de. *The Complete Works.* Translated by Donald M. Frame. Stanford, Calif.: Stanford University Press, 1958.

Morris, Herbert. *On Guilt and Innocence.* Berkeley: University of California Press, 1976.

Murdoch, Iris. *The Bell.* Harmondsworth, U.K.: Penguin, 1962.

———. *Existentialists and Mystics.* New York: Allen Lane, 1998.

———. *The Fire and the Sun.* Oxford: Clarendon Press, 1977.

———. *Metaphysics as a Guide to Morals.* London: Chatto and Windus, 1992.

———. *The Sovereignty of Good.* London: Routledge, 1970.

Nagel, Thomas. *Mortal Questions.* Cambridge: Cambridge University Press, 1979.

———. *The View from Nowhere.* New York: Oxford University Press, 1986.

Nietzsche, Friedrich. *On the Genealogy of Morals* (1887). In *Basic Writings of Nietzsche,* translated by Walter Kaufmann. New York: Modern Library, 1966.

Norton, Robert E. *The Beautiful Soul.* Ithaca: Cornell University Press, 1995.

Nussbaum, Martha. *Love's Knowledge.* New York: Oxford University Press, 1990.

Oakeshott, Michael. "The Tower of Babel." In *Rationalism in Politics and Other Essays,* rev. ed., edited by Timothy Fuller. Indianapolis: Liberty Press, 1991.

O'Hear, Anthony. "Guilt and Shame as Moral Concepts." *Proceedings of the Aristotelian Society* 77 (1976–77): 73–86.

Plato. *Apology* (c. 399 BC). In *The Collected Dialogues,* edited by Edith Hamilton and Huntington Cairns. Princeton, N.J.: Princeton University Press, 1989.

———. *Republic* (c. 370 BC). Translated by Robin Waterfield. Oxford: Oxford University Press, 1993.

Rawls, John. *A Theory of Justice.* Cambridge, Mass.: Harvard University Press, 1971.

Rogers, Elizabeth Frances, ed. *The Correspondence of Sir Thomas More.* Princeton, N.J.: Princeton University Press, 1947.

Sabini, John, and Maury Silver. *Emotion, Character, and Responsibility.* New York: Oxford University Press, 1998.

Santayana, George. *Three Philosophical Poets.* Cambridge: Harvard University Press, 1910.

Sartre, Jean-Paul. *Being and Nothingness* (1943). Translated by Hazel E. Barnes. New York: Philosophical Library, 1956.

Schneewind, Jerome B. *The Invention of Autonomy.* New York: Cambridge University Press, 1998.

Shaw, George Bernard. *Man and Superman* (1903). New York: Heritage Press, 1962.

Sophocles. *Oedipus the King* (c. 441 BC) and *Oedipus at Colonus* (c. 407 BC). Translated by Robert Fagles. Both in *The Three Theban Plays.* New York: Viking, 1982.

Stevens, Wallace. *The Collected Poems.* New York: Vintage, 1982.

———. *The Necessary Angel* (1942). New York: Vintage, 1951.

Stocker, Michael. *Valuing Emotions.* New York: Cambridge University Press, 1996.

Strawson, Peter F. *Freedom and Resentment* (1970). London: Methuen, 1974.

Sylvester, R. S., executive ed. *The Yale Edition of the Complete Works of St. Thomas More.* 14 vols. New Haven, Conn.: Yale University Press, 1963.

Taylor, Charles. *Human Agency and Language.* Cambridge: Cambridge University Press, 1985.

———. *Sources of the Self.* Cambridge, Mass.: Harvard University Press, 1989.

Taylor, Gabriele. *Pride, Shame, and Guilt.* Oxford: Clarendon Press, 1985.

Tolstoy, Leo. *The Death of Ivan Ilych* (1886). Translated by A. Maude. New York: Signet, 1960.

Trevor-Roper, Hugh. *Renaissance Essays.* London: Secker and Warburg, 1985.

Trilling, Lionel. *Sincerity and Authenticity.* Cambridge, Mass.: Harvard University Press, 1971.

Velleman, J. David. "The Genesis of Shame." *Philosophy and Public Affairs* 30 (2001): 27–52.

Warnock, Mary. *Imagination.* London: Faber, 1976.

Wharton, Edith. *The Age of Innocence* (1920). New York: Library of America, 1985.

White, Alan R. *The Language of Imagination.* Oxford: Blackwell, 1990.

Williams, Bernard. *Moral Luck.* Cambridge: Cambridge University Press, 1981.

———. *Shame and Necessity.* Berkeley: University of California Press, 1993.

———. *Truth and Truthfulness.* Princeton, N.J.: Princeton University Press, 2000.

Wollheim, Richard. "Flawed Crystals." *New Literary History* 15 (1983): 185–191.

———. *On the Emotions.* New Haven, Conn.: Yale University Press, 1999.

———. *The Thread of Life.* Cambridge, Mass.: Harvard University Press, 1984.

Wordsworth, William. "The Prelude" (1850). In *Poetical Works.* Oxford: Oxford University Press, 1969.

Index